THE DEATH OF KINGS

The Death of Kings

Royal Deaths in Medieval England

Michael Evans

**hambledon
continuum**

Hambledon Continuum

The Tower Building
11 York Road,
London, SE1 7NX

80 Maiden Lane,
Suite 704,
New York NY 10038

ISBN 978-1-85285-268-9

Typeset by Carnegie Publishing, Lancaster
Printed in the United States of America
Book Club Edition

Contents

Illustrations

Preface

Between 1066 and 1485 eight kings of England died violently: in battle, by murder, or in suspicious accidents. These deaths fascinated medieval chroniclers and have continued to fascinate historians and readers ever since. Nor was a fascination with royal death unique to the middle ages. We only have to think of the death of King Charles I to realise its continuing hold on people's imaginations. Indeed a much more recent death, that of Princess Diana of Wales in 1997, with its talk of martyrdom and sainthood, and the princess's ability to attract veneration after death, was in some aspects very recognisable in medieval terms.

Many people have helped make this work a reality. At Hambledon and London, Tony Morris saw the potential in the idea and encouraged me to develop it, and Martin Sheppard proved the ideal editor, being both helpful and patient. My colleagues, notably Roger Smith, and students in the History Department of Canterbury Christ Church University College responded to many of my ideas and made helpful suggestions. David Crouch alerted me to the relevance and circumstances of the death of Henry the Young King and Nicholas Vincent pointed out to me the significance of his coronation robe. Lesley Wallis informed me, much to my surprise, that I was taking an anthropological approach to death. Leah Rutchick, Charlotte Newman Goldy and Danielle Westerhof allowed me to develop my ideas at the Kalamazoo and Leeds International Medieval Congresses and made helpful comments on them. Miriam Gill kindly allowed me to read her unpublished chapter on the veneration of Henry VI. The subscribers of Medfem-l (the Medieval Feminist email discussion group) were a marvellous source of information and ideas, especially for the chapter on queens. The section on death in childbirth and medieval obstetric practice owes much to their collective wisdom. In addition, countless audience members at talks I have given have helped me by their questions and comments.

Many other colleagues, friends, and fellow historians helped me along the way by listening to and discussing my ideas, and pointing me toward sources or incidents that I would never have otherwise encountered. They include Dominic Alexander, Jeanelle Barrett, Julia Barrow, Julie Chappell, Simon Constantine, Dana Cushing, Elaine Graham-Leigh, David Green, Stefania Michelucci, Bonnie Millar-Heggie, Miriam Müller, Jon Porter, Sam Riches, Kevin Sorrentino and Claire Taylor. I wish to thank the following institutions for permission to reproduce illustrations: the British Library (pl. 6); the National Gallery (pl. 5); the National Monuments Record (pl. 4); and the National Portrait Gallery (pl. 7). My history teacher at school Martin Burgess is to blame for making me a historian, as are Malcolm Barber, Anne Curry, Bernard Hamilton and Alison McHardy for making me a medievalist; for which I thank them all. Finally, I wish to thank my parents for their patience and support over the years. I dedicate this book to them.

Introduction

Medieval chronicles can be frustrating sources. To quote a modern editor of the twelfth-century monastic historian Henry of Huntingdon: 'Henry's account [of the reign of Henry I] is tantalisingly brief, being overloaded with moral reflections, fictitious speeches, and irrelevant poetry, and yielding little in the way of "facts".' [1] An historian can react to this problem in one of (at least) two ways: he or she may lament the lack of 'facts', transcribing what few there are, before looking elsewhere for enlightenment; alternatively, the historian can ask *why* Henry included so many 'irrelevant' details, and begin to examine them in Henry's own terms. The latter approach will enable the historian to work *with* the text, not *against* it. It is possible to comment about a text not only that 'There are still many things to say about it', but also that 'It still has many things to say to us'. [2] A medieval writer of history did not merely present a narrative of a series of 'facts' (if, indeed, any historian has ever done so), but sought to demonstrate, through the writing of history, the unfolding of divine providence in human affairs. We may see history as a linear progression of events from the distant past to the present day, but medieval people saw history as a struggle between God and the Devil, which began with the fall of Lucifer, reached its climax with the incarnation of Christ, and would end with Doomsday. These events (although not their timing) were not open to speculation, having been described in the Book of Revelation. [3] In short, history had a purpose. Therefore moralising passages, quotations from scripture and the classics, and even apparently irrelevant anecdotes, should all to varying degrees be seen as integral to the text, and studied as such for their meaning and significance.

Chroniclers, whether monastic or secular in background, rarely if ever recorded the manner of a king's death (or its aftermath) in a neutral way. As we shall see, a violent death, in battle or by murder, was treated with strong political and moral overtones. So, for example, a chronicler who tells us that William II died without receiving the last rites was not simply recording a 'fact' in a disinterested manner, he was reflecting upon the moral make-up of the dead king, and his (slim) hopes of salvation in the next life. Conversely, for other reasons, the violence of the deaths of Edward II, Richard II and Henry VI was taken by some as proof of their sanctity.

Some death stories, especially those of kings or princes who were murdered or who disappeared in mysterious circumstances, are of doubtful origin. The 'facts' were and are hard to come by, and the chroniclers often resorted to reusing particular stories or motifs. These are known as *topoi*, images or ideas that recur in different texts. Even in the absence of clear 'facts', rather than dismissing these death stories as fabrications, we can learn a great deal about attitudes toward the murdered figure, and about the author and audience of the text, by studying the meaning in these *topoi*. To quote another modern historian:

> The paradox of the lie that might as well be true must interest anyone who seeks to understand texts in history or the historical influence of texts ... Were we to shun texts that rely upon devices of narrative rearrangement, interested selection of detail, and spurious self-authorisation, we would have to discard most of the written record. Yet, in other senses, the most blatantly made-up text cannot help but reveal truth. Fabulists and romancers conceive episodes within imaginary structures or value systems their audience embrace as true, and lies accepted as the basis for actions gain retrospective truthfulness through their influence on events.[4]

To use but one example of the use of fable or anecdote by a medieval chronicler, the famous story of King Canute (the historical Cnut, who reigned in the early eleventh century) attempting to turn back the waves first occurs in the writings of Henry of Huntingdon, some hundred years after Canute's death.[5] It is almost certainly a later legend, and can be discounted as evidence for the real character of that king, or for what really happened during his reign. Yet Henry of Huntingdon was a serious historian who cannot be dismissed as a mere fabulist. So why did he include stories such as this? The answer lies in the fact that he was writing not just about events or 'facts' but about morality and providence. As the proverbial schoolboy knows (or once did) this is a moral tale about the king of England's powerlessness against the greater power of the supreme king of the universe. It is not a true story, but its power as a metaphor has made it the only reason for Cnut's name being remembered by anyone but historians of the eleventh century. The story is invariably included in children's history books (or at least the more traditionally-minded among them), and the image of King Canute has passed into the language to mean someone displaying futile resistance to forces beyond their control. The story of King Alfred burning the cakes is similarly famous, even though it too was not recorded until a century after the date when the event is supposed to have taken place.[6] It is ironic that, in the debate in the 1990s over the teaching of history in England, the episode was cited by many conservative critics of the national curriculum as one of the 'facts' of history that all English schoolchildren ought to learn.[7]

This book is therefore not only about death, or even individual deaths, but about wider issues of story-telling in history, and of what (in the words of Sellar and Yeatman's *1066 and All That*) makes history 'memorable'. Ironically, Sellar and Yeatman's satirical intention to record 'only the history that is memorable' hit unwittingly on a significant truth: that medieval chroniclers did just that, and that the more colourful anecdotes were there for a reason. I will therefore take more than simply a forensic approach to the deaths of kings. (This approach has been attempted recently in a fascinating book by Dr Clifford Brewer, a Fellow of the Royal College of Surgeons, who has tried to determine the exact causes of death.[8] For the reasons given above, however, the sources by their very nature do not lend themselves to this type of analysis, not only because of possible inaccuracy or lack of necessary detail, but because medical diagnosis was simply not the purpose of the chronicler's narrative.) Likewise, it is tempting to adopt a detective approach to some controversial or mysterious deaths, of which there were many. Those of William Rufus, John, Edward II, Richard II, Henry VI and Edward V have all raised questions, either among contemporaries or among modern-day historians or controversialists. The fate of Edward V and his brother (better known as the 'Princes in the Tower') has even led to two societies being formed to defend the good name of Richard III.[9]

I will address some of these issues, especially in the case of those later medieval kings who were deposed and murdered by their enemies, where the telling and retelling of death-stories, and the political bias of the sources, had a profound effect upon the account of the death. The nature of the records, however, again makes the exact circumstances of these deaths difficult to determine, not least because political murder was, almost by definition, carried out in private. There were no dramatic assassinations of English kings. Unlike the murder of deposed kings such as Edward II, Richard II and Henry VI, assassination tended to be a public act, designed to some extent to publicise the political demands of the assassins. The most famous assassination in medieval England, the murder of Thomas Becket, although carried out in the enclosed space of Canterbury Cathedral, was arguably a 'public' act, performed before witnesses in a semi-public space. By killing Becket in his cathedral the assassins were very obviously killing the archbishop, not just the man.

It is important to bear in mind that the deaths of kings were no ordinary deaths. Politically, the death of a king was an event of huge significance, meaning a change of ruler with all that this implied for the making or breaking of policies, alliances and political careers. If the death was unexpected, or if the dying king had left an uncertain succession, the death could be the prelude to political conflict or civil war. Such was the case following the deaths of Edward the Confessor, William II and Henry I. Conversely, political conflict could hasten the deaths of kings, as befell Edward II, Richard II and Henry VI. The death of a king was also an important point of symbolic transition between two reigns, with the ceremonies of funeral and coronation emphasising the continuity of the dynasty and of the royal office. Some kings demonstrated this continuity by being buried in their coronation robes.[10]

Medieval kings were not special merely because they were politically supreme. They were also seen as placed above the mass of ordinary people by virtue of their anointing. A medieval king played a quasi-priestly role: he was ordained by God to rule, and there was biblical authority for the belief that 'the powers that be', however corrupt, tyrannical or incompetent they might be, were 'ordained by God'.[11] This was emphasised by the coronation ceremony, which was con-ducted by the church, and especially the anointing with holy oil, a practice based on the example of Old Testament kings of Israel.[12] Kings were believed to possess special powers that emphasised their status as divinely-ordained, notably the practice of touching for the 'King's Evil'. The belief that the common skin disease scrofula could be cured by the touch of the king first appeared in France, attached to the Capetian kings. The kings of England from the mid thirteenth century onwards were understandably keen to promote the belief that they enjoyed the same power. By virtue of their anointing, kings were able to borrow the power to perform miracles from God and the saints. One anonymous twelfth-century political theorist, defending the sacral nature of kingship against the assault on royal power over the church by Gregorian reformers, argued that the king, although a man in his mortal body, was divine by God's grace from the moment that he was anointed.[13]

This idea implied a tension or duality in the nature of kingship, which is often described as the concept of the king's two bodies. In early modern times this represented the distinction between the king's physical body and the body politic, but in the high middle ages the distinction was more that between the mortal body of the king and the immortal body of kingship. The death of a king therefore represented merely the handing over of kingship to the next generation. The individual king might die, but the institutional king and kingship did not: *le roi est mort, vive le roi* in the famous formulation. The idea of the king (or the crown) as a public entity legally distinct from the private entity of the king as a person grew as personal kingship evolved into a state governed by institutions and comprising the three estates (or orders) of society.

Once in place, kings could only be removed by the judgement of God. This presented those who deposed a king with a practical problem, which was usually solved by the simple expedient of rapid and convenient death soon after deposition. There were legal or political arguments raised in favour of deposition in the fourteenth century, based on the king's incompetence, tyranny or dubious lineage, but ultimately no usurper could exist comfortably alongside a living predecessor, no matter how closely guarded he may have been.

When it came to the presentation of royal death in narrative accounts, the anointed nature of the king meant that his death could easily be interpreted in terms of divine providence. For example, the sudden and entirely unexpected death of William Rufus could only be viewed as divine judgement on an anticlerical tyrant. In reality, clerical historians were always quick to point out that kings, no matter how exalted they were, were only mere mortals in the eyes of God. Royal death provided the perfect opportunity for the chronicler to edify the reader with a dissertation upon the passing nature of worldly glory.

Finally, death, whether it befell a king, a churchman or a commoner, was an event that was viewed with great awe. In the medieval period, and in the later middle ages especially, it was seen as desirable to die a 'good death'. Toward the end of the middle ages, a popular genre of book appeared addressing the *ars moriendi* (art of dying).[14] The dying person was expected to make arrangements both for his soul and for the settling of his worldly affairs before death, as well as approaching death with a suitable serenity of mind, neither too eager to welcome its release nor too unwilling to leave this world for the next. For medieval Christians a sudden death was to be feared, as it did not allow the dying the opportunity to make their peace with God and with their fellow humans, to take confession and to prepare the soul. Later medieval guides to dying frequently contained illustrations of the dying man surrounded by demons and being tempted by various allegorical figures, though protected by Christ.[15] The high middle ages saw a greater willingness of chroniclers to dwell on the realistic details of death, in contrast to the older tradition (at least in clerical hagiography) of treating death in a sanitised, idealised manner.[16] Despite the fact that violent or unpleasant deaths will loom large in this book, some kings faced death in the recommended manner. The ideal model of a royal death in the later middle ages was that of Louis IX (St Louis) in Tunisia in 1270. He died on crusade, which in itself was meritorious. According to his contemporary biographers, he made a deathbed speech in which he gave advice to his son, Philip, on how to be a good ruler, and asked for masses to be said for his soul.[17] He thereby fulfilled both the religious and secular requirements of a good death.

It is impossible to devote equal space to every royal death, and some kings ended their lives in unremarkable ways. I will therefore concentrate on those deaths that stand out in contemporary accounts as the most meaningful. To put it simply, I will concentrate unapologetically on the *interesting* deaths, or – to paraphrase *1066 and All That* again – the *memorable* deaths, precisely because these deaths were the richest in symbolism and in political and moral repercussions. This book therefore has a thematic, rather than chronological, structure. This is in order to treat separately the different aspects of royal death. The deaths of Anglo-Norman and Angevin kings will, however, be dealt with in the first part of the book and there will be a greater concentration in later chapters on the deaths of kings in later medieval England, a reflection of changing political circumstances and historiographical traditions.

An idea commonly held among the mainly clerical chroniclers of the high middle ages was that death, especially sudden death, was an example of God's judgement. Any sudden or unexpected event might be interpreted as an act of God; if that event was as significant as a royal death, then contemporary commentators would begin to look for signs of the divine will at work. These signs were viewed in a framework of the belief in God's punishment for sin. They include the deaths by arrow wound (perhaps the ultimate, and literal, 'bolt from the blue') of Harold Godwinson, William II (Rufus) and Richard I (the Lionheart).

Death was also viewed as an example of the mutability of earthly fortune in the face of the eternal. We will see that royal death provided a perfect opportunity for ecclesiastical chroniclers to reflect on this theme, as the mighty of the earth were proved to be mortal like other men. In particular, some of the more gruesome fates suffered by royal bodies that had been pampered in life were used to great effect by these writers. This is shown in the deaths (and aftermath of the deaths) of William I, Henry I and John.

The death of a king was the occasion for power to be transferred from one generation to the next, and this created problems and tensions when an heir was impatient to succeed, or when there was ambiguity over the succession. The death of a royal heir could also cause major problems. Special attention will be given to the deaths of William Atheling, the son of Henry I, and of Henry 'the Young King', the son of Henry II, and to the curious case of the attempted murder of Henry I by his daughter.

In the later middle ages, we encounter another phenomenon, the royal murder. This fate was a surprisingly common one for kings in late medieval England, despite the horror with which regicide was viewed. Four medieval English kings met this end: Edward II, Richard II, Henry VI, and Edward V. We will look at some of the circumstances surrounding their deaths, and at the circulation of rumours surrounding them, providing chronicles with a series of recurring motifs. Their deaths will be compared to those of other important murder victims of the time, to demonstrate how this process of rumour developed. There was also the thorny problem of what to do with the body of a murdered king.

Other difficulties arose from royal murder, and from the ambiguities created by usurpation. One of these was the problem of what happened if the king was not universally acknowledged to have died. This led to legends of royal survival and the appearance of impostors who exploited such legends for their own ends. Harold, Edward II, Richard II and the last members of the Yorkist dynasty were all subjects of such stories.

Finally, there was a somewhat different form of royal survival after death, the concept of the royal martyr-saint. A combination of the horror of violent death, circumstances of political controversy, and the veneration paid to the king as God's Anointed could all combine to turn a dead king into a saint, at least at a popular level. There was an established tradition of Anglo-Saxon royal saints, and high medieval cults of royal 'martyrs' arose around Edward II and Henry VI, as well as around quasi-royal figures such as Simon de Montfort and Thomas, earl of Lancaster.

I have chosen to treat the English middle ages in a very traditional time span, from 1066 to 1485. This, like any attempt to periodise history, is necessarily arbitrary, but it can be justified on a number of grounds. Two of the themes running through the book are the medieval Christian attitude to kingship, and the medieval ecclesiastical tradition of history (although this was increasingly replaced by other more secular approaches toward the end of the middle ages). In a story so dominated by religious and ideological concepts, it seems reasonable to choose a period that corresponds to that of the domination of the high medieval Catholic Church. The late eleventh century marked the beginning of the Gregorian reform, when the church, led by reforming popes, sought to cleanse itself of corruption, and to free itself from any dependence on kings and other temporal rulers. Such a programme clearly affected attitudes to kingship. The ideas of the new reform papacy reached England at the time of the Conquest (perhaps not coincidentally, as William the Conqueror received a papal banner, and a papal commission of sorts), so 1066 is a natural starting-point. Likewise, 1485 marks the accession of Henry VII, the last unambiguously Catholic king of England before the Reformation that began in the reign of his son, Henry VIII. Henry VII's own death was marked by the saying of 10,000 masses to help his soul pass through purgatory, a practice that was typical of the spirituality of late medieval England.[18]

This is not to say that the themes addressed in this book are unique to this period. The tradition of royal martyrs stretched back deep into the Anglo-Saxon past to the martyr-kings of seventh-century Northumbria. At the other end of our timescale, the idea of royal sanctity reached its apotheosis with the seventeenth-century cult of 'King Charles the Martyr' in high Anglican circles. It arguably lives on today in the near-saintly veneration of the dead Diana, Princess of Wales.

Nor are the themes of this book exclusive to England. England in the middle ages existed in a continental context. Its kings from 1066 to 1485 were drawn from French families. Until the loss of Normandy to the French crown in 1204, England was only part of a conglomeration of mostly French political entities, dubbed retrospectively the 'Anglo-Norman Empire' or, after the succession of Henry Plantagenet, count of Anjou in 1154, the 'Angevin Empire'. Even after 1204, the English crown was locked into the affairs of mainland Europe through war, diplomacy and the crusades. The retention, and at times the attempted expansion, of the mainland possession of Gascony ensured a continued conflict with France, which from 1337 onward became caught up in the English king's bid to gain the crown of France. Intellectually, too, England was part of the European mainstream, a fact of great importance in understanding English historiography. Reform ideas entered the English Church in the late eleventh and early twelfth centuries, and the ecclesiastics who are such an important source for events in the high middle ages were part of an institution, and of an intellectual tradition, that embraced the whole of western Europe.

Secular writers were also part of an international tradition. The twelfth-century Anglo-Norman author Geoffrey Gaimar was an early example of a writer of chivalric, secular work for an aristocratic audience, working in a tradition that embraced both history and literature. Indeed, there was no firm divide between the two in the middle ages; the notoriously unreliable, but very readable, fourteenth-century historian Jean Froissart perhaps represents the apogee of this tradition. He tells us that he began as a writer of poetry, before moving on to the higher calling of history.

His histories are full of chivalric derring-do, in which the brutality of the wars in France is described in places as if it were a courtly tournament. This tradition of writing was French in origin (the term 'Romance', used to describe one literary genre in this tradition, derives from the fact that it was written in the vernacular Romance language, rather than Latin, the language of the church and the classics), and international in scope.

There are also, for want of a better term, folkloric elements that span the ages and nations. For example, the motif of kings who cheat death is an extremely common one in many cultures, as we shall see. Likewise, the phenomenon of royal martyrs was not confined to England. A modern, non-English example of this is the current move in the Russian Orthodox church to canonise Tsar Nicholas II, executed by the Bolsheviks in 1918. The parallels with England's King Charles the Martyr are obvious, and illustrate the continued allure of kingship in many cultures.

Lastly, the modern perception of medieval kings and of their deaths is in many ways shaped by post-medieval writers. Perhaps the most important of these was William Shakespeare. Nine of his plays focus on the reigns of medieval kings of England: *King John*, *Richard II*, the two parts of *Henry IV*, *Henry V*, the three *Henry VI* plays, and *Richard III*. The last eight of these give a more or less continuous (if incomplete) history of England from the 1390s to 1485. Shakespeare's portraits of medieval rulers such as Henry V and Richard III have probably made a far more powerful impact on the imagination than any number of history books. Whatever academic historians may write about these two kings, they have been fixed in the public imagination by Shakespeare as the epitomes of patriotic heroism and of murderous intrigue respectively. Wholly fictional episodes, such as the one in which the rival factions in the Wars of the Roses pick roses in a garden to choose their badges, appear in twentieth-century children's history books such as L. Dugarde Peach's Ladybird histories,[19] while semi-fictional characters such as John Falstaff are more widely recognised than the various historical lords who stride across the stage of the history plays. Shakespeare dealt with several royal deaths, notably those of Prince Arthur, Richard II, Henry VI, the Princes in the Tower and Richard III, and our modern perceptions of these deaths are shaped by his treatment of them.

1

Death and Burial

In January 1066 Edward the Confessor, the last king of the ancient Anglo-Saxon dynasty of Wessex, lay dying at Westminster. His death was to plunge his kingdom into crisis and lead to its conquest by William of Normandy, one of the great turning points in English history. The circumstances of Edward's reign had helped create this crisis. Whether by choice (later tradition maintained that he had remained celibate throughout his marriage) or involuntarily, he had remained childless, leaving a disputed succession. Much of his reign had seen the ascendancy of Godwin, earl of Wessex, whose daughter Edith was married to the king. Her brother Harold Godwinsson, who succeeded Godwin as earl of Wessex, was an obvious candidate as Edward's heir.

William, duke of Normandy, also had a claim to the throne as he was related to Edward through Emma of Normandy, Edward's mother. More importantly, Edward had strong emotional ties to Normandy, where he had spent the years of his exile during the period of Danish rule in England. Finally, in a much-disputed episode, William claimed that Harold had sworn on holy relics to recognise him as Edward's successor. The Conquest of 1066 was therefore not simply a foreign invasion, it was also a succession dispute between Harold and William, arising from Edward's death. Edward himself died a peaceful death, and was interred in his own foundation of Westminster Abbey. He was later venerated as a saint, not least because his reign represented (in retrospect if not reality) a golden age of peace before the turmoil of the Conquest. Soon after his death, stories began to circulate of miracles that he had performed in life, or which were said to occur at his tomb.

On Edward's death, power passed to Harold. Nationalistic mythology has retrospectively turned Harold into the 'Last English King', slain while nobly and patriotically defending his kingdom against the foreign invader. The truth is more complex. Harold had no obviously convincing dynastic claim to the throne. He possessed no royal blood, and was connected to Edward's dynasty only by marriage. Edward's great-nephew, Edgar Atheling, had a far stronger claim by blood to the crown, but was only a boy in 1066. Harold's appeal rested on the important practical consideration that, as its most powerful nobleman and a proven war leader (he had defeated the Welsh prince Gruffudd ap Llywelyn in 1063), he possessed many of the attributes desirable in a king. The invasions in 1066 by Harald Hardrada (the king of Norway, who also hoped to make himself king) and William of Normandy can be seen as interventions by other contenders whose claims to the throne were no more tenuous than that of Harold. Norman propaganda was at pains to stress that William was the legitimate claimant, ousting an oath-breaking usurper.

Harold defeated and killed his first rival, Harald Hardrada, at the battle of Stamford Bridge in Yorkshire in September 1066. We again should be wary about viewing this battle as the 'English' king Harold patriotically defeating a foreign foe. Hardrada fought alongside Harold's disaffected brother, Tostig, and there was a long tradition, which Hardrada doubtless hoped to benefit from, of the people of the North identifying more with Viking rulers in York than with the distant southern kings of Wessex. Yorkshire formed the heart of the Danelaw – that area in the north and east of England that had been occupied and settled by the Danes – and many of its people had Scandinavian ancestry.

While he was dealing with the Norwegian invasion, Harold's other enemy, William of Normandy, landed on the south coast. Harold raced back south, but was defeated and killed by William at Hastings on 14 October. Harold's death in this battle is perhaps the most famous in English history. There is controversy still over the exact cause of his death, with some accounts saying that he was hacked down by William's knights, others that he died of an arrow wound. Recent study of the Bayeux Tapestry seems to confirm the traditional arrow-in-the-eye story. With him died his two brothers, wiping out at a stroke those who might have lived to avenge him and to cause trouble for William. His sons, seeking refuge in Ireland, continued the struggle for a while but were never a serious threat to William. There is also doubt over the site of Harold's burial, with the sources disagreeing over whether he was buried by the seashore in Sussex or taken for burial at Waltham Abbey in Essex. His dead body was mangled almost beyond recognition, creating sufficient doubt over its identity that legends developed that he had cheated death and gone to live incognito as a hermit.

The experience of the Norman Conquest demonstrates the profound political impact of a king's death. The Conquest may not have been the total, qualitative break in the course of English history that it was once made out to be; there were many aspects of continuity with Anglo-Saxon England after the Conquest in government, law and society. Nor did the verdict of Hastings lead to an overnight revolution; it took several years for William to impose his rule on the kingdom and to place his men in key positions in the church and the aristocracy. Before 1066, Norman influence had already grown in the reign of the strongly Normanised Edward the Confessor, while Danish rule from 1016–42 meant that the experience of foreign rule in England was neither a new nor necessarily a disastrous one. Nevertheless, the profound impact of the Conquest cannot be denied. By the time of the Domesday survey in 1086, there were only two Anglo-Saxon tenants-in-chief (that is, members of the highest rank of the aristocracy) remaining in the kingdom.[1] England after 1066 ceased to exist primarily within the Viking orbit around the North Sea. It became a part of the French-speaking world, which would soon come to embrace places as distant as Sicily and the Holy Land. Frankish ideas of kingship, and the influence of the church reform movement emanating from Rome, were to have a profound impact on England. This is not to deny that England had strong links with the Continent before 1066 (exemplified, for example, by the pilgrimages made to Rome by a number of Anglo-Saxon rulers), or that the penetration of continental ideas might have happened without the Conquest. Nevertheless, England in 1100 was a very different country to the England of 1065.

The death of Edward in January 1066, and that of Harold on the battlefield of Hastings, did not of course in themselves cause the Norman Conquest. But in an age when the person of the king was so important to the wellbeing of his kingdom, these two deaths certainly were critical events in the history of the Conquest. While the death of Edward did not in itself provoke the Norman invasion, his lack of a universally accepted heir was bound to create difficulties sooner or later. His death

provided the trigger for the three claimants – Harold, William, and
Harald Hardrada – to make their bids for the throne. Likewise, Harold's
death was not the sole reason for William emerging as the victor in the
contest, as the overwhelming victory at Hastings was the foundation of
his success. Given that it took him until 1070 to end resistance, it is
interesting to speculate what the outcome might have been had Harold
or even one of his brothers survived Hastings to lead an Anglo-Saxon
fight-back. In the event, no convincing candidate emerged to unify
resistance against William.

The fact that both William's rivals, Harold and Harald Hardrada, were
killed on the field of battle illustrates not only the dangers facing kings
in an age when their role as warriors was central to kingship, but also
the efficacy of battle as a brutal means of resolving dynastic conflict.
We may consider William exceptionally lucky in having both his rivals
removed in this way, one at the hand of the other at Stamford Bridge.
Contemporaries, however, ascribed this outcome not to luck but to the
judgement of God.

William the Conqueror in turn died as the result of battle, in 1087,
although in his case death came less quickly and a good deal less
cleanly. Fighting against the king of France at Mantes in the Seine valley,
his horse was frightened by a spark from a building that his forces
were burning, and he was thrown violently against the pommel of his
saddle.[2] The internal rupturing this caused led to his death at Rouen
on 9 September 1087. In a scene symbolic of the passing of worldly
glory, he was abandoned by his followers as soon as he died, and his
body greedily stripped of its finery by his attendants.[3] In a macabre
aftermath his bloated body burst upon being placed in the tomb.

The death of the Conqueror, like that of Edward the Confessor, left
a divided and disputed succession. William's problem was not, however,
a lack of sons, but the fact that three ambitious ones were competing
for the inheritance. As William had been in possession of two realms,
his inheritance was divided among his sons. This was a common practice
in such circumstances at that time; England and Normandy were considered separate polities, governed by their own laws and customs, not
a single 'empire' to be passed on entire to the eldest son, Robert
Curthose. Robert therefore succeeded William only as duke of Normandy, while the second son, William Rufus, became king of England.

Deaths and Burials of Kings of England, 1066–1485

King	Date of Death	Age at Death	Place of Death	Burial Place
Edward the Confessor	1066	60–63	Westminster	Westminster Abbey
Harold	1066	c. 46	Hastings	By the sea near Hastings, or at Waltham Abbey
William I	1087	59?	St-Gervais Priory, near Rouen, Normandy	Caen Abbey
William II	1100	40–44	New Forest	Winchester Cathedral
Henry I	1135	67	Lyons-la-Foret, near Rouen, Normandy	Reading Abbey
Stephen	1154	>54	St Martin's Priory, Dover	Faversham Abbey
Henry II	1189	56	Chinon Castle, Touraine	Fontevrault Abbey
Richard I	1199	41	Châlus-Chabrol, Limousin	Fontevrault Abbey
John	1216	48	Newark Castle	Worcester Cathedral
Henry III	1272	65	Palace of Westminster	Westminster Abbey
Edward I	1307	68	Burgh-by-Sands, Cumberland	Westminster Abbey
Edward II	1327	43	Berkeley Castle, Gloucestershire (probable)	Gloucester Abbey (now Cathedral)
Edward III	1377	64	Sheen Palace, Surrey	Westminster Abbey
Richard II	1400	32–33	Pontefract Castle, Yorkshire (probable)	Langley Abbey, translated to Westminster Abbey, 1413
Henry IV	1413	46	Palace of Westminster	Canterbury Cathedral
Henry V	1422	34	Vincennes Castle, Ile-de-France	Westminster Abbey
Henry VI	1471	49	Tower of London	Chertsey Abbey, translated to St George's Chapel, Windsor, 1484
Edward IV	1483	40	Palace of Westminster	St George's Chapel, Windsor

King	Date of Death	Age at Death	Place of Death	Burial Place
Edward V	1483	12	Tower of London (probable)	Unknown*
Richard III	1485	32	Bosworth, Leicestershire	Greyfriars Church, Leicester

* Body may be one of two skeletons discovered in Tower of London in seventeenth century and reburied in Westminster Abbey

A third son, Henry, was also ambitious for his share of the inheritance. Robert's absence on the First Crusade (1096–99) allowed William to occupy Normandy too – quite legally, as Robert had leased it to him in order to obtain funds for his crusade.

Rufus's death in the New Forest on 2 August 1100 upset these arrangements. His was perhaps the most dramatic death of the middle ages, as the king was fatally shot with an arrow in a hunting accident.[4] Rufus's clashes with the church, and reputation for anticlericalism, provided ample fodder for the chroniclers to portray the death as an act of God. In modern times, the circumstances of his death have led to conspiracy theories, arguing that he was murdered, or even that he was killed as a human sacrifice.[5] The Conqueror's third son, Henry, became king on Rufus's death, aided considerably by the fact that he was part of Rufus's hunting party at the time, while Robert was still returning from the Holy Land. This fortunate timing for Henry, and his presence near the scene of the crime (if such it was), has added fuel to the theories that Rufus was murdered. Even if we accept that the death was accidental, it illustrates how an unexpected death, and the timing of that death, could have profound political consequences. Secure in his rule of England, Henry later defeated Robert at the battle of Tinchebray in 1106 to add Normandy to his domains. Had William lived, England and Normandy might have gone their separate ways, giving medieval England a very different history.

Henry I's own dynastic ambitions were dashed by death in 1120, when his only legitimate son William Atheling was drowned in the White Ship.[6] This tragedy was to have serious consequences. Henry's own death by natural causes (some kind of gastric complaint brought on by the

famous 'surfeit of lampreys'), on 11 December 1135, ushered in a period
of political instability, traditionally (and inaccurately) termed the Anarchy.[7] This was the reign of his successor Stephen of Blois (1135–54).
The death of William Atheling had left Henry's daughter Matilda (Maud)
as Henry's sole legitimate offspring. Despite her acceptance as heir by
the English barons in 1127, it was her cousin Stephen (another grandson
of the Conqueror through his mother Adela) who gained the throne in
1135, exploiting baronial doubts over the suitability of a female ruler, one
who, moreover, was married to the count of Anjou, a traditional enemy
of Normandy. The subsequent civil war between Stephen and Matilda
ultimately ended in compromise, as it was agreed that Stephen should
retain the throne until his death, when he would be succeeded by
Matilda's son Henry of Anjou (later King Henry II). The succession was
smoothed by the fortuitous and, according to contemporaries, providential sudden death of Stephen's eldest son Eustace in 1153, struck down,
it was said, for violating the shrine of St Edmund. For his part, Stephen
died a natural death even though he had suffered such a disturbed reign.
The chroniclers had little to say in the way of moralising commentaries
on his death,[8] which took place at Dover on 25 October 1154, as a result
of a violent seizure of the bowels. Indeed, he is credited with an exemplary
death, receiving the sacraments.[9] He was buried at his favoured abbey
of Faversham in Kent, alongside his queen, Matilda of Boulogne.

Henry II's rapid restoration of a stable regime on his accession
demonstrates the fallacy of the idea that Stephen had presided over a
state of anarchy. Through inheritance, the military actions of himself
and his parents, and marriage to Eleanor of Aquitaine (the heiress to a
duchy comprising about one third of the land area of the kingdom of
France), Henry built up a vast but disunified 'empire' stretching from
the Pyrenees to the Cheviots. The later years of his reign were troubled,
not least by the rebellious behaviour of his sons. Like William the
Conqueror before him, Henry tried to satisfy their ambitions by parti-
tioning his inheritance. His eldest son, Henry, was to receive the paternal
inheritance of England, Normandy, and Anjou. His second son Richard,
was made count of Poitiers and was to inherit his mother's duchy of
Aquitaine, while the third son, Geoffrey, became count of Brittany by
marriage. The fourth son, John 'Lackland', was to inherit nothing of
consequence.

The problems inherent in these arrangement soon showed themselves. The younger Henry was crowned king in his father's own lifetime in 1170, a practice that was unusual in England but not uncommon on the Continent. Henry II failed, however, to match the younger Henry's title with a significant share of power, provoking him into rebellion in 1173–74, and again in 1183. As in 1100, however, death intervened to simplify the inheritance and to maintain the unity of the king of England's lands. The young Henry died in south-west France in the course of his second rebellion, never to become king in fact as he was in name. The death of Geoffrey in 1186 left Richard as heir to the whole of his father's domains. Henry II himself died at his castle of Chinon in Touraine, on 6 July 1189, facing a rebellion by his surviving sons Richard and John. Several chroniclers presented his death as a poor reflection on the behaviour of his sons, and one claimed that the king's dead body bled in protest at being approached by his faithless son Richard. It was this same Richard, Henry's eldest surviving son, who succeeded him as king of England and sole ruler of the vast Plantagenet domains in France.

After this inauspicious start to his reign, Richard I went on to become the crusading hero known as Richard Coeur de Lion or Richard the Lionheart. As befitted a warrior king, he died of a wound received in action, but not while fighting the infidel. While besieging the castle of a rebel vassal at Châlus-Chabrol in the Limousin, he was struck by an arrow fired by one of the defending garrison, and died of septicaemia some days later on 8 April 1199.[10] The ironic nature of his end, killed by a common soldier while fighting in an obscure action, received much comment from contemporaries.

He was succeeded by his brother John, much of whose reign was characterised by military defeat and domestic discord. Although Richard's death, childless, left John as the sole remaining son of Henry II, he did not enjoy an undisputed succession. His nephew, Arthur, count of Brittany, the son of Geoffrey Plantagenet, was now nearing adulthood, and his supporters, in alliance with the king of France, Philip II, made trouble for John in the north-west of France until 1202, when Arthur was captured, and then subsequently murdered. Although John weathered this storm, it was the first of several occasions on which the king of France was to cause him trouble. Philip conquered Normandy in 1204, the first of a number of setbacks that led to the virtual extinction of the Angevin Empire in France during the reign of John and that of his son.

John died campaigning in the east of England in the course of a civil war against rebel barons. It was an ignominious end; having recently lost much of his baggage train while crossing the Wash, John died of dysentery at Newark in 18 October 1216.[11] Like William Rufus, John was seen by clerical writers as an oppressor of the church, and his death was viewed by most of them as a fittingly providential end. A later tradition, promoted by the sixteenth-century playwright John Bale, had it that he was murdered by the monks with whom he was staying, making him an early martyr for royal authority against the power of the Catholic Church, and therefore a suitable predecessor of the Protestant Tudor monarchs.

John's death handed his son, Henry III, a difficult legacy. Henry succeeded, at the age of just nine, to a realm that was in the throes of civil war. The dangers of a minority were rightly feared in the middle ages, when political stability was so dependent on the abilities of the king. This was therefore another instance where the timing of a royal death had political consequences. John can scarcely be blamed for dying when he did, but the timing of his marriage to Henry's mother, Isabella of Angoulême, when he was already thirty-two but she was only twelve, meant that there was always a chance that John would not have an adult heir by the time he died. A king could not of course choose the time of his own death, but he did have a duty to try to produce an heir as early as possible. John and his brother Richard both failed in this respect.

Henry III's partisans restored royal power by 1217, but an even greater challenge to his authority occurred in the later part of his reign, with the baronial reform movement of 1258–64, and the subsequent civil war of 1264–65 against the partisans of Simon de Montfort, earl of Leicester, the leader of the reformists. For a time, England was a republic in all but name, ruled by a council of leading nobles and clerics, with de Montfort emerging as the republic's Cromwell, and Henry a captive in Earl Simon's train. The defeat and death of de Montfort at Evesham in 1265 restored royal authority, but created a popular cult of Earl Simon as a martyr. Henry died at Westminster on 16 November 1272, and was buried in the abbey there, which he had been responsible for rebuilding.

Westminster Abbey was the foundation of Edward the Confessor, England's royal saint, whose cult Henry had vigorously promoted.

Henry owed the restoration of his power largely to his son, Edward, the victor of Evesham. As Edward I, the latter spent much of his reign at war with the Welsh, the Scots and the king of France. His later reputation as the 'Hammer of the Scots' reflects his bellicosity but exaggerates his success. He died on 7 July 1307, heading north on another expedition to attempt to subdue Scotland, which, after a deceptively easy conquest in 1296, had proved a troublesome country to hold down. He had been stricken by illness the previous summer, and on the 1307 expedition he was troubled with dysentery and suffered pain in his legs and neck. These ailments necessitated the despatch of a number of exotic medicines to the king at Lanercost Priory in Cumberland. He rode out of Carlisle on 3 July, but died on the 7th at Burgh-by-Sands, a few miles short of the Scottish border, in the arms of the servants who raised him from his bed. There are colourful stories surrounding Edward's wishes for his body after death, as he is said to have requested that his heart be embalmed and buried in the Holy Land, and that his bones be carried into battle against the Scots.

Contemporary sources make it clear that Edward was concerned with the political arrangements following his death. He entrusted the welfare of his son, the prince of Wales and future Edward II, to the earls of Lincoln and Warwick, asking them also to prevent the return of Piers Gaveston.[12] This young man, whom Edward I had banished, was the favourite and probably the lover of the prince, and his influence was to have a baleful affect on the political stability of England in the early part of Edward II's reign. An element of hindsight may therefore be at work in the chronicler's accounts of the older Edward's careful arrangements. Edward, prince of Wales, was twenty-three in 1307, hardly a minor needing the supervision of adults.

Edward II's misrule ultimately led to his deposition in 1326–27 by his queen, Isabella of France, and her lover, Roger Mortimer, and to his subsequent murder at Berkeley Castle, probably in February 1327. The nature of his death in the secrecy of imprisonment makes the exact circumstances of his murder impossible to determine, but it led to colourful stories circulating as to how he died. The most famous of these was that he was killed by having a red-hot iron thrust into his bowels through the anus, so that no external wounds would be visible to show that he had been murdered.[13] This mode of death may also have been a comment upon his probable homosexuality. There were also rumours that he had escaped and gone to live obscurely in exile, while others, believing him to have been martyred, revered him as a saint.

This was the first time since before the Conquest that a king of England had been murdered. That it did not have a more serious impact on the stability of the kingdom was in part down to the fact that the crown passed to his eldest son, Edward III, so no succession crisis or dynastic dislocation occurred. After a three-year period in which Isabella and Mortimer held effective power in his name, Edward III seized personal power in 1330. He spent much of his reign engaged in warfare, after proclaiming himself king of France in 1337 (a title he claimed through his French mother). In contrast to his active early life, his last years and death were an anticlimax. He seems to have suffered from senility in his later years, and was criticised for allowing himself to be manipulated by his mistress, Alice Perrers. At his death, at Sheen on 21 June 1377, it was claimed that Perrers greedily stripped the rings from his fingers, after he was abandoned by his courtiers.[14]

Edward III, his eldest son, Edward, Prince of Wales (the 'Black Prince') having died the previous year, was succeeded by his grandson Richard II. The new king was only ten years old at the time of his accession. His reign was a troubled one. Having faced down the Peasants' Revolt of 1381, the adult Richard was confronted with a series of challenges from the nobility, who were alienated by his autocratic tendencies and his overreliance on favourite advisers. He successfully overturned the restrictions that were imposed on him by reformist Appellant lords in the 1388, but was overthrown in 1399 when he made the mistake of alienating his most powerful subject, his cousin Henry of Bolingbroke, duke of Lancaster, first by exiling him and then by confiscating his inheritance on his father John of Gaunt's death. Henry invaded, claiming at first to be merely reclaiming his inheritance, but going on to declare himself king, as Henry IV. Richard, whose arbitrary rule had led to comparisons being made between him and Edward II, suffered a similar fate to his great-grandfather. After his deposition, he was confined in Pontefract Castle, and died, presumably murdered, in the early months of 1400. Richard was never venerated as a saint in the manner of Edward II, whose canonisation he had unsuccessfully promoted, but like Edward there were rumours of his survival, and one adventurer even claimed to be Richard.

Richard's deposition had more far-reaching effects than that of Edward II, as it gave rise to a disputed succession, though the full effects of this were not felt immediately. Henry of Bolingbroke's claim to the throne was problematic as, even with Richard dead, there were others who arguably possessed a stronger title. He faced a number of revolts in the first decade of his reign, one of which led to the creation of a 'martyr', when Henry had Richard Scrope, archbishop of York, executed in 1405. Hostile commentators claimed that Henry's long fatal illness began on this date. He died of a slow wasting disease (possibly diabetes) described by some as 'leprosy', which his critics took to be proof of his moral degeneracy.[15] He breathed his last on 20 March 1413, at the royal palace of Westminster. Adam of Usk, a chronicler with a penchant for portents and omens, recorded that he died in the 'Jerusalem Chamber' of the abbot's residence at Westminster, 'whereby he fulfilled his horoscope that he would die in the Holy Land'.[16] The handover of power from Henry IV's reign to that of his son, Henry V, was a difficult one, and is often remembered via Shakespeare's *Henry IV Part 2* for the incident in which the younger Henry put on his father's crown before the latter had died. This incident, however, derives from a later Burgundian source, the chronicler Enguerrand de Monstrelet, and would appear to be a legend illustrating Prince Henry's ambitions in hindsight.[17] Whatever tensions there were between father and son, Henry IV had founded a dynasty, known to history as the Lancastrians.

Henry V, after facing rebellions early in his reign, helped legitimise his position by success in war. He resumed Edward III's struggle for the French crown, with great success; it was hard to portray the glorious victor of Agincourt as a usurper. Such was Henry's success that he came close to achieving Edward III's dream of gaining the French crown. The treaty of Troyes of 1420, concluded with the ruling faction around the French king, Charles VI, recognised Henry (or his successors) as the heir after Charles's death. Ironically, Henry's own death occurred just a few months before that of the French king, on 13 August 1422. His aim to establish a dual monarchy of England and France was frustrated by the youth of his heir (Henry VI), who was only nine months old at his accession, and the fact that the treaty of Troyes had been concluded with only a faction within France. Charles VI's son, the Dauphin, disinherited by the treaty, was proclaimed King Charles VII by his supporters and fought on, to an ultimately successful conclusion.

Henry V's death therefore came at a crucial, and in view of the subsequent collapse of his ambitions, poignant time. There was also irony in his manner of death: the great warrior king died on campaign, but not in the heat of battle. During the siege of Meaux in the Ile-de-France, the English camp was struck by an outbreak of dysentery (infectious disease was always a deadly menace in medieval sieges, for the attackers in the close confines of their encampment as much as for the defenders holed up in the town). The king himself contracted the disease, from which he died on 30 August. Henry's body was already weakened from years of campaigning; according to Thomas Walsingham, he had suffered from an 'old distemper, which he had contracted from excessive and long-continued exertion [and] fell into an acute fever with violent dysentery'.[18] The *Brut*, a London chronicle, credited him with making a good death, making arrangements in his will for the government of England and France, and for the education of his son and heir.[19]

As with the death of John, Henry's premature death left a minor as king. In this case, the danger was potentially even greater as his son, Henry, was only nine months old, leaving the prospect of a very long minority. However, compared to the young Henry III in 1216, the infant Henry VI enjoyed many advantages; where Henry III had inherited a kingdom in the throes of civil war, with French forces on its soil, his namesake became king of an England which was united, and which was fighting a successful war against the French on their territory. Two adult uncles and a council were on hand to guide the kingdom and its young king, and a respected nobleman, the earl of Warwick, had been appointed his tutor. The government during the minority was not without its problems, particularly the conflict between the council and the king's uncle, Humphrey, duke of Gloucester, but by and large it worked. In the event, the problem of the child-king's long minority proved to be the least of the country's ills. As an adult, Henry showed himself to be an incompetent ruler. To make matters worse, from 1453 onwards he suffered bouts of severe mental illness that rendered him incapable of governing. A tendency to mental illness may have been inherited from his grandfather, Charles VI of France. If so, this was an irony, as the marriage of Henry V to Charles's daughter had been a great political coup, intended to cement the unity of the French and English crowns. The crisis caused by Henry's illness, and by his factional favouritism when lucid, added to recriminations over the loss of the last English possessions in France, and led to civil war in the 1450s (the beginning of the so-called Wars of the Roses).

Later historians, particularly those writing in the Tudor period after peace had been restored, interpreted these wars as divine retribution on the kingdom for the murder of Richard II. This interpretation was taken up by Shakespeare, and his dramatisation of the conflict has been more influential in shaping popular perceptions of this period than has the actual history.[20] Today, we do not see history as the unfolding of the divine will, but the idea that the Wars of the Roses were a long-term result of the murder of Richard II is not without its merits. Although the wars were not purely dynastic, embracing as they did arguments over the nature of government, clashes between different interest groups and local feuds, the rival claims of the houses of Lancaster and York enabled the conflict to become one that made and unmade kings. By laying claim to the throne in 1460, Richard, duke of York, was reopening the unfinished dynastic business of 1399–1400. He was a descendant of the third son of Edward III, whereas the Lancastrians could claim descent only from the fourth son, Henry IV's father John of Gaunt. The deposition and murder of Richard II therefore cast a long shadow over Henry's Lancastrian dynasty.

At first, the faction led by the duke of York claimed to be fighting only against the king's evil advisers, but an attempt by York to seize the throne in 1460 showed that the war was beginning to threaten Henry's throne. The following year, York's son, Edward, earl of March, seized power and deposed Henry, to become King Edward IV. Henry spent the next decade as a fugitive in the north of England and in Scotland, and then as Edward's prisoner. A failed attempt to restore him led to his murder in the Tower on 22 May 1471, almost certainly on the orders of Edward IV, and possibly at the hands of Edward's brother Richard, duke of Gloucester. Like his ancestor Edward II, Henry became the focus for an incipient martyr-cult on account of his murder.

Edward IV himself was the only English king to die a peaceful death in the second half of the fifteenth century. After the murder of Henry VI had removed the threat of domestic strife, Edward was able to enjoy twelve years of peace. And enjoy it he did, gaining a reputation as a womaniser and carouser. This lifestyle was widely blamed for his early death, at the age of only forty-two. He became increasingly fat in his later years, was accused of gluttony and of having an insatiable sexual appetite. He died on 9 April 1483 after being seized by an unidentifiable sickness, described by some sources as a quartan fever.[21]

Edward's premature death set the scene for probably the most controversial event in the history of medieval England, the murder of the 'Princes in the Tower'. These were Edward's two sons, Edward, prince of Wales, and Richard, duke of York, who were only twelve and ten years old respectively at the time of their father's death. Arrangements therefore needed to be made for the government of the kingdom during the young Edward V's minority. His uncle, Richard, duke of Gloucester, seized the opportunity to make himself Protector, mainly by exploiting the unpopularity of the family of the young king's mother, Elizabeth Woodville, who were seen by the nobility as grasping *parvenus*. Having made himself king in all but name, Richard then set about seizing the crown for himself. He was able to disinherit Edward and his brother on the spurious grounds of their illegitimacy. After this coup, the princes were confined to the Tower of London, where they disappeared. Their fate seems to have mirrored that of their predecessors Richard II and Edward II, who were first deposed, then kept under close confinement, then murdered. In contrast to that of their forebears, the fate of the princes was never revealed, and their bodies were never given a funeral, creating controversy and uncertainty that has lasted to this day, when the guilt (or otherwise) of Richard III in the death of his nephews is still hotly debated. The truth will never be known, but most historians agree that the balance of probabilities overwhelmingly suggests that Richard had them murdered.

Richard himself died violently in 1485, killed on the battlefield of Bosworth, a fate that was presented by hostile contemporaries as a suitable punishment for his killing of his nephews.[22] The victor of the battle, Henry Tudor, who became Henry VII, presented Richard's death as an example of divine favour, and himself as the avenger of the murdered princes, a picture that shaped Shakespeare's portrayal of Richard as a scheming murderer and tyrant. The ambiguity over the fate of the princes dogged Henry in turn, as he was faced by the impostor Perkin Warbeck, who claimed to be the missing Richard, duke of York, as well as by another royal impostor, Lambert Simnel, claiming to be a nephew of Edward IV.

This brief survey suggests how dangerous it was to be a king in medieval England. Of the twenty kings whose deaths are covered in this book, nine died violent deaths (if we include William I, who died in the course of military action, even though he was not struck down directly by the enemy), of whom four (Edward II, Richard II, Henry VI and Edward V) were murdered, and two (Harold and Richard III) were killed in battle against rival claimants to the throne. Only the death of William II was an accident, although even this has been disputed by those who believe he was murdered to the benefit of Henry I. Richard I died fighting his enemies in southern France, so his death was no reflection on the political situation in England, although it did result from the problems the Angevin rulers were faced with when trying to impose their rule on their vast dominions in France.

The length of their reigns reflects this dangerous life. Between the death of Edward the Confessor in 1066 and that of Richard III in 1485, nineteen kings reigned for a total of 419 years, giving us an average reign of about twenty-two years. This is a respectable length for a reign, given the shorter life expectancy of medieval people. Two kings, Henry III and Edward III, enjoyed reigns of fifty years or more, although both these kings came to the throne as minors, the latter after the murder of his father, so they cannot necessarily be held up as examples of royal longevity. Nevertheless, a number of other kings enjoyed long reigns after ascending the throne as adults: thirty-five years for Henry I; thirty-five for his grandson Henry II; and thirty-five years again for Edward I.

If we break down the period into two roughly equal halves, a rather different picture emerges. Between January 1066 and 1272 ten kings died, four violently, but none of them was murdered. Only Harold died by enemy action in a battle for the throne. This period covers nine reigns, with an average length of nearly twenty-three years. The second half, from 1272 to 1485, encompasses ten reigns, with an average length of about twenty-one years. This period saw four royal murders, and the overthrow and death of Richard III in battle. Looking at the dates from another perspective, we are given an even clearer picture that the twelfth and thirteenth centuries were relatively stable, while the fourteenth and fifteenth centuries were much more dangerous for kings. The period from the coronation of William the Conqueror to the death of Edward I in 1307 saw nine reigns with an average length of over twenty-six years. From 1307 to the Battle of Bosworth in 1485, a further nine reigns had an average length of less than twenty years – and this in a period that includes the fifty-year reign of Edward III.

A comparison with the kingdom of France in the same period is instructive. Every medieval kingdom developed along its own trajectory, but in many ways the kings of France were faced with similar problems to their English counterparts. France too had its conflicts, notably the Hundred Years War with England, which lasted on and off from 1337 to 1453. Some periods of this conflict were also characterised by civil war and social conflict, and the French kings suffered many vicissitudes. John II was captured by the English in 1356, and Charles VI (reigned 1380–1422) suffered bouts of insanity, like his tragic grandson Henry VI of England. Yet no French king died by violence in this period.

A comparison of the length of their reigns also suggests that the French monarchy enjoyed greater stability. Between 1060 and 1483, eighteen kings ruled France, with an average reign of twenty-three and a half years, a figure comparable to, indeed slightly longer than, that of their English counterparts. If we compare the figures for kings in the later part of the period, we see a marked contrast. Only six kings reigned in the period 1328–1483 (giving an average reign of twenty-six years), despite the fact that this was an era of war and social upheaval (as was also the case in England). The pattern of long reigns also characterised later periods of French history; between the accession of Henry IV in 1589 and the overthrow of Louis XVI in 1792, five kings reigned for 203 years, an average reign of over forty years.

There is no single obvious reason why French kings fared better than their English counterparts. They, too, were faced with noble opposition and civil war. Indeed, in some ways the English kings were in a better position, as the Anglo-Norman rulers inherited a relatively strong and centralised state from their Anglo-Saxon predecessors. The French kings of the eleventh and twelfth centuries had to fight hard to establish themselves against the virtually independent rulers of the great feudal lordships that comprised the kingdom of France (of which the king of England, in his capacity as duke of Normandy, and later count of Anjou and duke of Aquitaine, was one). The English kings were also able to do most of their fighting against foreign foes overseas, whereas France faced the threat of English invasion in the fourteenth and fifteenth centuries.

To some extent, the kings of France simply enjoyed better fortune. The only major point of dynastic discontinuity for the medieval French monarchy came in 1328, when the failure of the offspring of Philip IV (reigned 1285–1314) to produce a male heir brought about a succession crisis which led to Philip VI establishing the Valois dynasty. The conflict over the succession gave Edward III, a grandson of Philip IV through his mother, the opportunity to stake his claim to the French crown in 1337, a claim which was the theoretical cause of (or at least the pretext for) the Hundred Years War. With this important exception, however, both the Valois and the Capetians who preceded them generally enjoyed a smooth succession, with fathers replaced as king by their eldest surviving son. There was little opportunity for the sort of succession conflicts which provoked the civil wars of Stephen's reign or the Wars of the Roses in England. When crises did occur, such as the minority of Louis IX (1226–34), which provided the opportunity for a serious aristocratic revolt, and the madness of Charles VI, the French monarchy proved strong enough to withstand them.

In an age when the personal qualities of a monarch were important, the survival of a king might come down to the abilities or personalities of individuals. For example, the undiplomatic personalities of Edward II and Richard II contributed to their downfall and murder by provoking aristocratic opposition. In contrast, French rulers such as Louis IX and Philip IV were able to build a strong monarchy without provoking dangerous opposition from the nobility. Likewise the madness of Charles VI in France ultimately had a different impact to that of Henry VI in England, although in both cases the short-term result was civil war. Whereas in England this led to dynastic conflict and the resulting murder of two kings, in France the abilities of Charles VI's successor,

Charles VII, helped France to restore royal authority. Charles VII was no doubt aided by the fact that his rival claimants for the throne, the Lancastrian kings of England, were foreign invaders, allowing him to take advantage of the nascent national sentiment embodied by Joan of Arc.

A comparison with other European dynasties shows the English kings in a more fortunate light. In Germany (or, to be more precise, the Holy Roman Empire), the period 1060 to 1493 saw twenty-one kings or emperors rule Germany over 414 years (excluding an interregnum of nineteen years in the thirteenth century), giving an average reign of a little less than nineteen years. In Sicily, between 1060 and 1285 (after which the kingdom was divided into two separate states), there were thirteen rulers, with an average reign of seventeen years. In both these realms, there was often bitter conflict over the crown in this period, going some way to explaining the short life expectancy of kings. In both Germany and Sicily, the ambitions of the papacy and of foreign powers contributed to the instability. The conflict between the papacy and the secular power in Germany led to the frequent deposition (either formally or in fact) of emperors by the pope, often accompanied by the encouragement of internal opposition. Although these events created great instability, they rarely led to the death of kings or emperors up to the middle of the thirteenth century. Perhaps the most famous death of a medieval German emperor was that of Frederick I Barbarossa in 1190, when he drowned while crossing a river in Syria on the Third Crusade. He therefore died serving the highest cause in the eyes of a medieval Christian, something that no English king was able to do.

A rather different picture emerges after the death of Frederick II in 1250. From this point on, the imperial authority was weak and the empire beset by conflict over an increasingly meaningless imperial title. A period of instability at the turn of the fourteenth century saw the deposition and death in battle of Adolf of Nassau in 1298, and the murder of Albrecht of Habsburg in 1308. As in England, the later middle ages were a more turbulent time, leading to the death of kings.

The medieval kingdom of Sicily was in many ways linked to the politics of the empire, especially after 1194 when the German emperor Henry VI acceded to the crown of Sicily through marriage to its heiress. The papacy was determined not to have both the empire (which theoretically controlled the north of Italy) and the kingdom of Sicily (which covered the whole of the south) ruled by the same dynasty. Papal encouragement of rivals to Henry's Hohenstaufen dynasty made Sicily a bone of contention between rival powers (including England) in the thirteenth century. The papacy claimed overlordship of the kingdom, and with it the legal right to appoint or depose its rulers. The German Hohenstaufen kings were eventually ousted by the French duke Charles of Anjou in 1266–68, leading to the execution of the last Hohenstaufen claimant, Conradin, in 1268. Conradin had himself been deposed as a child by his half-brother Manfred in 1258, an indication of the dynastic instability of the kingdom. Despite these events, there is still no parallel to late medieval England's record of four kings deposed and murdered in less than two hundred years. It seems that while England was not a particularly unstable kingdom, it was unusual in the number of violent deaths its kings suffered.

In this area, England most closely resembled its northern neighbour Scotland, which if anything was an even more dangerous country of which to be king. The kings of Scotland were faced with a factious nobility over which they were never entirely able to impose their authority, and frequent conflict with their more powerful southern neighbours. The story of how the early medieval Scottish kings met their ends is a violent and bloody one, especially in the years between 1040 and 1094. The period 1040–94 was particularly bloody: Duncan I was killed in 1040 fighting the usurper MacBeth; MacBeth was killed in turn in the aftermath of battle in 1057, and his stepson Lulach killed in an ambush the following year; Malcolm III Canmore, who overthrew MacBeth, was killed while invading England in 1093, to be succeeded by his brother Donald III, who was deposed and blinded by Malcolm's sons, one of whom, Duncan III, was briefly able to make himself king in 1094, before being killed by Donald. With the exception of Alexander III, who died in a riding accident in 1286, no more Scottish kings died a violent death until the fifteenth century, when a series of Stewart monarchs met unfortunate ends. James I was murdered by opponents from the nobility in 1437, while his son James II was blown up by his own cannon at the siege of Roxburgh castle in 1460. James III was murdered by his Scottish enemies in the aftermath of the battle of Sauchieburn in 1488, and James IV died fighting the English at the battle of Flodden in 1513. In a macabre aftermath,

James's embalmed body was taken to England and kept in the monastery of Sheen, where his head was removed and used as a football by workmen.

The figures for the reigns of Scottish kings suggest that there is no necessary corollary between the length of reign and the violent death of a king. The period 1058 to 1488 in Scotland saw twenty monarchs reigning for 418 years (excluding two interregna, that of 1290–92, when there was a disputed succession, and that of 1296–1306, when Edward I conquered the country). This gives us an average reign of nearly twenty-two years, comparable to, and in some cases better than, that in other kingdoms. Even including the disturbed years 1040–58, the average comes out at nearly twenty years. To demonstrate the fact that violent death and long reigns were not incompatible, the first four Jameses, all of whom died by violence, managed reigns with an average length of twenty-seven years. This was in large part because the premature death of their predecessors meant that they became king at an early age. Although royal minorities did not make for political stability, they might result in long reigns if the king survived to come of age. In England, the half-century reigns of Henry III and Edward III are examples of a similar situation, while even the disastrous reign of Henry VI lasted thirty-nine years (forty-nine if we include the ten years between his first deposition in 1461 and his second, final and fatal overthrow in 1471). In post-medieval Scotland, the fifty-eight-year reign of James VI (1567–1625) began with the deposition of his mother Mary when he was only a year old.

The average length of English royal reigns in the period 1066–1485 does not differ dramatically from that for post-medieval monarchs. The risk of a ruler dying by violence was reduced after the middle ages, as kings were less likely to be war leaders (George II was the last British king to lead his troops into battle, at Dettingen in 1743). As their real political power declined, they were also less likely to become victims of political turmoil. The obvious exception to this was Charles I, executed in 1649. If we exclude Jane Grey, whose brief 'reign' in 1553 led to her execution by Mary I, no other post-medieval monarch died by violence. Even James II, who was overthrown in the Glorious Revolution of 1688, was able to flee into exile. The nearest to a violent royal death after 1649 was that of William III, who died in 1702 after being thrown from his horse when it stumbled over a molehill, and Frederick, prince of Wales (the eldest son of George II), felled by a cricket ball in 1751. These deaths neatly encapsulate how monarchy had become a far less militarised and more sedentary affair after the middle ages. Despite the relative safety enjoyed by later monarchs, they have not enjoyed noticeably longer reigns. Twenty-one kings and queens on the throne since 1485 have reigned with an average length of less than twenty years, excluding the eleven years of the English Republic (1649–60), and counting the present queen's reign at fifty years.

Moving in the other chronological direction, we can compare the reigns of the kings of the high middle ages with those of their Saxon and Danish predecessors. It is difficult to pinpoint a time when a 'kingdom of England' first appears, but if we start with Athelstan (arguably the first Anglo-Saxon king to exert effective authority over the whole of 'England'), thirteen kings ruled England between 924 and 1066. This does provide us with a real contrast with later kings, as we find an average reign of only eleven years. This was a disturbed period in English history, which saw Danish invasions, succession disputes, and wars to unify England (or, from a northern perspective, wars of conquest by the Wessex monarchy against the neighbouring kingdoms). The period saw a king killed by a robber (Edmund the Elder in 946), one the victim of a political murder (Edward the Martyr in 978), and another killed on the field of battle (Harold).

Violent death, however, was not in itself the reason for such short reigns, as a number of kings not killed by human agency had reigns of less than ten years' length: Edmund the Elder (939–46), Edred (946–55), Edwy (955–59), Edward the Elder (975–78), Edmund Ironside (April-November 1016), Harald Harefoot (1035–40) and Harthacnut (1040–42). The short life-expectancy of these early kings of England may be attributable to other factors, such as disease (a number of the Wessex line of kings died young, pointing perhaps to some hereditary ailment), or simply accidental reasons (Harthacnut is said by the Anglo-Saxon Chronicle to have died of convulsions after overindulging in drink).[23] Whatever the reason for these short reigns, a picture emerges of a time when it was more dangerous to be a king of England than was to be the case in later centuries. It must be remembered, however, that for the Anglo-Saxon and Danish kings we are using a shorter time period and a smaller sample, so the short figure for the average length of a reign may not be statistically significant. We should also beware, when attempting to analyse historical data, of being selective in the time periods we choose. If we were to begin our list of Saxon kings with Alfred the Great (reigned 871–99), and end it with the death of Edward the Confessor (thereby conveniently discounting the short reign of Harold Godwinsson, who was not of the direct royal line), we would arrive at a figure of fourteen kings in 195 years, with an average reign of a somewhat healthier fourteen years.

To summarise, we can say that the high middle ages were not an exceptionally bad time to be king, nor England an exceptionally difficult country of which to be a ruler, if we judge by the length of the rulers' reigns. It would seem, by comparing these across time and across different kingdoms, that a reign of about twenty years was fairly typical for any monarch. Whatever changes time and circumstance may render to the nature and rate of human mortality, the length of a biological human generation was broadly the same, and an hereditary office such as kingship, over time, reflects this. Perhaps of greater significance is the number of medieval kings of England who died by violence. Here we see a marked difference to some (but not all) European monarchies. In comparison to later periods, the middle ages were a violent time for the kings of England.

A list of the places of death of the medieval kings of England is an interesting mirror of their activities and the geographical spread of their rule. After the Conquest, several 'English' kings died in France, an indication of the fact that the centre of their power lay in Normandy or Anjou rather than England. Of the first six after the Conquest, William II 'Rufus' and Stephen were the only two kings to die in England, and both of these were rulers of England only (Rufus's brother Robert Curthose was the duke of Normandy, while by the end of Stephen's reign Normandy had been lost to Geoffrey of Anjou). William I and Richard I died defending their French possessions, on the eastern border of Normandy and in the Limousin respectively. Henry I and Henry II both died in the heart of their French lands, the former at Rouen in Normandy, the latter at Chinon in the Touraine, in the heartland of the Plantagenet possessions. Subsequently, all medieval English kings died (or were killed) in England, with the significant exception of Henry V, who died while on campaign in France. This pattern reflects the changed nature of the English king's power, as the loss of Normandy, Anjou and Poitou in the early thirteenth century deprived them of most of their French lands.

A survey of places of death within England reveals that kings usually died in royal residences, especially in the later middle ages when government had become more settled, and royal authority was less itinerant. Four medieval kings died in royal palaces in the south east of England; Henry III, Henry IV and Edward IV at Westminster, and Edward III at Sheen in Surrey. Henry VI and Edward V also died in a royal palace, the Tower of London, but for the more sinister reason that this had become the prison in which they were murdered. The same applies for Edward II and Richard II, imprisoned and killed in the strongholds of Berkeley and Pontefract.

Some locations of royal death, away from London or its environs, were the result of military necessity, leaving aside the obviously military circumstances of Richard III's death in battle at Bosworth. John died at Newark in the course of his campaign against rebel barons in the north. Edward I's presence at Burgh-by-Sands in Cumberland is explained by the fact that he was heading north on an expedition against the Scots. As we have seen, some of those kings who died in France were engaged in military action that took them away from England (in the case of Henry V), or at least from their ancestral lands in northern France (Richard I).

The sites of royal death can be divided into secular and sacred places. It was deemed important to die a 'good death', an idea particularly emphasised in the late medieval *ars moriendi* literary genre, which set out the desired circumstances and state of mind in which a dying person should meet their maker. In these circumstances, it might be expected that kings would choose to end their days in religious houses, among the relics of saints whose prayers, it was hoped, would speed their soul through purgatory. In reality, the political responsibilities of kings prevented them from entering religious orders towards the end of their lives (an option often taken up by widowed queens, who had few governmental or military obligations). We therefore see secular places of death predominating. William the Conqueror, fatally wounded at Mantes, had the time and opportunity to have himself taken to the priory of St-Gervais near Rouen, where he died. Stephen, stricken with a fatal bout of dysentery, died at St Martin's Priory in Dover. These were the only two kings in our period who died in religious houses, and it must be remembered that they did so as guests, not as members, of religious orders.

The choice of burial place of a medieval king was not something that was decided arbitrarily or on sentimental grounds. It was a decision loaded with religious and ideological significance. A number of concerns were taken into account in making the decision.

Perhaps the most important factor for any Christian was the desire to be buried *ad sanctos*, among the saints. In an age when the cult of saints and the veneration of their relics was central to religious practice, it was believed that, by being buried in the presence of the saints, some of their sanctity might 'rub off' on the deceased and ease his passage through purgatory. Equally, there was a desire for the religious houses themselves to attract royal burials, and the prestige associated with them.[24] In the early middle ages, the church had attempted (according to the Council of Mainz in 813) to limit burial inside churches to 'bishops and abbots, or worthy priests, or faithful laity'.[25] While they might fall into the category of 'worthy laity', the burial of kings within abbey churches is in fact an indicator of the sacral element of medieval kingship. The practice of burying kings, not in the ground like ordinary men and women but in raised tombs, mimicked the burial of saints, whose tombs were made accessible to the faithful.[26]

Before Westminster Abbey emerged as the prime site of burial, a number of different sites were chosen by the Anglo-Norman and Angevin kings. This reflects two further concerns: the desire to be buried in an abbey of one's personal foundation, and the desire to be buried in a church linked to the dynasty. William the Conqueror favoured his own foundation of Caen (he and his wife Matilda of Flanders had founded twin male and female houses in this city), Henry I chose to be buried in the abbey that he founded at Reading, and Stephen was laid to rest at the abbey of Faversham, of which he had been a patron. John's burial at Worcester reflects a personal devotion to St Dunstan (Worcester's patron saint) and St Wulfstan, a former bishop, who had been canonised in 1203, during John's reign. John was buried before the high altar, where his tomb can still be seen, the effigy depicting him between two clerics holding censers, a graphic representation of medieval man's hopes to be helped into heaven through the aid of the church and the saints. Wulfstan's remains were translated in 1218, so that John lay between him and another saint, Oswald.

The burials of Henry II and Richard I at Fontevrault in Anjou signify an identification with their dynastic roots in France, as it was the traditional necropolis of the counts of Anjou. Although no kings were subsequently buried there, John's second queen Isabella of Angoulême was interred there in 1230, and Eleanor of Provence, the wife of John's son Henry III, was buried in a house belonging to the same order in 1291, the same year in which her late husband's embalmed heart was taken to Fontevrault. These burials demonstrate a continuation of dynastic favour to Fontevrault, as well as personal favour by these queens (Eleanor of Provence entered the English Fontevrine house of Amesbury toward the end of her life).

We see the emergence of a consistent royal necropolis with the burial of kings in Westminster Abbey from the late thirteenth century onwards.[27] The concept of a necropolis, a house in which the members of a royal dynasty were to be buried across the generations, was a common one for many of the royal dynasties of north-west Europe. The model necropolis was Speyer Cathedral in Franconia, Germany, the burial place of the German emperors. Founded by Conrad II in 1030, seven kings and emperors were buried there between 1039 and 1309. In particular, the practice of the kings of France of being buried in the abbey church of St-Denis, outside Paris, was the example that the kings of England sought to emulate. This practice began very early, with the burial of the Frankish king Dagobert in 639. In 1263–64, Louis IX was responsible for constructing a series of effigies of the kings of France to lie in St-Denis, to demonstrate the importance of the necropolis as a symbol of dynastic continuity.[28]

Henry III's development of Westminster was therefore in part an act of competition with Louis IX of France, whose foundation of the Sainte-Chapelle in Paris to house the crown of thorns led to one of the glories of Gothic architecture. In addition, Henry's promotion of the cult of Edward the Confessor as a dynastic saint for the English kings is evident in his choice of burial place, in the presence of Edward, in

Edward's own foundation.[29] Subsequently Westminster's pre-eminence as the burial place of the English kings was challenged only briefly by Canterbury Cathedral (where Henry IV and his uncle Edward the Black Prince were buried on either side of Thomas Becket), and by St George's Chapel, Windsor, which seems to have been intended as the necropolis of the Yorkist dynasty. The ascendancy of Westminster also reflects the growing 'Englishness' of the monarchy from Henry III's reign onwards, as the cult of the Anglo-Saxon St Edward was promoted. Richard I was the last king buried overseas, and John's reign represents something of a watershed, as the loss of Normandy in 1204 weakened the ties between the Anglo-Norman ruling class and its continental roots.

It is possible to see the royal tombs within the sacred geography of Westminster Abbey. All are buried in the choir, the holiest part of the church as it was closest to the high altar. Sixteenth-century monarchs were buried to the east of the altar in the Lady Chapel, which was rebuilt by Henry VII. At the heart of the choir, behind the high altar screen, is the shrine of St Edward the Confessor, dating from the time of his greatest royal devotee, Henry III. In 1269 Henry had Edward's remains translated to a magnificent new tomb, which was the centrepiece of a new building programme.

Subsequent royal tombs form an arc around that of the Confessor. Henry III himself was buried in an impressive tomb of porphyry (a stone bearing the imperial colour purple) and Purbeck marble in 1290. Henry's tomb, and the new shrine of the Confessor, were set in the midst of a magnificent Cosmati work (a kind of mosaic, made of pieces of coloured stone) pavement representing the spheres of the cosmos. This, and the tombs, were designed by Roman craftsmen, indicating Henry's alliance with the papacy and his imperial self-image.[30] In the eighteen years between his death and reburial in the new tomb, his remains rested on the site where Edward the Confessor had lain until 1269. Henry's sons Edward I and Edmund 'Crouchback', his daughter-in-law Eleanor of Castile, Edward III and Richard II were also later buried nearby. Edward III's will stated that he should be buried at Westminster 'among our ancestors of famous memory, the kings of England', indicating that by the time of his death in 1377 Westminster had been identified as the proper burial place of kings.[31]

Richard II was initially buried at King's Langley in Hertfordshire, and had to wait thirteen years before being buried in his intended location at Westminster. His tomb in the abbey had been planned in his lifetime, the intention being that he would share it with his first queen, Anne of Bohemia, who had died in 1394. Richard and Anne were the first royal couple to be buried together in this way. Like Henry III before him, Richard's choice of Westminster as a burial-place reflected the special devotion he showed to St Edward the Confessor. Edward, alongside another royal saint, Edmund of East Anglia, is featured as a supporter of Richard on the Wilton Diptych, and Richard had his arms impaled with those attributed to the Confessor.

Henry IV's burial at Canterbury was related to his own interest in the cult of St Thomas Becket. Henry successfully acquired a relic of holy oil associated with this saint, which was used (not entirely successfully) to anoint him at his coronation. It may seem strange that a king whose hold on the crown was insecure, and who had come to power through usurpation, should not have tried to emphasise continuity by having himself buried at Westminster. Canterbury, however, also had its own important associations. Henry was buried alongside the shrine of Becket, who rivalled Edward the Confessor as a patron saint of England, and opposite his uncle, Edward, the Black Prince, whose burial there reflected his links with Kent though his marriage to its countess, Joan. As the centre of Becket's cult, the most important pilgrimage site in England, and the seat of the archbishop, Canterbury arguably outranked Westminster in holiness and prestige.

Henry V was buried immediately to the east of the Confessor, behind the coronation chair of Edward I, representing a return of Westminster to favour after his father Henry IV's burial at Canterbury. The younger Henry was responsible for the reburial of Richard II at Westminster, and choosing the abbey for his own resting-place was another way to emphasise dynastic continuity after the upheavals of his father's reign. He encouraged building work at Westminster in his lifetime, and in his will he requested to be buried there between the shrine of St Edward and the chapel of the Virgin (the Lady Chapel), where holy relics were kept.[32] This illustrates how, alongside the dynastic considerations of burial, there was also a continuing desire to be buried *ad sanctos*. This was especially true of Henry V, a defender of orthodoxy against the

Lollard heretics, critics of the cult of saints. Henry was to be the last king buried in the abbey until the Tudors.

The reason for this break was the favour shown by the Yorkist Edward IV to St George's Chapel, Windsor. This new foundation was probably intended as a necropolis for the dynasty; Edward himself was buried there, as was Henry VI on the translation of his remains from Chertsey by Richard III in 1484. Edward developed the chapel as a focal point for the Order of the Garter, which he promoted as a rival to similar chivalric orders in France and Burgundy. The dedication to St George was also fitting for a chapel dedicated to an order of knights, as this warrior-saint had come to be associated with chivalric virtues, and in the later middle ages was replacing the traditional royal saints, Edmund and Henry III's favoured St Edward the Confessor, as the patron of England.

The resumption by the Tudors of the practice of royal burial at Westminster suggests a conscious decision to emphasise the continuity of the new dynasty with the medieval past. Henry VII attempted, unsuccessfully, to have Henry VI canonised, and as part of this process intended to have the remains reburied in Westminster, where they would have become the focal point for the new Lady Chapel that was being built at the east end of the abbey. The translation, and the canonisation, of Henry VI never took place, but the Lady Chapel did become a burial place for Henry VII, his wife Elizabeth of York, and his granddaughters Mary I and Elizabeth I. His son Henry VIII, however, was buried in St George's, Windsor, a reminder that he was also the grandson of Edward IV.

The later middle ages saw a greater individualisation of tomb design, arguably reflecting a growing sense of the individual. In the early middle ages, rulers had been buried in sarcophagi with no effigy. Tomb effigies became popular in the eleventh and twelfth century, although these, as in the case of the Plantagenet tombs at Fontevrault, showed idealised images of the dead, not individual portraits. There were still strong elements of standardisation as late as the end of the thirteenth century, when Edward I had gilt-bronze effigies of the same basic design, with idealised images, made for Henry III and Eleanor of Castile.[33] In the thirteenth and fourteenth centuries, however, a greater sense of individualism certainly emerged. Edward III had a wooden funerary effigy

made, which still survives in Westminster Abbey, and which was based
on a death-mask. His son Edward the Black Prince (d. 1376) had the
form of his tomb specified in his will, even down to the wording of the
epitaph. The effigy of the Black Prince's son Richard II is probably the
first realistic portrait of an English king on an effigy; the contract drawn
up for the design of his tomb specified that the artist was to *contrefaire*
('make a likeness of'; the word is also the root of the English word
'counterfeit') the king and queen.

    Simple convenience might also be a reason for the choice of burial
site. William Rufus was buried at Winchester largely because it was the
closest major church to the site of his death in the New Forest, although
it also had royal associations, Winchester being the seat of the old
monarchy of Wessex and also the burial site of a number of pre-conquest
kings, including Cnut. Likewise, the burial of Stephen at Faversham in
Kent was geographically convenient, as he died at Dover. Edward II as
a deposed and murdered king still merited an honourable burial, but
one well away from the court at Westminster. Gloucester Abbey was
conveniently close to the probable place of his death, Berkeley Castle
in Gloucestershire. Likewise, for the burial of the murdered Richard II
and Henry VI, Langley (Hertfordshire) and Chertsey (Surrey) were
conveniently close to London, where Richard's body was publicly displayed and where Henry was murdered, without being too prominent.
Richard III was laid to rest in Leicester, close to the battlefield of
Bosworth.

    Conversely, many kings' remains were transported a considerable
distance to lie in their favoured resting place. When this occurred, the
viscera – the parts of the body that were removed in the embalming
process, and which were held to be the most corrupt and therefore likely
to rot and cause disease – were buried closest to the place of death.
Henry I was buried in England, despite dying in Normandy, while his
viscera were buried at Rouen. Richard I was killed at Châlus in the south
west of France, and his viscera were buried nearby, but his body was
interred at Fontevrault, far to the north. John's viscera were buried at
Croxton Abbey, near to Newark where he died, but his body was buried
at Worcester. Edward I was buried in Westminster, despite dying near
the Scottish border, although Froissart claimed that he requested that
his remains be carried by his army into Scotland. Henry V died in

France, but his remains were nevertheless brought back across the Channel for burial at Westminster. The burial of body parts in separate locations was also a way of emphasising the geographical spread of royal authority, as when Henry I had his body buried in England but his viscera in Normandy. Richard I went one better, resting in three places, his heart being buried at Rouen. The geography of his burial therefore spanned the three centres of his power in France, Normandy, Anjou and Aquitaine. It is perhaps significant, given that he only spent a few months of his reign in England, that he did not grace this kingdom with any part of his body. Henry V's burial shows that the practice continued into the later middle ages. In his case, it reflected his claim to the crown of France as well as that of England. Before his embalmed body was taken away for burial in England, his viscera were buried at St-Maur-des-Fossés in France, and his embalmed corpse was given a funeral service at the abbey of St-Denis, the resting-place of the kings of France.[34]

Finally, a king's view of himself and his kingship might be reflected not only in his plans for his own burial but in his treatment of the tombs of his predecessors. Henry III had Edward the Confessor's remains translated to a magnificent new tomb because he was personally devoted to the cult of that saint, but also because it reflected glory upon the English monarchy at a time when Henry was competing with Louis IX of France for the leadership of western Christendom. He also hoped some of Edward's sanctity would rub off on him, as he was himself buried in the vicinity of the Confessor's shrine. Richard II unsuccessfully attempted to have Edward II canonised, and had the latter's tomb at Gloucester decorated with Richard's personal emblem of the white hart on his visit in 1390.[35] Edward and Richard, and later Henry VI, were all buried in relatively obscure places after their deposition, only (in the cases of Richard and Henry) to be reburied in the royal necropolises some years later as a symbol of dynastic continuity. Edward II was probably not reburied similarly because the cult that had developed around him had proved so lucrative for the monks of Gloucester.

2

Death as Divine Punishment

Three celebrated royal deaths of the eleventh and twelfth centuries all occurred in that most dramatic of manners, death by arrow wound; a literal 'bolt from the blue'. The first was the most celebrated, but also perhaps the most disputed, the death of Harold at the battle of Hastings by the famous 'arrow in the eye'. The second also generated controversy, the death of William II 'Rufus' in 1100 in a hunting accident in the New Forest. Finally, Richard I, the 'Lionheart', died a lingering death of a wound received from a crossbow bolt at the siege of Châlus in 1199.

In the historical framework used by monastic writers, events did not simply happen; history reflected the unfolding of God's plan for mankind. Therefore royal deaths were not simply natural events, but occasions calling for moralising commentary for the edification of the audience. When the death was dramatic and violent, the idea that it may have been in some way divine retribution for the sins of the individual or of the nation had to be seriously entertained.

The death of Harold at Hastings, and its (supposed) manner, the king being struck in the eye by a Norman arrow, is probably the most popularly well-known death of any English king. Edward II's unpleasant murder enjoys a certain notoriety, but the 'adult content' of this death has prevented it taking the place that Harold's has in schoolbooks. Unfortunately, the chronicle descriptions of the battle do not agree on the mode of death of the English king, and some do not even mention his being struck by an arrow. The Norman William of Poitiers, writing in the 1070s in his *Deeds of Duke William*, makes little reference to Harold's means of death, merely saying that he 'perished'.[1] Guy of Amiens's *Carmen de Hastingae Proelio* (*Song of the Battle of Hastings*), another pro-Norman account from the years immediately after the Conquest, has Harold being hacked to death by a number of assailants.[2] William of Jumièges, another near-contemporary Norman historian, wrote only that Harold was 'pierced with mortal wounds', without specifying the nature of these wounds.[3] The Anglo-Saxon Chronicle is equally silent on Harold's exact manner of death.[4] None of the contemporary or near contemporary accounts of Harold's death mention his being killed by an arrow.[5] Wace, who wrote a verse history of the Normans in the mid twelfth century, says he was killed in this way, but he may have been influenced by seeing the Baycux Tapestry.[6]

The tapestry is itself ambiguous, showing two figures beneath the inscription 'Hic Harold Rex Interfectus Est (Here King Harold is killed)'. One figure is standing, and appears to be trying to extract an arrow from his eye; the second is falling, being struck about the thighs with a sword by a mounted Norman knight. There is a great deal of controversy over which of these figures is Harold, or whether they both represent the king. Perhaps the most convincing interpretation of this scene is that the two pictures should be read sequentially like panels of a cartoon strip, to mean that Harold was first struck in the eye by an arrow and then cut down by a swordsman.[7] It has been argued that the placement of the caption above both figures means that they both represent Harold. Furthermore, close analysis reveals a set of needle-holes in the linen background that seem to correspond to a now-lost arrow jutting out from the eye-socket of the falling second 'Harold'. It may be objected that the second 'Harold' is wearing different colour stockings from the first, but this need not invalidate the theory, as the different coloured wools were used for decorative, not realistic, purposes, and on occasions the same man or the same horse appears in consecutive scenes in different colours.[8]

It is also important to remember that the Bayeux Tapestry, like the work of chroniclers, was not simply a representation of what happened but was constructed to draw a moral lesson. It was not just an account of the Norman Conquest: a sizeable portion of the tapestry – just over a third of what remains – represents events occurring before the death of Edward the Confessor and the assumption (or seizure) of power by Harold. The reason for the inclusion of these earlier events – Harold's visit to Normandy, his participation in William's campaign against Conan of Brittany, and the crucial episode of Harold's swearing fealty to William on holy relics – is that they explain and justify subsequent events. Their representation had an obvious political purpose, in showing Harold to be a forsworn usurper, whose overthrow by William is justified, but they also had a moral purpose, demonstrating that the defeat and death of Harold was a divine judgement on him as an oath-breaker. In addition, William had been granted a banner (the *Vexillum Sancti Petri*) by the reforming papacy, while Harold had been crowned by Stigand, the corrupt and excommunicate archbishop of Canterbury. William of Poitiers refers to this 'unhallowed consecration',[9] while the Bayeux Tapestry identifies Stigand by name in the scene depicting Harold's coronation, thereby drawing attention to the illegitimacy of his elevation to the kingship.

The theme of divine favour to William is emphasised by the portent of the comet, a symbol of divine disfavour, which appears to Harold after his coronation, and which foreshadows the Conquest, represented in the Tapestry by the ghostly outlines of ships in the lower margin.[10] Astrological portents were considered highly significant, occurring as they did in the heavens, the realm of God rather than of Man. In 1133, a solar eclipse was seen as a portent of the death of Henry I; although Henry did not die until 1135, the eclipse, which occurred when Henry set off for Normandy, was seen retrospectively to portend that this was the last occasion on which he would cross the Channel. It was also significant that the crossing occurred on the anniversary of Henry's coronation. William of Malmesbury saw this as a 'jest' by God.[11] William also recorded an eclipse during the reign of Stephen, which foretold great losses for the king.

Pro-Norman accounts of the Conquest therefore claim that Harold's defeat and death constituted divine judgement on his seizure of the throne and his perjury, demonstrating that his oath to recognise William as the rightful heir to England outweighed the dying Edward the Confessor's conferment of the kingdom upon him. Even the Englishman Eadmer, writing towards the end of the eleventh century, saw the Conquest in these terms: 'their [the Normans'] victory must truly and without doubt be entirely ascribed to a miracle of God, who in thus punishing the crime of Harold's perjury, shows that he is not a God who will allow iniquity'.[12] Baudri of Bourgueil, in a verse describing a tapestry that may be that of Bayeux, writes:

> The propitious gods favoured the Normans
> By chance a lethal arrow pierced Harold

He ended the war, he indeed was the cause
He circled his head with impure gold
He himself offended the sceptre with his perjured hand ... [13]

William of Poitiers, writing around 1075, has Duke William addressing the dead Harold: 'Your end proves by what right you were raised through the death-gift of Edward'.[14] This chronicler presents the Conquest as the enactment of divine judgement, and its successful outcome as a proof of the justice of William's claim to the English throne.[15] The Anglo-Saxon Worcester chronicler saw the defeat at Hastings as God's judgement on the sins of the whole English people.[16] Even the hagiographical *Vita Haroldi*, written at Waltham Abbey in about 1205, felt the need to refute a series of omens that were said to represent God's displeasure with Harold. A tree was said to have borne no leaves since Harold took his celebrated oath to William, a symbol of divine displeasure at his perjury. Likewise, a legend that a stone statue of Christ at Waltham had bowed in Harold's presence was seen by some as a symbol of the imminent debasement of Harold and England, an interpretation that the *Vita* author was at pains to refute.[17]

Edward's nomination of Harold as his successor caused problems for the Norman claim. English sources record this event,[18] and even William of Poitiers could not deny that it had taken place. He has Harold's envoy to William claim that this cancelled Harold's previous oath to William.[19] The Bayeux Tapestry suggests that Edward bequeathed the kingdom to Harold, as it includes the scene from the *Vita Aedwardi* where the dying king confers the protection of his widow, Edith (Harold's sister), and the realm onto Harold. Edith is represented at the foot of Edward's bed, and Edward's fingertips touch those of Harold.

Faced with this strong case against their duke's claim to the throne, the Norman sources see Harold's death as clinching the argument, God adjudicating between the rival claims by dramatically striking down the usurper. The dramatic and sudden death is therefore appropriate in the case the Norman sources make against Harold, but is there anything specifically about blinding that would make this an appropriate death? The punishment of blinding, as well as being a practical means of ensuring a ruler's inability to rule and lead his vassals in war, was also rich in symbolism. Light and the power to see clearly were attributes of divinity in medieval thought and art; conversely, darkness and blindness were associated with sin, for example, in the famous biblical metaphor of 'the blind leading the blind'. Loss of sight was not just a physical handicap but a moral attribute as well. In the words of the medieval writer Petrus Berchorius, blindness 'connotes to us only something negative and never positive, and by the blind man we understand the sinner'.[20] In particular, and of great relevance in this context of broken trust, blindness was associated with infidelity. William the Conqueror used blinding and castration in place of the death penalty in his laws for England; blinding in particular was employed as a punishment for rebellion.[21]

We therefore see how history can be made with a moral purpose, rather than a strict adherence to 'the facts', in mind. The contemporary accounts of Harold's death made no mention of his being killed by an arrow, yet this explanation of his death, loaded as it was with moral symbolism, was stressed at the expense of more prosaic versions, to the extent that it is often remembered today as *the* means by which he was killed.

One of the most dramatic royal deaths among Anglo-Norman or Plantagenet kings was that of William II 'Rufus', killed while hunting in the New Forest in 1100, supposedly by accident, although some modern historians have proposed theories that he was murdered.[22] Hunting with his companions, William was killed by an arrow which, most accounts agree, was fired at a stag, but missed it (or passed over its back) and hit the king instead.[23] The king died quickly, and (according to most sources) without having the opportunity to make confession or receive the sacraments. He was buried in Winchester, the nearest major church to the New Forest.

Leaving aside for a moment questions over the exact circumstances of the death, let us examine the way in which it was portrayed by twelfth-century authors. The background for all ecclesiastical accounts of Rufus's death is his mistreatment of the church, and allegations of his contempt for the church and even for Christianity. In ecclesiastical histories, Rufus is anticlerical, blasphemous, philosemitic and contemptuous of the power of God. He is given to swearing oaths, of which his favourite was 'by the Holy Face of Lucca', in reference to a renowned relic. Rufus's most serious offence from the church writers' point of view was his quarrel with Anselm, archbishop of Canterbury, which led to the latter's exile. Anselm's biographer Eadmer, a monk of Canterbury and companion of the archbishop in exile, is a key, and understandably hostile, source for Rufus's reign.

The reign of William Rufus occurred at a crucial time in the development of relations between state and church, between *regnum* (kingship) and *sacerdotium* (priestly power), and his troubled relations with Archbishop Anselm were part of this problematic relationship. Before the eleventh century, western European kingship had embodied both secular and ecclesiastical authority; the king was viewed as a *rex sacerdos* (king priest). He was an appointee of God and, although a man of the world whose duties included fighting and reproducing, he enjoyed a quasi-priestly authority, an idea represented in iconography of the king being crowned by a hand emerging from heaven, without clerical mediation. In many kingdoms, the practices of coronation and anointing with holy oil were being introduced to reinforce this idea, ceremonies that were conscious imitations of the coronation of Old Testament kings of the Jews.

The *rex sacerdos* concept probably enjoyed its heyday at around the turn of the millennium, in the person of the Emperor Otto III (983–1002; effective ruler from 994). The idea of an 'Ottonian system' whereby the German emperors coopted the church into government, almost as a tenth-century civil service, has been challenged recently by historians, but nevertheless, the emperors enjoyed close and fruitful relations with the church. Otto III promoted his mentor Gerbert of Aurillac to the papacy, where he took the name of Sylvester II (999–1003), in honour of the Sylvester who was pope at the time of the Emperor Constantine's conversion. Otto and Sylvester proved formidable allies in pursuing complementary policies of christianising central Europe, and bringing it under the aegis of the German-Roman emperors.

This cosy relationship collapsed in the last quarter of the eleventh century. The conflict known to history as the Investiture Contest began over the issue of whether pope or emperor had the right to invest (in effect, appoint) bishops, but the impact was far more wide-reaching, both geographically and in principle. The principle was essentially one of how far the secular power could exercise authority over the church, and raised the whole question of the relative powers of *regnum* and *sacerdotium*. An increasingly self-confident and independent papacy, heading a church that was attempting to reform itself and return to what it saw as its true values, was asserting itself and attempting to throw off the domination of kings and emperors whom it saw not as priest-kings but as secular rulers who should confine themselves to lay affairs. The difficulty, in a society where churchmen were also royal ministers and great land-holders, was in defining where the dividing line should fall between lay and spiritual matters.

The clash between Rufus and Anselm was not strictly speaking part of the Investiture Contest, although the struggle was to be played out in England between the archbishop and Rufus's successor Henry I. The quarrel between Rufus and Anselm was over precisely the problems of conflicting lay and ecclesiastical authority outlined above. When Rufus demanded that the monastery cathedral of Canterbury, like his lay vassals, should contribute knights to the king's service, Anselm refused. His refusal to recognise the authority of the king over that of the church embodied the new ideas of the reformed Gregorian papacy. Anselm left England in 1097, and so was in exile and in despair at Rufus's continued ascendancy when news reached him of the king's death.

The whole affair of Anselm's appointment to the see of Canterbury in 1092 after a vacancy of three years, and his subsequent breach with Rufus, is indicative of the image of Rufus as one who was contemptuous of God and His church. The king's decision to appoint Anselm, a saintly scholar rather than a bureaucrat, was said to have been reached while William was on his death-bed. The king recovered unexpectedly, when he regretted his decision, the political consequences of which he would now have to live with. This uncharacteristic bout of piety gave Rufus a 'spiritual father' with whom he found it impossible to work.[24] If the sources are to be believed, this was typical of William's attitude towards God, to whom he turned *in extremis*, but otherwise regarded as someone who had done him no favours, and to whom he owed nothing.

Eadmer's stories of William illustrate this well. Supposedly, the king hated anyone to end their sentences 'God willing', as if it implied that God's power was greater than the king's. He believed prayer to saints to be useless, and was opposed to judicial ordeals (thereby anticipating the church's ban on them of 1215) on the basis that God lacked the knowledge to make judgements in the affairs of law. The king was accused of being overly sympathetic to the Jews, and of encouraging Jewish converts to Christianity to apostasise.[25]

Many interpretations have been placed on accounts such as these of William's apparent disdain for God. The most wild of these is Margaret Murray's theory that William was a pagan, a theory that was used to argue that his death was a human sacrifice, of which he was the willing victim.[26] Likewise, it is tempting for a modern, secular readership to defend William as some kind of precursor of modern rational thinking, with his religious tolerance, his lack of fear of the church's threats of damnation, and his scepticism about the efficacy of trial by ordeal. These accounts should not, however, be taken literally. They were anecdotes, and Eadmer admits that they were hearsay. They were included in his history to illustrate Rufus's blasphemy, but he could not vouch for any of the stories that he repeated.

This is not to say that Rufus's anticlericalism was all a construct of the ecclesiastical writers; his clash with Anselm was real enough, and of huge political significance. But we should be wary of taking opinions of Rufus expressed by his enemies in the church too literally. Quite apart from problems of personal and political bias, we can see the image of Rufus as a literary 'type', the prodigious, possibly satanic, king. A more famous example from the following century was the Emperor Frederick II, who, like Rufus, was portrayed as a sceptic, with an inquiring 'rational' mind, an enemy of the church, a friend of despised religious minorities, and quite possible an atheist. His enemies portrayed Frederick as a satanic figure, even going so far as to view him as the beast of the Apocalypse. Frederick's case is slightly different from that of Rufus, however; as the emperor, he was a more significant figure, and in thirteenth-century Italy there were apocalyptic ideas current that were not present in Anglo-Norman England. Rufus was never viewed with quite the degree of apocalyptic terror as Frederick, but church writers implied that William possessed a diabolical nature.

Orderic Vitalis sets Rufus's death firmly in the context of that king's oppression of the English church. He begins with a vision of a monk of Gloucester Abbey, foreseeing the king's death, which was interpreted thus by the abbot of Shrewsbury: 'England is given over to reprobates for destruction, because the land is full of iniquity.'[27] With the accuracy of prophecy enjoyed only with hindsight, Orderic has the abbot say: 'Behold, the bow of divine anger is bent against the wicked and the arrow swift to wound is taken from the quiver.'[28]

The scene is therefore set: God has punished the English for their sins by delivering them into the hands of the Normans. But now it is the Norman king who will suffer divine punishment. The arrow 'will strike suddenly; let every wise man avoid the blow by amending his life'. But William, adding pride (not to mention Anglophobia) to his other sins, ignores the warning, conveyed in a letter from the abbot of Gloucester: 'Does he [the abbot] think I act after the fashion of the English, who put off their journeys and business on account of the snores and dreams of little old women?'[29] Rufus of course ignores this warning at his peril, as he is later struck down and killed by an arrow fired by his hunting companion Walter Tirel. After his death, William's brother Henry, who happens to be in the vicinity, seizes the royal treasury and is declared king, to the acclamation of the English according to Orderic, as he 'had been nobly born in the kingdom'.[30]

The violence of the death, and its timing, show that William was, to Orderic's mind, killed as a just punishment for his sins in oppressing the church. Interestingly, Orderic goes on to use the unusual word *biothanatus*, meaning a sudden, violent death. This word also implies damnation, as he did not have time to receive the sacraments.[31] Furthermore, the literal meaning from the Greek is 'living death', further emphasising the element of eternal suffering. This is an unusual word in medieval Latin; it usually occurs with reference to suicide, including that of Judas.[32] Orderic is therefore bracketing Rufus with the most grievous of sinners. At the time that he was writing, however, the meaning seems to imply not suicide, specifically, so much as a death that occurred without the opportunity for making one's peace with God.[33]

Orderic uses the word *biot(h)anatus* on four other occasions in his *Ecclesiastical History*. On all but one of these occasions he does so to suggest damnation, and the word refers not to the death but to the dead man; that is, the sinner who has died is called a *biothanatus*. On the first occasion, it is translated in the modern English edition as 'those who die a violent death', but the sense is of 'those who are damned'; in a charter of Peter of Maule in favour of the monks of St-Evroul,

Peter is quoted as saying that anyone who violates the lands of the abbey will be condemned by God 'together with the reprobate and those that die a violent death (*cum reprobis et biotanatis*)'.[34]

The word next occurs in the description of a vision of the priest Walchelin, who sees the ghosts of dead sinners pass before him. One such ghost is referred to as that of an 'accursed reprobate (*execrabilis biotanati*)'.[35] This is again translated as 'reprobate' when it next occurs, when Orderic has a Norman count defend Henry I on the grounds that he saved the Norman church that had been 'wretchedly oppressed by reprobates (*biothanatis*)'. This, to my mind, is the only time Orderic uses the word without a sense of damnation. Finally, and significantly, he uses the term to describe the body of a 'man who had met a violent death (*corpus biothanati*)'.[36] This last example is especially interesting, as the *biothanatus* died in a fitting manner, 'struck down by the avenging and just hand of God', having used his castle as a centre for brigandage, to the oppression of the people and in defiance of the king. So, as in Rufus's death, there is the element of divine judgement.

At a more specific level, Rufus's death is a just punishment not only for his oppression of the church, but of his father William the Conqueror's destruction of native villages to make way for the royal hunting ground of the New Forest. Orderic was angry less about the eviction of English peasants than the destruction of churches that accompanied it. It would be misleading, as well as anachronistic, to view Orderic, who was of mixed Anglo-Norman descent, as an English nationalist; he was sympathetic to the English, but, as we have seen from the vision attributed to the monk of Gloucester, he regarded the Norman Conquest as a punishment for the sins of the English, and as the medium by which ecclesiastical reform was brought to England.[37] Neither was he a eulogist of the Norman kings. He seems to have been attempting to produce narrative history on the grand scale of Bede. As a writer in the monastic tradition of history, he wrote for the edification of his readers, trying to guide them to salvation by showing how God punishes the sinful.[38]

In this historical framework, the deaths of two sons and one grandson of the Conqueror in his forest was an ideal opportunity for moralising upon divine judgement and the fall of great men. As well as Rufus, Richard (another son of William I) and a son of Robert Curthose, also called Richard, were killed in hunting accidents in the New Forest. Richard, son of Robert, was, like his royal uncle, killed accidentally by an arrow.[39] The Conqueror's son was killed more gruesomely, 'crushed between a strong hazel branch and the pommel of his saddle'.[40] By these means 'the Lord plainly showed his anger that consecrated buildings had been given over to be a habitation of wild beasts'.[41]

The role of hunting as a symbol of the Norman king's arrogance can be seen in another chronicler's motif. Just as, according to the Anglo-Saxon Chronicle, William the Conqueror 'loved the stags as dearly as if he had been their father',[42] so too William of Newburgh employs similar imagery in the case of Henry I: 'through his delight in hunting he was ... more attached to wild beasts than was right, and in his public punishments distinguished insufficiently between killers of deer and killers of men'.[43] Just as William I was punished through the deaths of his sons for his imposition of the New Forest, so William of Newburgh is building up to the appropriate death which Henry I was to meet, dying of the famous 'surfeit of lampreys' after exhausting himself in the chase – the hunter turned victim.

It is interesting to note that the mode of death of the Conqueror's son Richard differs between the accounts of Orderic Vitalis and William of Malmesbury. The latter maintains that Richard died because 'he caught some sickness from breathing the foggy and corrupted air', while reserving a version of the riding accident story for the other Richard, son of Duke Robert, killed 'as some relate, hanged by the throat on the branch of a tree, when his horse ran underneath it'. William makes it explicit that these princes 'met their deaths by God's strict judgement'.[44] It is possible that Orderic used a version of the prince's death that fitted more neatly the notion of divine retribution; death by miasma lacks the drama of a bolt-from-the-blue death by arrow. On the other hand, we can also see how William of Malmesbury uses a motif of death from a biblical source. Richard's death suspended from two tree branches resembles that of Absolom, son of King David:

> Now some of David's men caught sight of Absolom. He was riding a mule and, as it passed beneath a great oak, his head was caught in its boughs; he found himself in mid-air and the mule went from under him.[45]

William of Malmesbury, in his *De gestis regum Anglorum* written during the reign of Henry I, deals with the death of Rufus in a similar manner to Orderic. Like Orderic, he begins with a moment of prophecy before the king's death, or rather three such prophecies. First, he relates a story from Eadmer, the biographer of St Anselm, of how Anselm, exiled in Marcigny, was informed by Hugh, abbot of Cluny, that 'the previous night the king had been brought before his Maker, where solemn sentence had been passed on him, and he had received the desperate verdict of damnation'.[46] This is not strictly speaking a prophecy, as it was a simultaneous vision of Rufus's death, rather than an anticipation of it, but it can still be classed with prophecies as a miraculous insight. Eadmer and William make it explicit that Rufus's death is a judgement from God, and that the king is damned (as, unknown to Anselm, he died unshriven).

William goes on to relate a story of the king's death foretold in a dream, but unlike in Orderic, the dream is the king's. The night before his death, 'he dreamt that he was being bled, and a spurt of blood shooting up to the sky overcast the sun and brought darkness upon the day'.[47] Then, as in Orderic, a monk is granted a prophetic dream; in this case, 'a certain foreign monk', who relates the story to the nobleman Robert Fitz Hamon. This dream portrays the king in suitably demonic terms:

> The king had come into a church, looking scornfully round on the congregation with his usual haughty and insolent air; he had then seized the crucifix in his teeth, gnawed away the arms of the figure, and almost broke off its legs. The figure endured this for some time, but at length gave the king such a kick with its foot that he fell backwards; and as he lay there, such a gush of flame came out of his mouth that the rolling billows of smoke even reached the stars.[48]

William of Malmesbury uses this dream differently to the monk's dream in Orderic. It does not foretell the death but rather explains its significance. Rufus's dream provides the prophecy of bloodletting; the monk's dream demonstrates that William is to die because of his oppression of the church. In the dream, he is represented as literally dismembering and consuming the body of the church.[49] The use of the phrase 'with his usual haughty and insolent air' to describe Rufus's bearing in the church tells us that this behaviour is in character for the king. To this 'realistic' behaviour is added the supernatural element of the king belching smoke and fire from his mouth, demonstrating his demonic nature. The smoke 'even reached the stars', a parallel with the king's own dream that his blood shot 'up to the sky', blotting out the sun.

The notion among church writers of Rufus as 'demonic' was still current in the thirteenth century. Matthew Paris cited a story that William of Mortain, earl of Cornwall, hunting in the New Forest shortly after Rufus's death, was confronted by a vision of the dead king riding a black goat, which announces that it is the devil, taking Rufus off to hell.[50]

The king's reaction to these portents is as dismissive as in Orderic's account, although the reason for this dismissive attitude is slightly different. Rufus does not ascribe the dream story to English credulousness but to clerical cupidity: 'He is a monk ... and has these monkish dreams with an eye to the main chance. Give him a hundred shillings.' But the end result is the same: the king, having ignored God's warnings, is struck down by His punishment.

William of Malmesbury's use of the imagery of divine retribution is all the more interesting given that he was not unfavourable toward Rufus elsewhere in his history. For example, he praises the king's magnanimity in allowing a defeated foe to escape punishment, comparing him to Caesar, although the historian William, keen perhaps to display his own classical learning, points out that his royal namesake could not have been deliberately following the divine Julius's example, as he was 'a man of no education'.[51] Furthermore, William of Malmesbury was generally discriminating in his choice of sources and not overly given to credulity. After relating Rufus's death, he tells us that the tower under which the king was interred subsequently collapsed, but is at pains to point that the building might have fallen down, through imperfect construction, even if he had never been buried there.[52]

This confirms that William of Malmesbury was located firmly in the tradition of monastic history, with its emphasis on writing history in order to explain the working of God's plan for the world. Therefore, although he may be viewed as more sceptical than Orderic, he too used the 'divine retribution' motif in recording the death of Rufus and the similar deaths in the New Forest of the two Richards.

The idea of Rufus's death as divine retribution is present in all the chronicle accounts of his death. Similarly, all stress that he died without having the opportunity to make confession and obtain absolution for his sins, and therefore in a state of mortal sin. Orderic's use of the term *biothanatus* to express this idea has already been mentioned. The earliest chronicle reference to the death, in the Peterborough (E) version of the Anglo-Saxon Chronicle, is very brief, mentioning only the bare facts of his death, but finds time to include a portent story – blood welling up from the earth in a village in Berkshire – and the divine retribution motif: 'he … was abhorrent to God, just as his end showed, because he departed in the midst of his injustice without repentance and any reparation'.[53]

Eadmer's account of Anselm's learning of the king's death, on which William of Malmesbury's version was based, puts great stress on Rufus's damnation. The abbot of Cluny dreams that 'the king had been accused before the throne of God, judged, and had sentence of damnation passed upon him'.[54] The point is that the king is, or will be, damned – the abbot did not say explicitly that Rufus had died. Set in its original context (if we are to accept the reported words, Eadmer having been present), we could see this as the abbot's attempt to reassure his exiled friend, Anselm, that some day Rufus would receive his due punishment in the next world, even though he may appear to have the upper hand in this one. Unless we believe the dream to have been genuinely miraculous, Abbot Hugh had no way of knowing of Rufus's death – his words only become a miraculous vision of the king's death with the benefit of hindsight. Damnation, not death as such, was the important part of Hugh's message. This is reinforced by Eadmer in his *Historia novorum*; apart from the variation that the king may have accidentally killed himself by falling upon an arrow, he gives more or less the 'standard version' – Rufus was killed as an act of divine judgement, and in a state of mortal sin: 'impenitent and unconfessed, he died instantly and was at once forsaken by everyone'.[55] He goes on to add that Rufus had been favoured with good fortune by God, in an attempt to have him amend his ways, but that when that failed 'since he refused to be disciplined by ill-fortune or to be led to right-doing by good fortune … the just judge by a death sharp and swift cut short his life in this world'.[56]

By way of contrast, we may compare this emphasis on damnation to the description by Orderic of another son of William the Conqueror, named Richard, who was also killed in the New Forest. In this instance, the writer was at pains to point out that the dying prince had the opportunity to confess and receive the sacraments.[57] We can see from this the importance that the monastic chronicler placed on the receipt of the sacraments at death – as would be expected in a society with a dominant Christian world view – and the significance of the absence of this element in the stories of Rufus's death.

The motif of a sudden death, with denial of the sacraments as a means of divine vengeance, is also to be found in the story of the death of a English nobleman, Miles of Gloucester, during the reign of Stephen (1135–54). Miles, according to the *Gesta Stephani*, was killed in a hunting accident much like that of Rufus: 'he had his breast pierced with a comrade's arrow while hunting deer and died instantly'.[58] The *Gesta* author viewed him as 'instigator of much evil' and notes that he died 'without a word of confession or profit from repentance'. Just as Rufus's death was seen by some as a judgement on his father's destruction of churches, so that of Miles was seen as punishment for his despoliation of churches during the civil wars, when he was alleged to have violated the sanctuary of the altar to which his enemies had fled.[59] This account occurs alongside similar stories of 'deserved deaths'.

A parallel to the story of an oppressor of the church dying unshriven can be found in the death of Thomas of Marle. Thomas was one of the troublesome castellans – independent-minded local lords who allegedly terrorised the population of northern France – who were brought to heel by King Louis VI of France (1108–37). Thomas's story was well-known to Anglo-Norman chroniclers, and was referred to by Henry of Huntingdon in his letter *De contemptu mundi*, where he says that the castellan died 'twisting his neck away from the Lord's body'.[60] Louis VI's biographer, Abbot Suger of St-Denis, provided an even more providential version of the story. He has the dying Thomas being offered the host and agreeing to accept it, but

> it seemed that the Lord Jesus would in no way allow himself to enter the most contaminated vessel of a man who was thoroughly impenitent. Just as soon as the scoundrel lifted up his neck, it twisted back and broke on the spot; bereft of the eucharist, he breathed forth his utterly foul spirit.[61]

Thomas's death was fitting, as he was an enemy of Louis, an oppressor of the community and an excommunicate. It is this last point in particular that the story may refer to, but the parallel with William Rufus, the enemy of the church, is evident.

The immediate aftermath of Rufus's death is also worth commenting on. The sense of damnation, of Rufus as forsaken by God, is echoed in the chroniclers' imagery of him as abandoned by human society, 'impenitent and unconfessed ... forsaken by everyone' in Eadmer's words.[62] Both Orderic and William of Malmesbury describe this. Orderic tells us that:

> Some of the humbler attendants covered the king's bloody body as best they might with wretched cloths and carried him like a wild boar stuck with spears from the wood to the town of Winchester.

He comments that the poor and the lower clergy reverenced the dead king, but that

> the doctors and prelates of the church, considering his squalid life and dreadful death (*biothanatus*), ventured to pass judgement, declaring that he was virtually past redemption and unworthy of absolution by the church, since as long as he lived they had never been able to turn him from his vices to salvation. In some churches bells that had often sounded long peels for the meanest of the poor and for common women were not rung for him.[63]

The motif of the king abandoned by his attendants on his death-bed is a fairly common one, standing as a metaphor for the passing of the king's power, and the fickleness of his followers who depart to fawn upon his successor. Similar scenes were described at the deaths of William I and Edward III.[64] The use of the death of Rufus as an exemplar for the great man humbled was repeated in late chronicles. William of Newburgh, writing at the end of the twelfth century, saw Rufus's death as punishment for 'his own wicked deeds, and [he] met an end worthy of his undisciplined arrogance'.[65] He went on to quote the thirty-sixth Psalm:

> I saw the wicked man raised high and exalted like the cedars of Lebanon, and I passed by, and behold he was not; I sought him out, and his place was not discovered.

An interesting parallel for the death of Rufus occurred in France, at around the time that Orderic Vitalis and William of Malmesbury were writing. In 1131 Philip, the son of Louis VI of France, was killed in an accident when riding through the streets of Paris. He died of the injuries sustained in his fall when a pig dashed out in front of his horse, causing it to rear up and throw him. The interpretation, and many of the details of this event, varied widely between different authorities. Suger, the abbot of St-Denis and the Capetians' chief propagandist, described this event as a great tragedy, and saw it as the devil's work, referring to a 'diabolical pig' that caused the prince's horse to stumble. Philip was carried by his companions to a nearby house where he died, amidst much mourning.[66] The chronicle of Morigny, while also seeing the pig as having been sent by Satan, differs from Suger in his description of what happened next, asserting, in a passage very reminiscent of accounts of Rufus's death, that the prince was abandoned by his companions and his body carried to a house by the poor people who found it.[67] This was not always a shameful turn of events, as the same element appears in stories of the death of St Olaf, king of Norway, where it seems to imply the pious humility of a saint.[68] The Morigny chronicle was written in about 1132, making it unlikely that the Morigny chronicler was simply copying Orderic. His purpose is very different from that of the chroniclers of Rufus's death, in that the prince is described as a 'simple and innocent child'. Orderic himself mentions the incident, but omits any mention of the pig or his abandonment by his companions. He does, however, add the detail that the prince died without confession or receiving the viaticum, also reminiscent of the fate of Rufus.[69]

Walter Map's later account (of Philip's death) is the most negative, and fits most closely the pattern of sudden death by divine judgement.

He ... degenerated from his father [Louis VI]'s ways and strayed away from his father's orders, and with proud brow and tyrannical pride was injurious to all. But it befell, at the Lord's command, that one day when, in company with many knights, he had put his horse to the gallop in that part of Paris called La Grève, a black pig rushed out of a dunghill on the bank of the Seine, and ran in among the feet of the galloping horse. The horse stumbled and fell, and the rider broke his neck and died; but the pig suddenly plunged into the Seine ... Therefore his father Louis the Fat, or rather the Lord who had delivered France out of the mouth of a lion, set in his place the kind and merciful Louis [later Louis VII], as he put Daniel in place of Saul.[70]

Map retains the story of the pig, adding the detail that it was black, a demonic colour, like the black goat on which Rufus was said to have been carried off to Hell, and adding the dunghill for bathos. However, he reverses the sense of the story to that in Suger, by making the death a divine judgement, not a diabolical act. The association of the pig with Satan, or with an ignominious death, also echoes Orderic's description of William as 'a wild boar stuck with spears' (a particularly ironic fate for Rufus, who had set out into the forest as the hunter, and left it as the prey).

Only one account of the king's death fails to mention that Rufus died unshriven. Significantly, it is the Anglo-Norman history *L'estoire des Engleis* of Geoffrey Gaimar, a work sympathetic to, indeed adulatory of, Rufus, who was 'well loved ... honoured by his folk'.[71] As a metrical history, written in the vernacular, this was a far more secular work in form and tone than that of the monastic histories. In Gaimar's work, William's companions (who are named, another departure from the monastic chronicles) are on hand (rather than having fled in terror, or to make the most of the crisis). William becomes a faithful son of the church, asking for the host, the *corpus domini*. He is unable to receive the sacraments because they are too far from a church, not because Rufus is anything less than a perfect Christian ruler. Besides, William had received 'pain beneit le dimaigne de devant' (the blessed bread the previous Sunday), emphasising his devotion to the eucharist.[72] It should be stressed that regular receipt of the eucharist was rare, even among the clergy, so that William's having received it the previous Sunday is seen as especially meritorious, especially as lay communion was infrequent in this period, with excessive lay devotion to the eucharist viewed almost with suspicion. William's eating the body of Christ in Gaimar's account makes an interesting counterpoint to William of Malmesbury's dream-story of the king chewing at a statue of Christ. Yet it is worth bearing in mind that Gaimar predates the establishment of the feast of Corpus Christi, and the attendant veneration of the consecrated host, by over a hundred years.[73] Until the thirteenth century *pain bénit* was not viewed with quite the same awe as being the body of Christ as it was to be in later times, and was quite commonly distributed among the laity at the end of mass.[74] So Rufus's receipt of *pain bénit* may not have been as remarkable as it first appears. Nevertheless, the effect that Gaimar wished to produce is clear, and the examples of the death-stories of William Rufus and Thomas of Marle may even be seen in the context of the growing cult of the consecrated host.

Some theories have been advanced in modern times suggesting that Rufus's death was not quite the accident it seemed.[75] These are often dismissed as conspiracy theories,[76] and it is not my intention here to delve into them, but it would appear that such theories, whatever their veracity, were already in circulation in the middle ages. A gloss on Orderic's account of the death reads 'De obitu seu interitu Guillelmi Rufi regis Anglorum (On the death or killing of William Rufus, king of the English)'.[77] Orderic's own wording could be read as implying that there was some intent in Tirel's actions. The words ascribed to the king and Tirel are heavily ironic, as the reader knows what is to occur: 'It is only right', says the king, handing Tirel two arrows, 'that the sharpest arrows should be given to the man who knows how to shoot the deadliest shots.' Later, the king, after laughing scornfully at the abbot of Gloucester's warning about the monk's dream, addresses Tirel again: 'Walter, do what is right in the business you have heard', to which he replies, 'So I will, my lord'.[78]

Is Orderic implying that Tirel murdered the king? The comment that Tirel was regarded by Rufus as the deadliest shot may suggest that his shooting the king was no accident; likewise, Tirel's promise to 'do his best' may be taken as a promise to do God's work by slaying the tyrant. On the other hand, we may equally be seeing a literary device at work. Rufus's entrusting the bolt that killed him to his best archer ironically foreshadows his death, and builds up narrative tension, in much the same way as do the dream portents, and William's scornful refusal to pay heed to the warnings that they contain. The king's death, we are led to believe, has been brought about by his own actions. Significantly, Tirel's words, 'So I will, my lord', are immediately followed by the words: 'So scorning the warnings of his elders, forgetting that pride comes before a fall ...'. The references to Tirel's shooting should therefore be seen in the context of the portents, and of Rufus's sinful pride. Tirel does 'do what is right' in slaying Rufus, but the context in Orderic's

narrative suggests that the author believes him to be the unwitting tool
of divine judgement. Orderic is probably not accusing Tirel of murder;
significantly, William of Malmesbury omits any such exchanges between
Tirel and the king.

William Rufus was not the only medieval king of England to be struck
down by an arrow. Richard I met a similar end at the siege of Châlus
in 1199. Venturing out without wearing his full armour, he was wounded
in the shoulder by a crossbow bolt fired by one of the defenders on the
walls. The blow was not immediately fatal, but the shaft of the arrow
broke off when attempts were made to remove it, leaving the head
lodged in Richard's flesh. The surgeon being unable to extract the bolt
cleanly, infection set in, and Richard died a slow death, eleven days after
receiving the wound.[79] The circumstances were, therefore, in many
senses very different to those of Rufus's death. Rufus was killed in an
accident, Richard in battle; Rufus was hated by the church, Richard was
a crusader and loyal son of the church; Rufus died suddenly, Richard
at agonising length; Rufus's death was (if the church authors are to be
believed) regretted by none, while Richard was mourned by many.

Richard was by no means the ideal Christian warrior king. He was
often accused of sexual immorality, charges which have been uncon-
vincingly interpreted by some modern commentators as evidence for
his being a homosexual. In 1195, he was confronted by a hermit who
reminded him of the fate of the city of Sodom.[80] Conversely, the
Aquitainian nobles who rebelled against him in 1183 complained that he
seduced women and then handed them on to his soldiers.[81]

Richard died on an obscure military expedition at the siege of Châlus-
Chabrol in the Limousin in April 1199. This campaign was in the context
of two struggles in which the Angevin kings were constantly engaged
in the French lands: the struggle with the Capetian kings of France and
that with their own vassals in Aquitaine. These two struggles frequently
overlapped, as the nobility of Aquitaine made common cause with their
ultimate overlord, the king of France. This had been the case in 1199
but, by the time of the siege of Châlus, Richard had made peace with
the Capetian king, Philip II, but had continued to wage war against his
rebellious vassals in the south west. One such was the viscount of
Limoges, to whom Châlus-Chabrol belonged.

According to a number of sources, notably the English chronicler Ralph of Coggeshall and the Limousin monk Bernard Itier, Richard was further attracted to attack Châlus by rumours that a great treasure was stored there. In Coggeshall's version, Richard went out unarmoured to observe the siege and was struck in the left shoulder by a bolt from a crossbowman who was defending the walls. He attempted to extract the bolt, but the shaft broke off, leaving the iron head buried in his flesh. The effects of his wound were aggravated by the heavy-handed intervention of a surgeon who cut deep into his flesh in an attempt to remove the bolt. Knowing that he was dying, Richard had time to make his peace with God and with Man. The castle fell, and Richard forgave the bowman who had caused the fatal wound. The king died, probably of septicaemia, on 6 April.

The poignancy of a virile, warrior king being struck down in his prime was expressed in the accounts of friend and foe alike. Geoffrey of Vinsauf bewailed the king's death, and railed against death itself, in a passage that reflects the standard didactic point that earthly glory is passing:

> Do you not realise whom you snatched from us? ... Nature knew not how to add any perfection; he was the utmost she could achieve. But that was the reason you snatched him away. If heaven allow it, I chide even God ... O Lord ... you could have done this more graciously, and with less haste ... But by this lesson you have made known how brief is the laughter of earth, how long are its tears.[82]

An interesting variation, which is stressed by those chroniclers hostile to Richard, is that he was waging war in Lent, so was acting blasphemously. Clearly, then, the 'bolt from the blue' could be viewed in this context as an example of divine punishment, an echo of the death of Rufus. The poet William the Breton has the Three Fates cutting off Richard's life because he is a rebel (against Philip, his overlord in France), greedy, disrespectful of God and of the Lenten fast, a breaker of treaties and a rebel against his own father (Richard having rebelled against Henry II before becoming king).[83] Even sources less hostile to Richard admit the element of divine judgement. For example, Gervase of Canterbury has the crossbowman pray to God to direct his aim. Gervase's interests are more parochial: the purpose of the death for him is that Richard on his death-bed was able to repent of his sins, including the harm that he had done to Gervase's church of Canterbury.[84]

It was long a commonplace among historians that Richard's end was inglorious in comparison to his great crusading feats. The man who had fought Saladin in the name of liberating the Holy Places was killed in a minor battle that was occasioned by his pursuit of treasure. Chroniclers were only too quick to point out the irony of the unheroic circumstances of his death. Roger of Howden recorded a number of epigrams moralising on Richard's death; in one of these Richard is a lion slain by an ant. In others he dwells on Richard's sins, which include cupidity, and on the power of death; in an allusion to the siege, Howden says that just as men conquer fortresses, so death conquers men.[85] For Ralph of Coggeshall, Richard died a humble death in an obscure place, as he had returned too soon from crusade and was driven by greed. God did him a favour, by striking him down before he could commit even greater sin. For Ralph, the death was an act not of divine vengeance so much as divine mercy, as Richard's slow death allowed him time to confess his sins.[86]

A number of additional points may be made about the inglorious nature of his death as it occurs in the account of Ralph of Coggeshall. The irony of his death is obvious, but also it is surely significant that he was killed by a humble foot soldier, in contrast to his previous wars against great figures such as Saladin and the king of France. The crossbowman was a mere footsoldier; the bow was considered an unknightly weapon, used by footsoldiers or mercenaries. The theme of the great man slain by a lowly one was popular among chroniclers, as a variation on the theme of the passing nature of worldly glory. We have seen above how the theme of humiliation was employed in the nature of William Rufus's death, abandoned and left to the lowliest of his followers. Two examples from William of Newburgh suffice to demonstrate this: in his description of the civil wars of Stephen's reign, he describes the deserved deaths of Geoffrey de Mandeville, earl of Essex, and his followers, who had been terrorising the churches and people of East Anglia. Mandeville himself was killed by an arrow, fired by an 'insignificant footsoldier', while his cohort Robert Marmion was killed in battle by a 'mean minion of the enemy faction'.[87] In a passage glossed as being about the 'wicked life and appropriate death of Geoffrey de Mandeville',

William of Newburgh described how his death was a punishment for his sack of Ramsey Abbey, the walls of which sweated blood as a portent of Mandeville's imminent end.[88]

According to Coggeshall, the crossbowman who slew Richard was not even properly armoured, but was defending himself with a frying-pan in place of a shield when captured. This reflects the different equipment used by a footsoldier and that of a knight, further emphasising the archer's lack of social status; he had no shield not because he was neglectful, but because a shield would, in normal circumstances, be of no use to a crossbowman. His lack of proper armour ironically echoes Richard's neglect in venturing out without his armour. This neglect could, furthermore, be seen as arrogance, strengthening the interpretation of the story as an example of a fitting, divinely ordained death. There are interesting parallels with descriptions in crusading chronicles of women joining in with the defence of cities under siege, and using whatever household equipment they could lay their hands on as armour or weaponry.[89] Even if Coggeshall is not consciously 'unmanning' Richard, by implying that he was killed by a 'feminine' soldier, there is still a note of irony at such a great king struck down by a foe so ill-equipped for warfare. A further parallel may be seen in accounts of the death of Simon de Montfort the elder, the father of the rebel killed at Evesham, who was said by some to have been killed in 1218 at the siege of Toulouse by a stone launched from a catapult operated by women.[90] Finally, the crossbow, with its capacity for accurate, clinical killing of aristocrats by footsoldiers, was considered a cruel, subversive, unchivalrous and faintly disreputable weapon; indeed its use was condemned by the papacy.

There has been a recent (and convincing) challenge to this accepted version of events.[91] Once again, it would seem that the death story was manipulated for the purposes of providing an appropriate end for a king who was thought to be a poor ruler, who neglected his kingdom in favour of adventure and who was a brutal warmonger. The conflict that led to Richard's death has traditionally been viewed as a 'sordid quarrel' in contrast to his great crusading deeds.[92]

It has been argued that the origins of the 'treasure trove' story demonstrate that it has to be read critically. Treasure was an element which often featured in legend and folklore, for example in the common folk-tale motif of a great treasure guarded by a dragon or similar fantastical creature. Richard's striving for a hoard of treasure, in preference to more prosaic explanations for his actions grounded in the politics of France and Aquitaine, does seem to have a fairy-tale quality to it. Coggeshall only admits that there were 'some people who say' that Richard went to Châlus in search of treasure. Bernard Itier, the main source for the story, was a monk at St-Martial in Limoges, a house associated with the viscount of Limoges, Richard's enemy, against whom the siege of Châlus was ultimately directed. William the Breton's hostile version, which includes the condemnation of Richard for fighting during Lent, also mentions the treasure.

There is an alternative, and more positive, reading of Richard's end. Not all kings were seen as having died miserable or damnable deaths like that of Rufus. Some died an exemplary death, or something approaching it. As we have seen, Gaimar's account of Rufus's death shows the king willing to accept the sacraments and make confession. This was ideally how a Christian would hope to end his life, and more favourable chronicle accounts usually allowed that they had done so. As well as making his peace with his creator, a man was also expected to put his secular affairs in order.

Henry I was credited by William of Malmesbury with making a good end to his life. His account stands in contrast to that of the negative one of Henry of Huntingdon. According to William, Henry I died surrounded by clergymen, including the archbishop of Rouen, whose letter to the pope describing the king's exemplary death William quotes. He describes how Henry made his confession, received the eucharist, and was anointed with holy oil. Having made his peace with God, he also settled his earthly affairs, confirming his daughter Matilda as his heir, and arranging for the payment of his debts and of alms.[93] In contrast to Henry of Huntingdon, who claimed that the dead king's body quickly began to decompose, William states that it was disembowelled 'lest it should rot with lapse of time and offend the nostrils of those sat or stood by it'.[94]

Likewise, Stephen was credited by Gervase of Canterbury with an exemplary death, receiving the sacraments on his death-bed.[95] Henry II was said by Roger of Howden to have made confession and received communion toward the end.[96] Henry, the Young King (the eldest son of Henry II), was also credited by a sympathetic observer with making a pious end, doing penance and lying on a bed of ashes with a halter around his neck. So it was not always the case that a king met a bad end, at least in a spiritual sense. Later medieval kings such as Edward I and Henry V were also credited with 'good' deaths, taking the time to set their affairs to right and to compose their souls. Edward, for example, advised his lords to see to the welfare of the kingdom under his son, while Henry took the opportunity to settle the affairs of the realm, hear prayers read to him, express the regret that he had never been able to go on crusade, and repent of his unjust treatment of his stepmother Queen Joan, whom he had dispossessed on trumped-up charges.[97]

Despite the accusations against Richard I as a blasphemer and rebel, many accounts of his death (primarily the Anglo-Norman chroniclers, who might be inclined to be more sympathetic than their French counterparts) present it in an exemplary fashion. It must be remembered here that Richard's death was unlike that of Rufus in that it was a lingering one, allowing him ample time to make his peace with God and Man. Ralph of Coggeshall mentions that Richard's confession was heard by the abbot of Le Pin, and that he received unction before death. He also summoned his mother, Eleanor of Aquitaine, to his bedside, and, after the castle had fallen, summoned the archer who had killed him, in order to express his forgiveness of him.[98] His actions therefore fit the idealised pattern of setting right the affairs of both the spirit and of the world before death. Howden confirms the story that Richard forgave the archer, but adds that he was then flayed alive by Richard's men after the king's death.[99] Gervase of Canterbury includes the story of Richard's forgiveness of the archer, but adds a local touch, that Richard repented the harm that he had done to the church of Canterbury.[100] The Winchester Annals repeat this story, adding the detail that Richard's sister Joan ordered the execution of the archer.[101]

The distinction between Richard's supposedly wicked life and his pious death was probably played up for moral effect by the chroniclers. This device was certainly used by Howden, whose epigrams commented that Richard had been brought down after a sinful reign. In his account, however, Richard dies the death of a good Christian, forgiving the crossbowman who had inflicted his mortal wound.[102]

A much later incident demonstrates the longevity of the idea of divine intervention bringing about the death of a king. The reign of Richard III occurred centuries later, but descriptions of his death contain elements that are strikingly similar to those of his Anglo-Norman ancestors. Richard was defeated and killed by his rival for the throne, Henry Tudor, at the battle of Bosworth in 1485. A key element of Henry's propaganda against Richard was the latter's alleged murder of the 'Princes in the Tower', Richard's young nephews Edward V and Richard, duke of York. Although the full-blown caricature of Richard as the irredeemably evil villain of Shakespeare was a product of later writers such as Edward Hall and Thomas More, even near-contemporary accounts sought to portray Richard as a tyrant brought down by divine justice, just as twelfth-century chroniclers had treated William Rufus. Like Rufus, Richard was afflicted with terrible visions that presaged his death. On the eve of the battle of Bosworth, he dreamt of being surrounded by demons. In Shakespeare's play, this is transformed into a scene where he is confronted by the ghosts of his murdered victims, which, in his jaundiced view of Richard, include not only the Princes in the Tower, but Henry VI, Henry's son Edward, prince of Wales, and Richard's brothers the duke of Clarence and Edward IV.[103] Ominously, when he rose and went to mass, no priest could be found, so we are left to assume that he, like Rufus, died unshriven.[104] He is presented by hostile commentators as diabolical; for John Rous, 'like Antichrist to come, he was confounded at his moment of greatest pride',[105] while the Crowland Continuator, who related the story of his dream, concluded that his subsequent defeat was 'a glorious victory granted by God to the earl of Richmond [Henry VII]'. This judgement was not confined to English writers: for the Frenchman Philippe de Commines, Henry's relative obscurity, and lack of a very convincing claim to the throne, made him appear as one raised up by God against Richard. The Spanish diplomat Diego de Valera, in a letter to the Catholic Monarchs Ferdinand and Isabella, commented that 'our lord did not permit [Richard's] evil deeds to go unpunished ...'[106]

Like Rufus in Orderic's chronicle, Richard is shamed in death by comparison to a hunted animal; his dead body was slung ignominiously over the back of a horse and carried off the battlefield. In the words of Jean de Molinet, he was carried 'hair hanging as one would bear a sheep'.

The *Great Chronicle of London* described how the body was stripped, 'naught being left about him so much as would cover his privy member', and was trussed to the back of a horse 'as a hog or other vile beast, and so, all bespattered with mire and filth, was brought to a church in Leicester for all men to wonder at, and there lastly irreverently buried'.[107] *Fabyan's Chronicle*, another London account, probably compiled by the same author as the *Great Chronicle*, describes how the body was 'spoyled and naked, as he was borne, cast behynde a man, and so caryed unreverently overthwarte the horse back ...' Richard's end was fitting for one who 'ruled mostwhat by rygour and tyrranye, when he in great trouble and agonye reygned or usurped' the kingship.[108] These chronicles were written in the early years of the sixteenth century, under the Tudors, and tend to be pro-Lancastrian and pro-Tudor and therefore anti-Yorkist in outlook.[109] Polydore Vergil repeats the story, adding the comment that this was 'a miserable spectacle ... but not unworthy for the man's life ...'.

This is not to suggest that any of the above writers were attempting deliberately to copy the twelfth-century accounts of Rufus's death, or even than they knew of them (the so-called 'Crowland Continuator', for example, who at first glance might be thought to be writing in the tradition of high medieval monastic chronicles, appears not to have been a monk at all, but a lawyer and royal councillor, writing under a pseudonym). Rather, it demonstrates that they continued to draw on a similar stock of images to demonstrate God's providential purpose at work in the affairs of men.

We have seen the popularity throughout our period of the idea that sudden, violent death was visited upon a king as a means of divine judgement. The symbolism of death by a sudden blow such as an arrow wound was simply too powerful for the chroniclers to resist. In the particular case of death in this manner there is the added element of the apparently random nature of such a death. Unlike, say, a blow with a sword, which was deliberately aimed by the assailant to kill an intended victim, the firing of arrows in medieval battles had a random element; they were not generally aimed at a particular person (the crossbowman who killed Richard I is an exception, in that he took aim), so to be struck by one was an example of ill-luck, or of providence, rather than the intention of the archer who fired it. The deaths of Harold, killed by a random arrow if we accept the Bayeux Tapestry version, or of Rufus in an accident, were therefore arguably more providential than the death of Richard, who was deliberately killed by the act of a man. Although God's design was to be seen in all things, according to the chroniclers, Harold's or Rufus's deaths were by their nature more 'acts of God' than that of Richard.

The mode of death, however, is not the full story. The state of the king's soul at the time of death, and the immediate aftermath of his death, were of paramount importance to the chronicler's purposes. The circumstances of the deaths of William Rufus and Richard I were similar, but the emphasis on the former's unpreparedness to meet his maker, and his subsequent damnation, may be contrasted with the assurances of more sympathetic chroniclers that Richard had met a good death, the slowness of which allowed him time to repent his wicked life and make his peace with God, friend and foe. The spiritual state of the dead king was the often reflected in the subsequent treatment of his body, with Rufus's and Richard III's bodies being treated irreverently (although in the latter case, this was due primarily to his defeat in battle by a rival for his throne).

We have touched upon the treatment of the dead bodies of kings by man. But chronicle accounts also often dwelled upon the physical state of the body, demonstrating what nature (or God) had done to the deceased, and what this too might reflect about him.

3

The Corruption of the Body

Telling stories is perhaps an underrated part of the historian's discipline, but it was central to the art of the twelfth-century monastic chronicler. As the authors of *1066 and All That* understood, the 'memorable' incidents of history are precisely those striking stories – often of dubious historical truth – that owe their provenance to the penchant for story-telling of medieval chroniclers. With this in mind, we must consider royal deaths not in the light of their political repercussions but by looking at the stories that were told about them by chroniclers. One common motif occurs in several stories of royal death, that of the corruption or dismemberment of the body, and it carried strong moral and religious overtones.

One such incident concerns the death of William I, 'the Conqueror' in 1087. William was severely wounded in the abdomen in the course of the siege of Mantes in September of that year, while campaigning against the Capetian king of France, with whose lands Normandy shared its eastern border. William's horse was startled by a beam falling from a burning building, and threw him heavily against the pommel of his saddle. He died of an internal rupture that this caused. The cause of his death, and the fact that in his later years the Conqueror had become notoriously fat, are directly relevant to the gruesome aftermath.

In his description of the death of William, Orderic Vitalis dwells at some length on one particularly unpleasant incident during his funeral at Caen:

> Next, when the corpse was placed in the sarcophagus, and was forcibly doubled up because the masons had carelessly made the coffin too short and narrow, the swollen bowels burst, and an intolerable stench assailed the nostrils of the bystanders and the whole crowd. A thick smoke arose from the frankincense and other spices in the censers, but it was not strong enough to conceal the foul ignominy. So the priests made haste to

conclude the funeral rites, and immediately returned, trembling, to their own houses.[1]

The description by Henry of Huntingdon of the corpse of Henry I demonstrates a similar interest in the corruption of the dead king's body:

> The remainder of the corpse was cut all over with knives, sprinkled with a great deal of salt, and wrapped in ox hides, to stop the strong, pervasive stench, which was already causing the deaths of those who watched over it. It even killed the man who had been hired for a great fee to cut off the head with an axe and extract the stinking brain, although he had wrapped himself in linen cloths around his head: so he was badly rewarded by his fee. He was the last of many whom Henry put to death. They took the royal corpse to Caen, and it lay there for a time in the church in which his father had been buried. Although it had been filled with much salt and wrapped in many hides, a fearful black fluid ran down continuously, leaking through the hides, and being collected in vessels beneath the bier, was cast away by attendants who grew faint with dread.[2]

We are immediately struck by the chroniclers' emphasis on the stench and corruption of the dead body, but in particular by the apparent relish with which they dwell on particularly nauseating details; the bursting of the body in the case of William, and the emission of 'a fearful black fluid' from the body of Henry. In both cases, it may be noted, the writer stresses the fact that the foulness emanated from out of the dead body itself.

What are we to make of these accounts? The most obvious point is that the two accounts were written by monastic chroniclers, so there is a stress on the idea of *contemptus mundi*, the dwelling on the corruption of the earthly body of the king to draw the reader's attention away from worldly pomp and glory and towards a contemplation of the life of the spirit. Indeed, Henry of Huntingdon wrote a letter to a friend entitled *De contemptu mundi*, which among other things dealt with the supposed crimes of Henry I, and declared 'regia res scelus est' (the business of kingship is felony).[3] In a letter to Henry I himself, Henry of Huntingdon had described the 'succession of the most powerful kings' so that the king might 'see and consider how the names of the most terrible kings will have come to nothing ... Consider whether this transient, indeed vanishing, kingdom ... should be lovingly cherished, or should the other, which is by far the better and never passes away, be sought and the other despised?'[4] Huntingdon applies this idea to his description of the embalming of Henry I:

> See, then, whoever you are reading this, how the corpse of this mighty king, whose crowned head had sparkled with gold and the finest jewels, like the splendour of God, whose hands had shone with sceptres, while the rest of his body had been dressed in gorgeous cloth of gold, and his mouth had always been fed on the most delicious and choice foods, for whom everyone would rise to their feet, whom everyone feared, with whom everyone rejoiced, and whom everyone admired; see, what that body became, how fearfully it melted away, how wretchedly cast down it was! See, I say, the outcome of events, upon which final judgement always depends. And learn to hold in contempt whatever is put to such an end, whatever is reduced to nothing in this way.[5]

The reference to the shining of royal jewels was repeated in a more reverent tone, but with a similar moral message that heavenly kingship was greater than that on earth, by the chronicler Thomas Wykes to describe the magnificent burial of Henry III in 1272, who 'was adorned with the most precious garments and a royal diadem as was fitting ... so that he shone forth with greater splendour dead then before when he was alive'.[6]

Orderic writes in similar terms about William I's end, alluding also to his earlier account of how the king had been abandoned by the attendants at his death-bed:

> A king, once powerful and warlike, feared by many peoples in different lands, lay naked on the ground, abandoned by those who owed their birth and position to him ... His bowels, nourished with so many delicacies, shamefully burst, revealing to wise and foolish alike how vain is the glory of the flesh. All who beheld the corruption of that foul corpse learnt to strive earnestly through the salutary discipline of abstinence to earn better rewards than the delights of the flesh, which is earth, and will return to dust ... Rich and poor are of the same nature; both alike fall victims to death and decay. Therefore put not your trust in false princes, O sons of men, but in the true and living God who is the creator of all things.[7]

This is standard ecclesiastical moralising; the stress on the passing nature of worldly glory, on the fact that death and decay come to rich and

poor alike, and a call on the reader to forsake this world and consider
the next. There are interesting elements in the two accounts that require
further comment. First, in both a link is drawn between the deceased
king's indulgence in food and his sorry state after death. William's
bowels, we are told, had been 'nourished with so many delicacies', and
the implication is that they burst because of this, or at least that their
bursting was a fit reward for William's self-indulgence in life. A dispas-
sionate reader may conclude that the bowels may have swollen up
through a combination of the internal rupture that killed him, and the
body's having spent several days in transit from Mantes to Caen in the
heat of August. Furthermore, Orderic tells us that the attendants had
been attempting to 'double up' the body to make it fit into the sarco-
phagus when the accident occurred – in other words, it was William's
height, not his corpulence, that was responsible for the ill-fitting coffin.
Yet it serves Orderic's moralising purpose better to emphasise the
bloated body of the dead king, rather than his stature. The choice of
word to describe William's fatness is also revealing: he describes the
body as *pingue*, and intriguingly, although he does not repeat Huntingdon's story about Henry I, he also refers to that king's body as
pinguissimus.[8] Orderic's modern translator renders the word in both
cases as 'corpulent', but it seems to me to have been chosen not to
denote size but to imply a sense of the body as fatty or oleaginous, as
if to invoke disgust in the reader.

The prelude to Henry of Huntingdon's account of Henry I's embalming is the famous story that he died of a 'surfeit of lampreys'.[9] We are
told that he ate lampreys against doctor's orders, as, according to Henry
quoting Ovid, 'we always strive for what is forbidden and long for what
is refused'.[10] Again there is a clear moral message: the king died because
he sought after what was forbidden or dangerous, just as mortals seek
after the pleasures of glory of this world when they should put the minds
on seeking after the next. Henry's sinful gluttony, like William I's, was
reflected in the decayed state of his body after death, as if the forbidden
meat, the 'delicious and choice foods' eaten by Henry, or the 'many
delicacies' consumed by William, had turned into poison, which had
despatched the king and now continued to poison those who stood
around his dead body. The motif of death as punishment for gluttony,
in a context of reflection on the transience of worldly power, occurs

elsewhere in Henry of Huntingdon's writings. In a letter to Henry I himself on 'the succession of the most powerful kings',[11] the writer had reminded the king of the fate that befell the Emperor Vitellius, 'a man devoted to gluttony', who was slain by the Romans.[12] Some medieval versions of Vitellius's death held that his bowels were torn open, another echo of the same theme.[13]

Gluttony was one of the Seven Deadly Sins, and obesity was therefore an external expression of sin, as demonstrated in Huntingdon's description of the French kings Philip I and Louis VI, 'whose god was their stomach, a deadly enemy indeed'.[14] Such a lack of self-control was clearly a poor quality in one who was born to rule, and Henry claims that these two kings lost all their battles. Furthermore, gluttony was often regarded as the worst of the sins, as it led to further sin; in medieval ideas of physiology, it was believed that an excessive intake of food increased the body's heat, which in turn led to lust. The belly and viscera were associated with appetite, vice and disease; Roger of Wendover reported that the monks of Châlus were insulted by the burial of Richard I's viscera in their abbey.[15]

This type of imagery reoccurs in a later account of the death of a king of England, that of John in 1216. Like William Rufus, John had a history of conflict with the church. The disputed election to the archiepiscopal see of Canterbury had led to a breach with Pope Innocent III, which resulted in England being placed under an interdict from 1208 to 1214. John used Innocent's actions as an excuse to plunder the resources of the English church in this period. For these reasons, John was viewed in a highly negative light by clerical chroniclers.

John died in the north, while campaigning against rebel barons. His oppressive government, and his failure to regain Normandy (lost to the French in 1204), provoked baronial opposition, leading to the concession of Magna Carta by the king in 1215. This did not, in fact, end the conflict. John was able to persuade the pope, with whom he had been reconciled in 1214, to declare the charter null and void, at which point the barons resumed their rebellion. John marched north, as many of the rebel barons had their estates in Lincolnshire and Yorkshire.

John was seized with fever at Swineshead in Lincolnshire, shortly after the famous misfortune that had befallen him when he lost his baggage train while crossing the Wash. As told by Roger of Wendover, the king, like Henry I before him, hastened his own end through foolish self-indulgence: 'His sickness was increased by his pernicious gluttony, for that night he surfeited himself with peaches and drinking new cider, which greatly increased and aggravated the fever in him.' [16] John struggled on to Newark, where he died, receiving the cucharist from the abbot of Croxton. The abbot, perhaps significantly, was John's physician, so the king's flouting of medical advice may be linked in the person of the abbot-physician with his flouting of the church earlier in the reign. Another monastic historian, Ralph of Coggeshall, was more explicit in attacking John through describing his manner of death, claiming that John's illness, dysentery, had been brought on by his self-indulgence in food at Lynn a few days earlier: 'But at this place, as it was said, from an excessive voracity by which his belly was always insatiable, he gorged himself to the point of intoxication, by which his greedy belly flowed with dysentery.' [17] Again, we see the link being drawn between the king's self-indulgence, and his death through corruption within, particularly in the belly. In case we have missed the point, Ralph describes a terrible storm at Newark that accompanied his death, accompanied by 'horrible and fantastical visions'.[18]

A similar motif was employed in describing the death of Falkes de Bréauté, a hated former captain of John's, in 1226. According to Matthew Paris, Falkes perished as a result of eating rotten fish, and died 'black, stinking, and intestate'.[19] This was divine judgement on Falkes for having attacked Matthew's own abbey of St Albans some years earlier.

Given the associations of dysentery, it is not surprising that later generations believed John had been poisoned by the monks of Swineshead. Shakespeare, in his *King John*, has the king suffer this fate.[20] Shakespeare presented John as a tyrant, the murderer of his nephew, in some ways the forerunner of Richard III. An earlier Tudor playwright, John Bale, in his play *Kynge Johan* (written *c.* 1548), includes the death by poison, but makes John a martyr for England at the hands of the Roman Catholic Church, a thirteenth-century Henry VIII.

A late medieval example illustrates the continuity of the imagery of gluttony. Edward IV died in 1483 of uncertain causes. He had a reputation for sexual licence and self-indulgence, however, and it was widely held by contemporaries that he died at the relatively young age of forty largely because of his life of overindulgence. In particular, his sexual activities were remarked upon, as he was accused of seduction and of keeping a number of mistresses. Given this reputation, and the medieval association of an excess sexual appetite with an excess appetite for food, it is not surprising to see that his death was widely blamed on his gluttony. The Italian priest Dominic Mancini, reporting the English events of that disturbed year to the archbishop of Vienne, observed that:

> In food and drink he was immoderate: it was his habit, so I have learned, to take an emetic for the delight of gorging his stomach once more. For this reason ... he had grown fat in his loins ... He was licentious in the extreme: moreover it was often said that he had been most insolent to numerous women after he had seduced them, for, as soon as he grew weary of dalliance, he gave up the ladies much against their will to other courtiers.[21]

Mancini also viewed Edward's ill-considered marriage to Elizabeth Woodville as another example of the king's carnal appetites. Mancini's character portrait of Edward is in the tradition dating back to the classical historian Suetonius of providing a 'pen-picture' of a ruler. It was conventional for rulers to be praised for their moderation in food and drink, an image used by medieval biographers, such as Einhard in his *Life of Charlemagne*.[22] Mancini's inversion of this theme suggests Edward was a bad ruler, as does his dwelling on the king's sexual vices, another echo of Suetonius, who gleefully described the extreme sexual behaviour of the tyrannical emperors Tiberius, Caligula and Nero. Edward's dietary and sexual immoderation are also linked in Mancini's statement that he became 'fat in the loins'.

Given this picture of Edward, it is not surprising to find so many sources claiming that his death was caused by his overindulgence. Mancini himself did not do so, blaming it on despair at hearing of a Franco-Burgundian alliance (which was hostile to English interests on the Continent), or on a chill that he caught while fishing in a boat.[23] Others, however, were less kind. The French writer Philippe de Commines said that he died of apoplexy following a surfeit of food (an echo perhaps of Henry I's surfeit of lampreys). Commines's compatriot Thomas Basin wrote that Edward had eaten an excess of vegetables on

Good Friday – an ironic comment that he had died at a time of fasting, implying that he was incapable of restraining his appetite even when red meat was off the menu. Jean de Roye blamed Edward's overindulgence in wine, adding the charge of drunkenness to that of gluttony. The English chronicler Edward Hall, by contrast, patriotically asserted that Edward had died of an 'incurable quartan' fever contracted in France in 1475.[24] The Crowland Continuator commented that he had 'indulged too intemperately his own passions and desire for luxury', but allowed that he died a good death, making a will and performing penance before his death.[25]

We can see that monastic chroniclers used the same elements in describing aspects of the deaths of these kings. The similarity of these accounts suggests they ought to be seen as part of a genre, rather than as literal descriptions of the events they purport to relate, especially as none were eyewitness accounts. The elements of bodily corruption, self-indulgence of the flesh, and moralising reflections on the way of all flesh, make the accounts appear highly stereotyped. They also, however, reflect particular moral judgements against the individual kings concerned.

In the case of Henry of Huntingdon and Henry I, we can see elsewhere in his writings that Huntingdon was very critical of the king. In his *Epistola ad Walterum de contemptu mundi*, Henry had – somewhat inaccurately – related the story of how the king had caused his nieces' eyes to be put out.[26] Huntingdon is probably referring in fact to the occasion when Henry allowed his granddaughters' eyes to be put out, an incident that will be looked at in detail later. The events were certainly shocking, but Henry of Huntingdon chose to put the worst possible interpretation on Henry's actions. The king was in fact acting on an appeal by a vassal, whose own son had been blinded by the girls' father. Did the writer therefore have a personal animus against his ruler? It would seem not; this incident is related as part of a moral treatise, and elsewhere, giving a balance-sheet of Henry's reign, the chronicler is broadly supportive, comparing Henry's firmness favourably to the vacillations of Stephen.[27] Similarly, Orderic Vitalis's account of William I's death does not seem to reflect a particular enmity toward the conqueror: the Anglo-Norman Orderic criticises the Norman oppression of the

English, but also justifies the Conquest on the grounds of the decadence of the English church.[28]

Orderic's attitude could be summarised as 'what is good for the church is good for England'. An illustration of this can be seen in his view of the deaths of two of the Conqueror's sons in separate accidents in the New Forest, discussed already. Orderic makes the point that this was divine retribution for the king's razing of English villages to make way for the forest, but it was less the destruction of the villages *per se* that concerned him than a concern that churches had been destroyed: Rufus's death illustrated that 'the lord plainly showed his anger that consecrated buildings had been given over to be a habitation of wild beasts'.[29] He noted with apparent satisfaction that 'the doctors and prelates of the church' considered him 'beyond redemption', and that many churches refused to ring their bells for the dead king.[30] Whatever their faults, William I or Henry I did not receive similar treatment, as they were not viewed specifically as oppressors of the church.

If there is no specific political explanation, then to understand the full implications of the imagery employed by Orderic and Henry of Huntingdon we need to consider the moral symbolism surrounding the image of decay. Here is a modern historian's comment on Huntingdon's account of the state of Henry I's body, as it was retold by the fifteenth-century historian John Capgrave:

> [Capgrave] expected his readers to understand a moral criticism. Because it had long been an agreed proof of sanctity that the deceased holy person's body resisted decomposition so far as to smell sweet rather than to putrefy, a corpse that stank might be taken as evidence of the opposite kind of life ... A question such as 'But did Henry's corpse *really* smell?', might have seemed to him to miss the point of his description.[31]

By making the bodies of Henry and of William corrupt and stinking, the chroniclers are suggesting a moral corruption associated with them. By employing this motif, Orderic and Henry of Huntingdon were tapping into a very old literary tradition in classical and biblical sources, in which tyrants met with slow, unpleasant and malodorous deaths.

In the Apocryphal Books of Maccabees (2 Maccabees 9: 1–29), the persecuting King Antiochus meets a death that was both timely and

sudden in its onset, and slow and unpleasant in its course. After his
army has been defeated by the Jews, Antiochus swears vengeance:

> But the all-seeing Lord, the God of Israel, smote him with a fatal and unseen
> stroke: the words were no sooner out of his mouth than he was seized with
> an incurable pain in the bowels, and his internal organs gave him cruel torture
> – a right proper judgement for one who had tortured the bowels of other
> people with many an exquisite pang.

The Greek king continues to curse the Jews and swears to destroy them,
so God sends another warning to him: he is flung from his chariot, after
which he has to be carried on a litter, 'a manifest token to all men of
the power of God'. From this point on, things become highly unpleasant
for the tyrant:

> Worms actually swarmed from the impious creature's body; his flesh fell
> away, while he was still alive in pain and anguish; and the stench of his
> corruption turned the whole army from him with loathing. A man who
> shortly before had thought he could touch the stars of heaven, none could
> now endure to carry, such was his intolerable stench.

Only then does Antiochus repent of his promise to slaughter the Jews,
admitting that 'Right is it that mortal man should be subject to God,
and not to deem himself God's equal.'

Similarly, the persecutors of Christ and the apostles met equally
unpleasant ends. Herod the Great was punished for his slaughter of the
Innocents:

> Finally, when Herod was seventy years old, he fell ill with a deadly disease,
> being tormented by high fever, an itch all over his body, incessant pain,
> inflammation of the feet, worms in the testicles, a horrible smell, and shortness
> and irregularity of breath.[32]

This description was not simply the invention of Christian moralists,
but was taken quite faithfully from the account of Josephus, the Jewish
historian of the first century AD.[33] For good measure, the biblical writers
applied a similar death to other persecuting Herods: Herod Agrippa,
after having killed Stephen and imprisoned Peter, was struck down
by an angel, and 'was eaten up by worms and died'.[34] Like Antiochus,
the specific crime for which he was punished was blasphemy, having
compared himself to God.

A very similar fate was assigned to the Emperor Galerius, one of the persecuting pagan emperors of the early fourth century. According to the Christian apologist Lactantius, Galerius was like Herod eaten up by worms from the penis upwards, and like Antiochus was reduced to such a stench that none dared approach him. The disease became worse after Galerius prayed to his 'idols', and the worms spread to inside his vital organs. 'The smell pervaded not just the palace but the whole city ... He was consumed with worms, and his body dissolved and rotted amid insupportable pain.' [35]

An early medieval precedent, which mirrors very closely the unpleasant end of the biblical Antiochus, was the death of the Frankish king Charles the Bald in 877. According to the *Annals of St-Bertin*, he was struck down with fever, and then poisoned by his Jewish doctor under the guise of giving him medicine. After his death, his body was disembowelled, and attempts were made to preserve it with wine and aromatic herbs. It was to be carried to the royal necropolis of St-Denis for burial, but the bearers were unable to withstand the stench of the decaying flesh. They wrapped the body in skins and placed it in a barrel, and when that did not work, they buried him hastily at the abbey of Nantua in Burgundy.[36] The story is repeated in the *Annals of St-Vaast* and the *Annals of Fulda*, where the anti-Semitic story of the doctor is omitted in favour of the explanation that he died of dysentery.[37] We can see many elements of similarity with the death of Antiochus, notably the statement that the body's bearers could no longer stand the stench, but also with the later accounts of English kings that have been considered.

These examples were not limited to biblical or classical and artistic sources, but also occurred in contemporary chronicles. The *Gesta Stephani* records the similarly unpleasant death of Robert fitz Hildebrand. For the twin crimes of treachery and adultery, he was suitably afflicted:

> a worm was born at the time when the traitorous corrupter lay in the unchaste bosom of the adulteress and crept through his vitals, and slowly eating away at his entrails it gradually consumed the scoundrel, and at length, in affliction of many complaints and the torment of many dreadful sufferings, it brought him to his end by a punishment he richly deserved.[38]

The author then explains that this is God's punishment on account of his treason and adultery, and because he had burned the church of St Ethelfleda, who, perhaps significantly in the context, was a virgin.

The imagery of putrefaction continued into the later middle ages, illustrating how long-lived this motif was. Indeed, the late fourteenth and fifteenth centuries had a fascination with the idea of death and decay, as shown by the popularity of the cadaver tomb, which depicted the decaying corpse of its occupant, often underneath an effigy of him or her in their worldly finery. These tombs expressed the idea of *memento mori*, reminding the living that they too would be dead some day, and that death and decay came to all social classes. The same idea was expressed in another popular late medieval artistic image, the Dance of Death, in which Death, represented as a skeleton or as a decaying cadaver in a winding sheet, dances with representatives of each social class.[39]

As we have seen, the story of Henry I's putrefying corpse was recorded by Capgrave, but the imagery reappears for a later medieval king, in the case of Henry IV. Putrefaction, if the chroniclers are to be believed, accompanied both the beginning and end of his reign. According to Adam of Usk, Henry was stricken with an

> infection which for five years had cruelly tormented [him] with festering of the flesh, dehydration of the eyes, and rupture of the internal organs [which] caused him to end his days ... The festering was foreshadowed at his coronation, for as a result of his anointing then [with rancid oil], his head was so infected with lice that his hair fell out, and for several months he had to keep his head covered.[40]

The incident of the holy oil was doubly ironic, first, because the anointing was central to the idea that the king ruled by a divine mandate; and, secondly, because Henry himself had acquired the oil, believed to have been provided by Thomas Becket, himself. The St Albans Abbey chronicler Thomas Walsingham tells the story.[41] Becket, in exile in France, had donated a phial of holy oil to an abbey in Poitiers, along with a written prophecy that whoever was anointed with that oil would go on to recover Normandy and Aquitaine, and drive the Infidel from the Holy Land. Like all the best prophecies, this was retrospective, as in Becket's day the Plantagenet possessions in France were yet to be lost and the Holy Land was still in Christian hands. Richard II found the phial and the prophecy, and eagerly asked the archbishop of Canterbury to reanoint him with the oil. The archbishop refused, saying that it was necessary for a king to be anointed only once. Following his detention by Henry's supporters in 1399, Richard handed the oil over to the archbishop, recognising that God had intended another to be king. It was therefore Henry who was anointed with this oil. Adam of Usk's story stands in marked contrast to that of the generally pro-Lancastrian Walsingham, as if the very oil of St Thomas (who had been martyred for defying a tyrant) were rebelling against the usurper Henry. Adam has often been described as a 'Lancastrian' chronicler, but this is to overstate the case. He supported Richard's deposition but was by no means an enthusiast for Henry.[42] His story of the oil supports the view that he had his doubts about Henry's legitimacy, whereas Walsingham presents Henry as chosen by God and St Thomas. There is also a telling contrast between the putrefaction evident in Henry, and in the oil used to anoint him, and the idea of anointing as a cleansing ritual. A thirteenth-century work recording the form of the coronation rite specifies that the coif worn on the king's head for the anointing was to be worn for seven days, and that on the eighth day the coif was to be removed, and the king's hair formally washed and styled 'in reverence of his cleansing'.[43]

Henry IV was a king against whom accusations could easily be made, as he was a usurper in the eyes of many. His overthrow of Richard II created legends that the former king had survived, and even produced an impostor claiming to be Richard. The opposition to Henry also produced a political martyr in the shape of Archbishop Scrope of York, whom Henry had executed for his part in a rebellion in 1405. The dead prelate was hailed a saint by his supporters. It was widely claimed that Henry's long, terminal illness began on the day of Scrope's execution. This illness, a disfiguring and unpleasant skin disease, was held by some to be leprosy, a disease that was associated with sin, especially sexual sin, a judgement that may have influenced those modern authors who have concluded that he suffered from a venereal disease. Capgrave recorded that 'the Kyng after that tyme [the execution of Scrope] lost the beaute of his face. For as the comonne opinion went, for that tyme until his deth he was a lepir and evyr fowlere and fowlere.'[44] A late fifteenth-century chronicle records an ongoing memory of the supposed leprosy and sinfulness of Henry, 'whom as it is said God touched and was a lepre er he dyed'.[45] This author suggests that the 'leprosy' was a punishment for Henry's not paying proper respects to the tomb of Richard II, so the disease is again associated with his killing of an opponent, in this case Richard rather than Scrope. Given the traditional belief that 'King's Evil' (the skin disease scrofula) could be cured by the touch of a king, the irony of the king whom many considered a usurper suffering from a disfiguring skin disease would not have been lost on contemporaries, especially as the disease was conferred by the 'touch' of God. According to Adam of Usk, Henry had been tormented for five years by rotting of the flesh, by a drying up of the eyes and by a rupture of the intestines.[46]

The attitudes of ecclesiastical authorities towards the body, its decay and its resurrection were of great importance to the cult of saints. To take but one example, the descriptions of the dead bodies of kings can be contrasted with the early thirteenth-century miracle story of the aptly named Christina the Astonishing, who died, but who was miraculously restored to life in the middle of her funeral service. The revived Christina found the smell of the congregation offensive, and attempted to escape it by levitating to the roof of the church. She was persuaded down by the priest, and related to the astonished congregation that she had died, visited purgatory and been recalled to life. She was afterwards blessed (or cursed) with a particularly acute sense of smell, and spent much of her life attempting to avoid the smell of human beings by hiding up trees, in the rafters of churches or in ovens.[47] The very name Christina is redolent of sacred and perfumed oils. According to Jacobus de Voragine, writing of her namesake St Christina, the name 'suggests *charismate uncta*, anointed with chrism. She had the balm of good odour in her relationships with others, and the oil of devotion in her mind and benediction in her speech.'[48] The association of stench with ordinary, non-saintly mortals contrasts with the association of saints with a sweet odour of sanctity: by about 1200, a common motif in saints' lives was the production of fragrant oils from their bodies. Conversely, saints' bodies did not produce the bodily fluids associated with mortality and mutability: Elizabeth of Spalbeck miraculously did not produce any saliva or mucous, while Lutgard of Aywieres did not menstruate. These female saints frequently fasted, or lived only on the nourishment of the consecrated host, a further contrast to the gluttony ascribed to a number of dead royal males.[49] Stench (*fetor*), by contrast, was associated with Hell, and was often included among the Seven Plagues of Hell.[50] Male saints as well could be sensitive to foul odours: Godric of Finchale appeared to a devotee in a dream, revealing that he had been disturbed by the stench of the latrines near his grave.[51]

William of Newburgh's account of Henry I's death makes a neat point about the contrast between the king and the holy man. Describing how the stench of the decaying corpse killed a bystander, William remarks sardonically that 'just as the body of the dead Elisha gave life to a dead man, so the body of the dead man brought death to a living man'.[52]

There are numerous examples of miracle stories relating to saints' bodies that were found to be incorrupt upon their discovery or translation. Theodore of Echternach, writing in around 1104, argued that

> No substance of flesh is more noble than the flesh of the saints, for the more it is subject to the spirit the more it is free and glorious in the very resolution of corruption ... From nature it is putrid and corruptible, but from grace and merits it remains for a long time without rot even contrary to nature, and it repels the greedy worms.[53]

This was a tradition with a long history. Sulpicius Severus, the fifth-century hagiographer of St Martin of Tours, first established the motif of the clean, only semi-carnal, body of the saint, and his work became the archetype for subsequent saints' lives. In the thirteenth century, the hagiographer of St Hugh of Lincoln could describe his body as 'like Martin's, clearer than glass, whiter than milk'.[54]

Kings, however, could also be saints; the two roles were not incompatible, even if there were tension between them. The archetypal royal saint was Charlemagne, whose body was said to be incorruptible. When his tomb was opened by the Emperor Otto III in 1000, his corpse was found seated on a throne, robed and crowned as in life, the book of the Gospels open on his knees. His body was well preserved, with the exception of his nose, which had decayed, and which Otto replaced with a gold replica. In contrast, Charlemagne's less holy (and less successful) grandson, Charles the Bald, possessed a body that decayed very rapidly after death in a manner similar to that of Henry I.

One example of an incorrupt saint's body, that of St Edmund, is particularly relevant, as he was both a king and an English martyr, so the contrast between his fate and that of the two Anglo-Norman kings is particularly striking. The cult of Saint Edmund was well established, and had produced two hagiographies, by the beginning of the eleventh century. His story would presumably have been known to the two Anglo-Norman historians, especially Henry of Huntingdon, for whom the East Anglian saint's cult must have had a local resonance as it originated at Ramsey Abbey in Huntingdonshire. According to the *Passio Sancti Edmundi* of Abbo of Fleury, written in the late tenth century, Edmund was beheaded by the Danes, but his head was discovered and miraculously re-attached to the body. Furthermore, the body remained uncorrupt; the hair and nails continued to grow, and were groomed by a holy woman who cared for the body.[55] Abbo maintains that, at the body's translation to Bury, it was found to have a thin red line around the neck, 'proving' the story of Edmund's beheading. An account of Hermann, a monk of Bury, in about 1100, and the later more famous account of Jocelyn of Brakelond, also refer to the body's incorrupt state.[56] Abbot Samson, in the translation of 1198, had satisfied himself of the body's intact state by feeling through the shroud. (An earlier abbot, who had impiously put the re-attached head to the test by tugging at it firmly, had been afflicted with palsy in the hand that had dared to abuse the saint.) [57]

Another English saint-king, Edward the Confessor, was found to have an incorrupt body on his first translation in 1102. One aspect of his sanctity is relevant here, that of his miracles, one of which appears to be the first example in England of the belief in the king's power of curing scrofula by touch. In this instance, the cleanliness of the king's body is stressed, in contrast to the accounts of the deaths of William I and Henry I; but of course Edward, as a saint, had acquired the purity that these kings lacked. In the miracle of the cure of a woman with scrofula, the disgusting nature of her disease is stressed; her swollen face is full of pus and worms, which are drawn out by the king's healing hands. We learn that her husband had become so repelled by her appearance that he refused to sleep with her, adding the denial of children to her other woes; after the cure, they resumed marital relations, and she had many children. By contrast, the king is shown as clean; in this, as in other miracles, the recipient is cured by the application of water in which Edward has washed, implying that even his filth is pure.[58]

It is well established that scrofula – a swelling of the glands of the face and neck – was known as the King's Evil (*morbus regius*) before it was believed to be curable by the touch of a king. The expression seems to have been extended to include other unpleasant disfiguring diseases, including leprosy. The term dates back to classical times, the belief in the disease's cure by a royal touch to the eleventh century at the earliest. The association of the disease with a royal cure seems to have followed its naming, not the other way around. The horrible vermicular death of Herod contributed to its naming; it was a disease of kings. So, ironically, it was the negative, worldly, corrupt element of kingship that gave its name to a disease that was believed curable only by the saintly, sacerdotal element of kingship.[59]

The stress on the incorrupt nature of the saint's body contrasts with the corruption in the accounts of Henry I and William the Conqueror. There was also a second element of contrast, that of the indivisibility of the body. King Edmund's body differed from those of William and Henry. Not only did it not decay, it was restored to wholeness, whereas those of the Anglo-Norman kings were broken up, by accident (in the case of William) or by design (in that of Henry). Henry of Huntingdon's account may reflect monastic disapproval of the breaking up of the body for burial, a practice that would eventually be condemned by the papacy at the end of the next century.[60] This practice had been gathering pace during the twelfth century and was not restricted to royal burial, as shown by the practice of breaking up the bodies of saints to supply relics. There was, however, an older tradition stressing the integrity of the body, and horror at its dispersal. Hence Abbo's account of Edmund's martyrdom, in which the Danes, having killed the Saxon king, threw his head and body into the woods to deny him a decent burial, only to have them miraculously rediscovered and reassembled. Abbo's *Vita* may itself borrow elements from that of St Denis, the patron saint of the French kings, who survived beheading long enough to walk, head in hand, the two miles from Montmartre, the site of his martyrdom, to St-Denis, the site of his burial.[61]

The accounts of the burials of William the Conqueror and Henry I, and the horrible incidents surrounding them, can therefore be viewed as a kind of anti-hagiography. Like authors of saints' lives, who drew on common images and topoi to emphasise their subjects' sanctity,

Orderic and Henry of Huntingdon drew on images that stress the lack of sanctity of their subject. By using images of decay and dispersal of the body, they reversed the very bodily qualities associated with sainthood. They did so not so much to attack the dead king himself, as both were political realists who appreciated the political stability imposed by the Anglo-Norman kings; rather, the accounts were designed to emphasise the mutability of earthly pomp and the vanity of kingship.

The symbolism of dismemberment and the separation of parts of the body also had important political implications. From early times, dismemberment could be taken to represent the destruction of the victim, not only as a physical entity but as a political one. In later medieval England, as we shall see later, the practice of quartering the bodies of those executed for treason became common, as the idea of treason as a political concept developed. This acted both as an example to others and as a symbol of the bodily and political destruction of the traitor.

An early example of the dismemberment of a defeated king is to be found in accounts of the death of King Harold. As we have seen, the depiction of Harold's death in the Bayeux Tapestry is notoriously ambiguous, and its meaning has aroused much debate among historians. The section in which Harold's death occurs is often interpreted as a 'cartoon strip' sequence, showing the king first being wounded by an arrow in the eye and then cut down by a horseman. Many eleventh- and twelfth-century accounts of his death, possibly influenced by the tapestry itself, follow this interpretation, and it is in this context that many of the dismemberment stories are told. Typically, Harold is said to have been so badly hacked about by the Norman knights that his body was dismembered, or was at least unrecognisable.

In William of Poitiers' account, Harold's body was badly mutilated, and was with difficulty recognised and recovered by William. The Norman duke refused Harold's mother's request for the return of the body, and contemptuously buried it by the seashore.[62] Guy of Amiens' Latin poem, the *Carmen de Hastingae proelio*, written in 1068, describes Harold's body as being deliberately and systematically cut up by the Norman knights. This is the earliest account of Harold's death.[63] The author describes how each one cut off a certain part of body:

The first of the four, piercing the king's shield and chest with his lance, drenched the ground with a gushing stream of blood. The second with his sword cut off his head below the protection of his helm. The third liquefied his entrails with his spear. The fourth cut off his thigh and carried it some distance away.[64]

The death of Harold and the defeat of the Saxons is made plain in the carving up of his body (in much the way, we might add, that the kingdom itself was carved up among William's followers, although Guy does not make this judgement). The conquest of England is therefore enacted in the *Carmen* upon Harold's dismembered body. The order of the blows struck against Harold is in descending social status, and the wounds were applied quite specifically to parts of the king's body. Therefore William himself strikes the fatal blow to the chest: as the heart was viewed as the seat of the soul, it was appropriate that William should strike this most important of organs. The blows struck by his followers begin with the neck, and work their way down to an ignoble blow to the thigh (possibly a euphemism for his genitals being severed). [65]

In the *Carmen*, William exhibits a more forgiving aspect than in William of Poitiers' account, and effectively reconstitutes Harold, by collecting together the pieces of his body and wrapping them in a cloth of purple, the colour of imperial authority, before giving him a respectful funeral by the seashore.[66] Guy seems to be having the best of both worlds here; having described the symbolically and politically powerful act of dismemberment, he allows William to exhibit the kingly prerogative of burying his predecessor. The act of burying the previous king was important in the transfer of royal authority to the new monarch; even if the old king had been of questionable legitimacy, and had been deposed or even killed by his successor, the aura conferred by anointing was still powerful and still needed to be properly transferred to the new king.[67] It is important to note here that, while William struck the fatal blow, he was not himself involved in the ignoble process of dismemberment. The reconstruction of Harold's body, and his receiving an honourable burial, also has an ideological purpose; just as the dismemberment symbolised conquest, so his burial is an act of reconciliation, as he is buried by a part-Norman, part-English companion of Harold. William wished to be seen as the legitimate king of England, ruling according to the laws and customs of the realm, not as a foreign invader. Eleventh-century England had been ruled previously by Danish kings and by Edward the Confessor, who had been brought up in exile in Normandy, so the idea of a foreign king was not unprecedented. William's burial of his predecessor helped to smooth the transition of power and emphasise dynastic continuity.[68] He assumed the royal title only *after* Harold's burial.[69] By burying his predecessor, he acted like a son officiating at his father's funeral, an idea to be seen later in the reburial of Richard II by Henry V.

The political symbolism of dismemberment can also be seen in the later medieval practice of hanging, drawing and quartering of traitors. This punishment was first carried out in England on Dafydd ap Gruffudd, the brother of Prince Llywelyn of Wales. Dafydd was one of the leaders of the Welsh revolt of 1282–83, the defeat of which sealed the fate both of his brother and of an independent Wales. The concept of treason was itself a new one, a reflection of changing political ideas in the later middle ages. It developed in the later thirteenth and early fourteenth centuries, becoming enshrined in a statute of 1352. The older concept of the tie between a subject and his king being based on personal loyalty evolved into a relationship where the king represented the state, and breaking of faith with him was not merely a case of personal disloyalty but of treason. The concept of 'the king's two bodies' meant that, although the king in his mortal body might die like any man, his political 'body' was immortal. In this political 'body' we can see the ancestor of the modern state, and in the concept of treason the idea of disloyalty to that state. The baronial rebels of Henry II's reign and earlier were usually punished by confiscation of their lands, a blow from which many families were able to recover in the next generation. The later medieval traitor, however, was likely to be subjected to the most horrific death, as well as losing his lands. In the full horror of hanging, drawing and quartering, the victim was first hanged and cut down before losing consciousness, then disembowelled and his viscera burned before his still-living eyes, before finally being beheaded, after which the dead body was divided into four parts which were taken away and displayed in different parts of the realm.

This gruesome punishment demonstrates once more the principle that it was not enough to kill an enemy, it was necessary utterly to destroy him. On a practical level, of course, the horrors of a traitor's death were intended to act as a greater deterrent than just death itself: not only was it an agonising death, but it was one that stripped the victim of any dignity. The division of the body into segments, and the denial of burial, might also be seen as an attempt to prevent subsequent veneration of the dead man's remains. If there were no burial-place and no tomb, it would guard against the development of a cult centre. This was often not the case, however as the dispersal of an executed man's remains could act to spread his cult, in the same way that a saint's cult could be spread by the dispersal of his or her relics. The quartering of the body was also political theatre; and the despatch of the quarters to the four corners of the kingdom was a demonstration of the king's power. The king was seen to affirm his authority over the whole kingdom in the very act of destroying one who would deprive him of that authority. For example, after his beheading, the head of Archbishop Scrope of York, who had rebelled against Henry IV in 1405, was placed on the walls of York, as if to demonstrate that the city was not the archbishop's but the king's, and that rightful authority had been restored.[70]

The destruction or dissolution of the condemned man's body had another powerful message; if there were no body, it would be as if he had never lived. In medieval religious thought, bodily dissolution and reconstitution were symbolic of damnation and salvation. Religious art of the time often shows scenes of the general resurrection, in which the bodies of the saved are reconstituted and revivified, even to the extent that beasts such as lions and wolves vomit up body parts that they had consumed.

An example of the state's power being enacted on the bodies of defeated rebels in this manner is given in the following description of the fate of the rebels of 1381:

He [Justice Tresilian] condemned (according to the nature of their crimes) some to beheading, some to hanging, some to drawing through the cities and then hanging in four parts of the cities, and some to disembowelling, followed by the burning of their entrails before them while still alive, and then their execution and the division of their corpses into quarters to be hanged in four parts of the cities. Lord [sic] John Ball was himself captured at Coventry and brought to St Albans where, by royal command, he was drawn, hanged, and quartered so that the four parts of his body should be sent to hang in four different places [71]

The significant point to note here is the phrase 'according to the nature of their crimes', the terrible penalty of hanging, drawing and quartering being reserved for the ringleaders of sedition, including John Ball. Executions were often carried out in a manner that was considered apposite for the crime; for example, French 'brigands' (bandits or rebels, or possibly both) in the last period of English rule in Normandy (1415–50) were 'beheaded as traitors and the bodies hung from the gibbet as thieves'.[72]

Another example of the political significance of dismembering and reconstitution of the body can be seen in a dream attributed to Richard II by the chronicler Adam of Usk. Richard imagined that the tomb of the earl of Arundel, who had been executed for treason in 1397, was opened up, and the earl's severed head was found re-attached to his body.[73] This account refers to a popular belief recorded by Thomas Walsingham, and by the chronicle of Dieulacres Abbey, that Arundel's head had grown back onto its body, a story that circulated to the extent that the king had the earl of Surrey proclaim that it was not true.[74] The story is strikingly similar to the legend of St Edmund, with the distinction that it represents not the sanctity of kingship but its coming fall. Adam places the dream in the context of other portents of the deposition of Richard in 1399. The implication is that the ideas represented by Arundel and his fellow reforming lords, which were overturned by Richard's tyranny, will soon be victorious in the person of Henry IV. In this context, the concept of the body politic is embodied not in Richard, who has deformed that body by his personal and arbitrary rule, but in that of his baronial opponents.

There was also symbolism in the partition of the king's body after death. The burial of parts of the dead ruler's body in different places across his territories was an effective way of demarcating his power, in much the same way as the quartering of a traitor marked out the king's jurisdiction. The practicalities of the embalming process, as illustrated in Henry of Huntingdon's account of Henry I's death, made the swift removal of the viscera and brain necessary before corruption began to set in. The internal organs were often buried at or near the place of death, but the embalmed body could be carried longer distances to be interred at a site requested by the king before death. For example, Henry I's viscera were buried in Normandy, where he had died, at the abbey of Notre Dame du Pré, but his embalmed body was taken to England and buried at Henry's foundation, the abbey of Reading.[75] The need to bury part of his body in Normandy was a practical one, but the result was politically convenient. Henry in death was able to stay in both his two lands, much as in life he had fought hard to be both king of England and duke of Normandy.

This practice became commonplace in the twelfth century. The Young King Henry, whose death in 1183 is discussed in the next chapter, had his viscera buried in south-west France where he died, but his body was taken north for burial, and became the focus of a struggle between Maine and Normandy for its possession. Similarly, Richard I's remains were divided after his death in 1199. His brain, blood and viscera were buried in Charroux in Poitou, his heart in Rouen in Normandy, and his body in Fontevrault Abbey in Anjou, at the feet of his parents Henry II and Eleanor of Aquitaine.[76] In this way his remains were scattered between the three main territories of the Angevins' continental possessions, illustrating in a very literal way the king's presence as a ruler in all his lands. Perhaps significantly, given that he spent so little of his reign in England, no part of his body found its way to Richard's island kingdom.

The practice of separate burial of body parts continued well beyond the twelfth century. In the later middle ages, the church was increasingly disapproving of the practice, but to little effect. The St Alban's chronicler commented on the division of the body of Eleanor of Provence, Henry III's queen, in 1291. He wrote that the Franciscan Friars of London, in whose church her heart was buried, 'claimed for themselves somewhat of the body of any folk who died; like dogs at a corpse, where each is in greedy expectation of his own gobbet to devour'.[77] Henry III himself, who died in 1272, was buried in Westminster Abbey, close to the resting place of St Edward the Confessor. This was fitting, as Henry had promoted Edward's cult and had sponsored the rebuilding of the abbey. He also asked that his heart be buried in Fontevrault Abbey, the resting place of his mother (Isabelle of Angoulême), uncle (Richard I) and grandparents (Henry II and Eleanor of Aquitaine).[78] This choice reflected a continuing personal commitment of Henry to his Angevin roots, but also demonstrated a continuing claim to the dynasty's continental possessions (including Anjou) which had been lost to the Capetians in the early thirteenth century.

There are colourful stories surrounding Edward I's wishes for his body after his death in 1307. Legend had it that, in his will, Edward asked that his heart be embalmed and taken to the Holy Land, and that eighty knights be provided for to accompany it there.[79] This is psychologically and politically consistent with Edward's career. He had fought on crusade, and had often expressed an intention of doing so again. The practice of making provision for knights to fight in the Holy Land was also a common one at that time, as was the practice of separate embalming and burial of the heart, which was relatively easy to preserve and transport, and which had a special symbolism as the presumed seat of the soul.[80] The two decades after the fall of Acre – the last crusader possession in the East – saw a great deal of talk about the recovery of the Holy Land, if rather less action. Edward was a central figure in this; the French writer Pierre Dubois dedicated his treatise *De recuperatione Terre Sancte* to Edward in about 1308. So Edward's gesture is highly plausible. There may be some significance in the fact that his funeral service at Westminster Abbey was conducted by Antony Bek, the patriarch of Jerusalem, although this ecclesiastic, an Englishman, held his grand title in absentia and was a political servant of Edward's.

Another story, which again sounds psychologically plausible, is that Edward requested his body be broiled and the bones carried into Scotland on campaign. This is not, however, a contemporary tale, but comes down to us courtesy of Froissart,[81] writing in the second half of the fourteenth century, who was not the most reliable source even for the events of his own time. Froissart's histories were dedicated to recording chivalrous deeds, and this story of Edward the single-minded warrior king, continuing the struggle even in death, would doubtless have appealed to him. Whatever the truth of Edward's wishes, his son Edward II had his body buried in Westminster Abbey.[82] By this time, the dismemberment of the body and separate burial was being condemned by the ecclesiastical authorities. An indication of this may be seen in the fact that in 1312 the decapitated body of Piers Gaveston was buried with the head sewn back onto the neck.[83]

We have therefore seen the powerful symbolism associated with the body, especially that of a king, who embodied the realm in his person. The two related themes of decomposition and dismemberment of the body were employed by the chroniclers to great effect, as the mutability of the flesh was contrasted with the eternal nature of God. The hagiographical tradition that saints' bodies remained uncorrupted after death, on account of their flesh having attained a purer state than that of ordinary humanity, stands in contrast to the accounts of putrefaction of the corpses of William the Conqueror and Henry I. In this manner the reader was reminded by the clerical authors that kings also decay, and that earthly power and pomp are but transient.

In addition, there was a tradition that associated bodily decay with tyranny, based on scripture and on the classics. Clerical writers, knowing the fate of biblical tyrants such as Antiochus and Herod, applied the same motifs to more recent historical figures. While these comparisons were not explicitly applied to the Anglo-Norman kings, they were clearly a part of the mental furniture of the ecclesiastical authors and their audiences. Writers such as Orderic Vitalis and Henry of Huntingdon were not writing in direct opposition to the Anglo-Norman kings, whose role in bringing order and church reform to England they appreciated. Rather, they were making a more general point about the inferiority of earthly to heavenly authority. There were, nevertheless, examples from medieval England of tyranny proper, such as the rule of John and his lieutenants, or the robber barons of Stephen's reign, whose corrupt governance was reflected in a corrupt end. Finally, putrefaction was associated in a physiological sense with obesity and gluttony, sins which were a result of a lack of self-control, and were therefore signs of the inability of a ruler to properly govern himself or his realm.

The dismemberment of the body was closely related symbolically to its putrefaction, in that it represented the destruction of the flesh and the affairs of this world. It also had important political symbolism, whether carried out on the body of the king himself or those of his defeated antagonists. If the king's body symbolised his realm and his authority, its destruction had the opposite symbolism, as demonstrated in the accounts of Harold's mutilation by William the Conqueror's knights. By destroying the body of Harold, they enacted the Norman Conquest physically upon his body, and demonstrated the illegitimacy of his rule. William's later medieval successors inflicted a similar pun-ishment on traitors through the grim process of hanging, drawing and quartering. Conversely, William's reassembly and burial of Harold's body demonstrated the legitimacy of his own rule, as he restored the broken realm and publicly asserted his own just claim to rule.

4

Father and Son

The death of a king was a beginning as well as an end, marking the start of his successor's reign. Before this took place, however, there could be tensions between the old king and the new, tensions that were exacerbated by the fact that both parties belonged to the same family. The last years of a king's reign could often see political tensions as the heir became impatient to rule. We have encountered the legend that Henry V tried on the crown while his father, Henry IV, still lived, and a similar problem posed by the ambition of Henry II's sons toward the end of his reign.

There were wider issues of death in the context of the relationship between kings and their offspring, and three case studies from the twelfth century will illustrate some of these. The first is not an actual death but an attempted killing of Henry I by his daughter Juliana. This incident, and the horrified reaction of the chroniclers who described it, sheds interesting light upon attitudes to death and violence when it was administered by a woman, and attitudes to the killing of a king. The second incident, the drowning of Henry I's son William in the White Ship disaster, brought about the death of Henry's son and sole male heir. The main chronicle accounts of this tragedy illustrate how the personal grief of Henry was entwined with the political impact of this dynastic disaster. A medieval king could never be a private individual, as the principles of dynastic inheritance and personal kingship ensured that family and politics were inseparable. This point is reinforced by the third case study, the death of Henry, the 'Young King', eldest son of Henry II. He died in revolt against his father, caught between his position as a son, and his ambitions as a prince.

In his *Epistola ad Walterum de contemptu mundi*, Henry, archdeacon of Huntingdon, related a story of a terrible act of tyranny, as he told

of how the king of England Henry I had caused his own granddaughters'
eyes (or those of his nieces', as he wrongly had it) to be put out.[1] This
work, a moral treatise on the passing nature of worldly glory, portrayed
kings in a negative light, as Henry of Huntingdon believed that 'the
business of kingship is felony' ('regia res scelus est'). The truth, cruel
as it was, does not reflect quite so harshly upon Henry. Henry allowed
his vassal Ralph Harenc to put their eyes put out in revenge for their
father Eustace de Bréteuil having done the same to one of Ralph's sons.
It could therefore be argued that Henry was acting legitimately in placing
his duty as protector of his vassal before his own flesh and blood, and
that this was a remarkable example of honourable behaviour, but Henry
of Huntingdon chose to interpret the affair otherwise.

The fullest version of the tale is provided by the Anglo-Norman
monk Orderic Vitalis.[2] Juliana, an illegitimate daughter of Henry I by
a concubine, was married to Eustace of Bréteuil, also interestingly an
illegitimate son of William of Bréteuil, who was preferred to his legitimate Breton cousins on account of the preference of the people for a
Norman lord.[3] In 1119 Eustace withdrew his support from Henry, king
of England and duke of Normandy, in a dispute over control of the
castle of Ivry. Henry attempted to make peace by arranging an exchange
of hostages between Eustace and Ralph Harenc, the custodian of Ivry,
whereby Eustace was to keep the son of Ralph, and Henry the daughters
of Eustace, who were themselves his (Henry's) granddaughters. Eustace,
however, put out the eyes of Ralph's son and sent him back to his father
mutilated. Ralph appealed to King Henry, asking him to hand him the
daughters of Eustace so that he might be revenged on him. Henry did
so and Ralph put out their eyes and cut off their noses.

In response to this 'both mother and father were in great distress',[4] and prepared to make war on Henry. Juliana, organising the
defence of Bréteuil, found herself besieged by her own father. Under
the pretence of arranging a parley, she tried to kill Henry by a subter-
fuge, attempting to kill him with a crossbow. Orderic regarded Juliana's
ruse as a 'woman's trick' and an example of 'treacherous intent', proving
that 'there is nothing so bad as a bad woman'. Trapped in the besieged
castle 'the unlucky Amazon (*bellatrix*) got out of the predicament
shamefully as best she could' by leaping from the battlements 'shamefully, with bare buttocks, into the depths of the moat'. Eustace and

Juliana subsequently submitted to Henry, and Juliana ended her days as a nun of Fontevrault.[5]

This incident raises interesting questions of family relations and lordship, and about just violence and just authority. There are two key elements in the story: Henry's contribution to the blinding of his granddaughters, and Juliana's raising a weapon against her father at the siege of Bréteuil. The punishment of blinding was often employed in this period as a punishment short of inflicting death. William the Conqueror used blinding and castration in the place of the death penalty in his laws for England. Blinding was used there by William as a punishment for rebellion.[6] For members of the highly militarised nobility, a punishment that inflicted such a disability was as effective as death in rendering a man incapable of fulfilling his role of leadership. Blinding and castration were often associated, as a punishment that both physically disabled the victim and prevented him procreating, thereby rendering him both politically and dynastically harmless. Ralph of Coggeshall's account of the fate of Arthur of Brittany at the hands of King John in 1202 has John ordering that the young prince be blinded and castrated, although his gaoler Hubert de Burgh refuses to carry out these cruel instructions.[7] This version has come down to us via Shakespeare's *King John*, where Hubert cannot bring himself to blind Arthur, who later, however, is killed falling from a castle wall while trying to escape.[8] Shakespeare presents Arthur (who was fifteen at the time) as an innocent young boy, not as a young man in rebellion against his lord.

Blinding was also rich in symbolism, being associated with ignorance and sin.[9] In particular, and of great relevance in this context of rebellion and broken trust, blindness was associated with infidelity. As regards the cutting off of the nose, the disfiguring of the woman was often viewed as a female equivalent to castration, which like blindness was a disabling and unsexing punishment. By making her unattractive a woman was effectively desexed by losing her value in the marriage market. For example, the law codes of the Latin kingdom of Jerusalem stipulated castration for men, and disfigurement for women, as punishment for Christians who had sex with Muslims.[10] These decrees were introduced in 1120, coincidentally at around the time of Juliana's conflict with Henry, and shortly after Baldwin I of Jerusalem rid himself of a wife in 1108 by claiming that she had engaged in sexual relations with

Saracens. This aura of sexuality may not be directly relevant to the young offspring of Eustace de Bréteuil and Juliana, but it emphasises the atmosphere of betrayal in the events Orderic describes.

Henry I was himself not above the use of blinding and mutilation. He blinded the count of Mortain, who had fought against him at Tinchebrai in 1106,[11] and ordered blinding and castration as a punishment for thieves, and castration and the loss of the right hand for counterfeiters (the production of false or unlicensed coinage was a serious infringement of royal power).[12]

In Orderic's account of Juliana's actions, he treats Henry as the wronged party. Far from being treated sympathetically, as a mother defending her children from a cruel fate, Juliana's actions are portrayed as shameful, as she transgresses her assigned gender by taking up arms, and her role as daughter by resisting her father. The fact that Henry had connived in the blinding and mutilation of her daughters did nothing to soften the chronicler's harsh verdict. Juliana receives her just deserts for usurping a man's role and for acting treacherously against the king. As one historian has aptly put it, 'Although Juliana was desperate, was suffering, and had been violent in an acceptable way ... Orderic notes that Henry was taken totally by surprise by this action. Orderic goes on further and blames it on her female deceit.'[13]

How are we to explain Orderic's hostile attitude towards Juliana? At one level, it is because she had transgressed authority by fighting her father and her lord. Henry's actions, conversely, are justified because his public duty as a lord took precedence over his familial duties as father and grandfather. Juliana had not only rebelled against her father, but had been 'plotting to raise her hand against the Lord's anointed ...'.[14] Orderic showed great respect for anointed kings, regardless of the legitimacy of their claim to the throne: for example, once he was crowned and anointed, he accepted Stephen as king unquestioningly, putting aside any previous doubts over his rights.[15] Juliana, as a rebel, is condemned, while other fighting women such as Sibyl de Bordet and Mathilda of Boulogne, Stephen's queen, are praised, as they are acting in defence of rightful authority.

The lesson that legitimate authority has been challenged, but has triumphed, is emphasised by Orderic's description of Eustace's and Juliana's submission to Henry: 'You are my natural lord [said Eustace].

Therefore I come to you without fear as to my lord, to offer my service loyally to you, and to make full restitution for my misdeeds, as you in your just compassion judge to be right.'[16] Peace is restored, and familial relations are restored too. Whereas at the beginning of the passage the couple are referred to as 'Eustace and his wife Juliana', Orderic now tells us that the king showed mercy 'towards his daughter and son-in-law'.

It could be argued that Orderic's treatment of Juliana was determined by her illegitimate birth, and that this perhaps explains Henry's lack of fatherly and grandfatherly concern. This point is easily countered. No reference is made in this context to Juliana's birth out of wedlock; indeed, as we have seen, when peace was restored she was welcomed back into the family. Little or no distinction was made by Henry between his legitimate and his numerous illegitimate offspring. Although Juliana married a fellow bastard, Eustace was a good match, being an important Norman lord, and other natural daughters enjoyed high-status marriages.[17] The church reformers may have been promoting a distinction in status between children born in and out of wedlock, but the battle was far from being won, as demonstrated by Eustace's own accession to the lordship of Bréteuil.

Finally, how far is Orderic's account revealing of attitudes to women? The editor and translator of the standard English edition of Orderic's *History* argues that he did not have a stereotyped, negative view of women as a sex, tending to portray sin and sinners in gender-neutral ways. Curiously, her comments on Orderic's treatment of women omit any reference to Juliana.[18] If Orderic's writing is gender-neutral, and his attitudes are based purely on the question of right authority, why is he not more sympathetic to Juliana? Why does her own authority as a wronged mother and as the legitimate defender of her husband's property count for nothing? Orderic's unfavourable treatment of Juliana appears to be gendered.

It must be admitted that Orderic's treatment of armed women is by no means always structured in negative terms. For example, Sybil de Bordet, who defended the walls of Tarragona against the Muslims, is described thus:

> She was as brave as she was beautiful. During her husband's absences she kept a sleepless watch; every night she put on a hauberk like a soldier and carrying a rod in her hand, mounted on to the battlements, patrolled the

circuit of the walls, kept the guards on alert, and encouraged everyone with good counsel to be on the alert for the enemy's stratagems. How greatly the young countess deserves praise for serving her husband with such loyalty and unfaltering love, and watching dutifully over God's people with such sleepless care! [19]

For Orderic, Sibyl's actions were praiseworthy, as they were legitimised by her defence of the Christians against the Saracens, and were carried out on behalf of her absent husband.[20] In the earlier middle ages, the division between the lord's private role as head of household and his public one as war leader was less clear-cut, so it was by no means unheard of for women to take on roles of military leadership as proxies for their husbands, or by hereditary right as châtellaines.[21] For example, Nicola de la Haye, hereditary castellan of Lincoln Castle, held it for the king against rebel forces in 1217.[22]

Orderic's description of Sybil is gendered: she is beautiful as well as bold, and thus remains female, in contrast to the usual tradition of armour rendering the woman masculine.[23] Her role is also an auxiliary one of rallying the troops; she never forfeits her femininity by actually wielding a weapon in anger, and carries only a rod, not a sword or bow. Sibyl and other 'good' women in Orderic's history rally or assist male forces, but they do not take up weapons themselves. Generally speaking, in medieval chronicles and literature, women's role in war was that of assistance; accounts of armed and armoured women tend to be hostile propaganda from enemy sources; for example, in Arab sources for the crusades.[24] Juliana's use of the crossbow, however, condemns her in two ways; she is rendered unwomanly by using a weapon, but neither is she able to access the male virtues of knighthood, as she employs a treacherous 'female' trick, and uses a footsoldier's weapon.

Another notable example of warrior women can be found in Orderic's history, that of Helwise, countess of Evreux, and Isabel of Conches, two others of the few women who feature in Orderic's writing,[25] who fought one another in about 1090. Reading his description of Isabel, we might be led to believe that Orderic admires this warrior woman, whom he compares to the Amazons of old:

> [She] was generous, daring, and gay, and therefore loveable and estimable to those around her. In war she rode armed as a knight among the knights, and she showed no less courage among the knights in hauberks and

sergeants-at-arms than did the maid Camilla, the pride of Italy, among the troops of Turnus. She deserved comparison with Lampeto and Marpesia, Hippolyta and Penthesilea and the other warlike Amazon queens ...[26]

His treatment of the conflict between Helwise and Isabel shows Orderic capable of a stereotypical treatment of female folly and vanity. Orderic's admiration of the Amazonian Isabel is not the whole story. While admiring her courage, he deplores the conflict, which he sees as having been 'fomented by the malignant rivalry of two proud women'.[27] The war is presented as frivolous and feminine in its origins, as Helwise is angered by slighting remarks made about her by Isabel, the wife of Ralph de Tosny. Helwise persuades her husband, William, count of Evreux, to take up arms, 'so the hearts of brave men were moved to anger through the suspicions and quarrels of women'. The violence used by Helwise and Isabel, like that of Juliana, is viewed as illegitimate. They are not, like Sibyl de Bordet, defending their husbands' lands in his absence but have usurped male authority by taking the lead in violence. Like Delilah, Helwise's persuasive influence is a malign one.

The strange and shocking case of Juliana and Henry gives an interesting insight into the relative values of lordship and family in the aristocracy of twelfth-century Normandy, especially as they related to women. In the eyes of Orderic Vitalis at least, Juliana, despite the wrongs she had suffered, was acting in an unacceptable manner in resisting her father and her king. For Henry, the duties of lordship dictated that he must act ruthlessly, even to the extent of allowing a terrible punishment to be inflicted upon his own grandchildren.

The death of William Atheling, the son of Henry I, in the White Ship disaster on 25 November 1120, had a profound effect on the politics of England in the first half of the twelfth century. By killing Henry's sole legitimate male heir, the disaster created the dynastic uncertainty that would be the occasion of civil war after the king's death. This tragedy fits rather awkwardly into the chroniclers' scheme of providential death; there were no reported portents of the catastrophe along the lines of those that foretold the deaths of Henry I himself or William Rufus. The tragedy, on the contrary, appeared to be meaningless and senseless.

There are a number of comments that can be made about the way in which chroniclers described the disaster. Their accounts draw on a number of common themes of medieval writing, touching on ideas about youth and age, drowning and oblivion, and that old chestnut: the fall of the mighty before the ineffable actions of the will of God. There are six authors who described the White Ship disaster, but in this section I will concentrate on the three most substantial chronicle descriptions, those of Orderic Vitalis, William of Malmesbury and Henry of Huntingdon. All accounts ultimately derive from that of the sole survivor of the disaster, a Norman butcher named Berold or Beroud.

Orderic Vitalis saw the disaster as God's disapproval of the betrothal of Henry's illegitimate son Richard to the daughter of Ralph de Gael. This was an element in Henry's diplomacy following the defeat of a rebellion in Normandy. Orderic maintained that this was an unfitting alliance, as Ralph held his land against the will of the Normans; this refers back to the conflict between Henry and his daughter Juliana. Ralph had been her husband Eustace's rival for control of Bréteuil, and had been rejected as a Breton, in favour of a Norman lord, albeit an illegitimate one. By marrying his daughter to the king's son, he hoped to stabilise his own precarious position, and Henry hoped to consolidate his own rule in that part of Normandy. The match 'was ill-considered and of no effect, for God, who governs all things well, ordained otherwise'.[28] The subsequent disaster can best be described as a 'drunk-sailing' incident, nearly nine centuries before an over-the-limit Ritz chauffeur collided with a pillar in a Paris underpass. The master of the White Ship, one Thomas son of Stephen, asked Henry if he could have the honour of conveying him, as his father had carried William the Conqueror to England. Henry had made alternative arrangements, but allowed Thomas the honour of taking the prince and his brother and sister in his vessel. The delighted sailors received a gift of wine from the princes, with which they celebrated the honour that had been done to them. The combination of a drunken crew and passengers who, we are told, consisted of 'headstrong young men' was to prove fatal. Some more sensible passengers, including two monks of Tiron, chose to leave, perhaps fearing the worst, although it is more likely that this is Orderic's way of implying that God was about to desert the travellers.

The crew were, in Orderic's monastic eyes, guilty most of all of pride and rebelliousness. At an earthly level, they showed themselves to be insolent; the rowers and marines on the boat 'were showing off and, too drunk to know what they were doing, were paying respect to almost no one'. At a more elevated level, they were guilty of pride in taking on the elements – that is, God – in such a light-spirited manner. This criticism is coupled with criticism of their attitude to the clergy:

[They] had in their hearts no filial reverence for God, who tempers the raging fury of the sea and wind. So when the priests came there with other ministers carrying holy water to bless them, they laughed and drove them away with abuse and guffaws. All too soon they were punished for their disrespect.[29]

William of Malmesbury, who was less condemnatory of the conduct of the young men, nevertheless echoes Orderic's references to their youthful arrogance or frivolity. He tells us that Prince William had 'through his father's indulgence enjoyed all the sweets of kingship ...', and that the young noblemen joined him on the White Ship 'as though for a youthful frolic'.[30]

The framework is therefore one of youthful rashness leading to disaster. In medieval writings youth, especially the youth of a ruler, was viewed as dangerous if it was not tempered by the counsel of age and experience. The young ruler had to seek the guidance of his elder counsellors. It was considered dangerous for a young man to consort only with his peers, who would be as rash and inexperienced as him. The archetype for this was the Old Testament king Rehoboam, who ignored the counsel of his elders and listened only to that of his fellow young men.[31] This idea explains the insistence of the chroniclers on the fact that only the young men were on board the White Ship, and that the wise ecclesiastics had disembarked. Worst of all, the young men had been disobedient not to their earthly fathers but to their father in heaven, to whom they had failed to show 'filial reverence'.

The passage also reveals the contrast between the power of earthly kings and princes, and that of God the king of the universe. The untameable elements were a useful metaphor for the weakness of the former in face of the latter, a theme used in Henry of Huntingdon's story of Canute trying to turn back the waves.

The drowning was, then, a punishment for the sailors' and passengers' lack of respect for God, within a wider framework of a moralising commentary on that familiar theme, the passing of worldly glory and its insignificance before the eternal. One point in particular is interesting, that of the lack of respect shown to the clergy. The mocking of the priests and the disembarkation of the monks are highlighted, implying that the shipwreck was a direct result of the anticlericalism of those drowned, itself a microcosm of their greater disrespect for God. There is clear symbolism in the imagery of water; the young men reject the saving holy water offered by the priests, and so are drowned by the awful waters of the sea. In medieval biblical exegesis, the holy water of baptism was seen as a parallel to the waters of Noah's flood. The events of the Old Testament were interpreted by scholars on four levels; the 'highest' level of interpretation, the anagogical, saw the stories as prophecies of the coming of Christ and of events in the New Testament. Within this framework, the Flood and the baptism of Christ in the waters of the Jordan were corollaries, as both represented mankind saved by water.

Drowning was itself a death loaded with symbolism. The sheer might of the elements and the sea were a reflection of God's majesty, while the enveloping nature of the waters, and the loss of the bodies beyond hope of recovery for Christian burial, invoked horror and seemed to echo the fear of damnation. The ocean waters, as we have seen, featured in the Bible as God's means of punishment for man's sin, and delivery from drowning was a sign of the Lord's favour to His chosen ones, such as Noah.

The Book of Jonah is another biblical story featuring the providential symbolism of water. When trying to escape the mission God had set him, Jonah took ship, only for the Lord to send a storm. The crew of the ship drew lots and threw Jonah overboard, at which point the Lord relented and sent a whale (or great fish) to save him.[32] The swallowing of Jonah, and his subsequent release after three days and nights in the belly of the whale, were viewed as a parallel with the resurrection of Christ, and ultimately of mankind. Mouths often featured in medieval art, either swallowing the damned into Hell, or spewing out the bodies of the saved at the Resurrection.[33] Likewise, the motif of swallowing and disgorging features in the story of St Margaret, who was swallowed by a dragon but subsequently released from its belly unharmed, when it vanished as she made the sign of the cross.[34]

Descriptions of the fate of those on board the White Ship reflect a horror (or, in the case of more moralistic authors, grim satisfaction) at the fact that the victims were lost without the benefit of confession or a Christian burial. The idea of the dead being food for fishes, without benefit of the rescue afforded Jonah, was a popular one. Henry of Huntingdon has Prince William being 'buried in the bellies of fishes ...', and elsewhere remarks of the dead that 'almost all of them had no burial',[35] while William of Malmesbury commented that the 'pampered bodies' of young royals and nobles made 'a cruel feast for monsters of the deep'.[36] Orderic Vitalis, in a verse reflecting on the disaster, observed that

> He whom the king begot became food for the fishes ...
> Damnation threatens all those lost in deep waters
> Unless mercy from heaven is willing to spare them.[37]

The Anglo-Saxon Peterborough chronicle reflected that 'to their friends the death of these was a double grief: one that they lost this life so suddenly; the other that few of their bodies were found anywhere afterwards'.[38]

Another twelfth-century account illustrates this point. Aelred of Rievaulx's hagiography of Edward the Confessor, written in the middle of the century, included among its miracle stories one in which the king was, by divine favour, granted a vision of the king of Denmark drowning along with a fleet he had assembled for a planned invasion of England. This story is not to be taken seriously as history, but reveals the belief that the destruction of a fleet by the elements was God's judgement. Specifically, the Danish king was guilty of pride. In the supposed words of King Edward:

> the wicked king, too haughty to support himself, stumbled and slipped to his knees: he had carelessly overstepped himself, and fell from the prow: the deep closed over him, the waters covered his head ... The Lord struck the head of a wicked house and cursed his sceptre, and the whole of his army which was approaching like a hurricane for our destruction ...[39]

We see again the contrast between human power and the divine: the 'hurricane' raised by the Danish king was no match for the storm raised by God. Aelred comments that 'God was fighting for Edward ...'[40]

In a similar vein, William of Newburgh, writing of the civil war in Stephen's reign, dwelt on the just judgement passed by God on the barons who tyrannised the realm. The chief of these was Geoffrey de Mandeville, who died when struck down by an arrow during a siege, but even his lieutenants died premature deaths; one of them, Rainer, died in watery circumstances that were unambiguously a divine judgement. In a ship becalmed at sea, he, his wife and his 'ill-gotten gains' were cast off in a boat. While the ship, lightened of this burden, was able to resume its journey, Rainer's boat sank 'under the weight of the sinner'. Lest there be any mistake that this was a divine judgement, William pointed out that, when lots had been drawn to decide who should be cast off in the boat, the lots indicated Rainer three times.[41] Again, we are reminded of Jonah, selected by lot to be cast overboard, but Rainer was not saved by a whale.

One version of the story of Arthur of Brittany, killed by King John in 1202 or 1203, gives a different slant to the symbolism of water. The Margam Abbey chronicler claimed that John, 'drunk and possessed by the devil', killed Arthur with his own hand, then, to cover his tracks, had his body tied to a stone and thrown into the River Seine. The body was found by a fisherman, who recognised it; it was then secretly buried at the abbey of Bec. In this incident, John had hoped the all-consuming waters would cover his crime, but God allowed the body to be discovered and given a Christian burial.[42] The nature of water, which had consumed the bodies of the drowned, filled medieval people with horror, but stories such as this held out the comforting hope that God would recognise and find the bodies of His children.

To return to the story of the White Ship: the young men, filled as we have seen with pride and drink, egged on the captain and crew to attempt to overtake the king's fleet – another example of a lack of 'filial reverence'. The ship struck a rock, however, a result of the helmsman's drunkenness and the ship's excessive speed. The captain, Master Thomas, on hearing that the king's son was drowned, chose to go down with his ship rather than face the wrath of Henry I.[43] There was only one survivor who, fittingly for this narrative of the humbling of pride, was one 'Berold, who was the poorest of all and was dressed in a pelisse made of rams' skins …'. The reference to Berold and his means of escape, and to the crew's drunkenness, was included in the later vernacular verse account of the disaster in Wace's *Roman de Rou*, a history in Norman French of the dukes of Normandy.[44]

The immediate legacy of the White Ship disaster was a personal one for Henry, his famous grief after which he 'never smiled again'. According to Orderic, the barons were so afraid to tell Henry the news of the disaster that they had to persuade a young boy to do so. The chronicler presents Henry's grief in biblical terms:

> Jacob was no more grief-stricken from the loss of Joseph, nor did David utter more bitter laments at the slaying of Amnon or Absalom.

There appears to be no particular significance to the choice of fathers and sons in this passage; the relationship of Jacob and Joseph was a loving one, while the sons of David, by contrast, were slain by David himself (or by his soldiers) as a result of their own crimes or rebellions. So there is no direct parallel with the death of William; rather, Orderic is drawing on the stock of biblical motifs. The choice of biblical precursors is not entirely flattering to Henry or his sons. In all three cases, the death of the son was a poor reflection on his family: Joseph's supposed death (and actual sale into slavery) was the result of his brothers' enmity; Amnon's death was an unjust punishment inflicted upon him by his father, David, at the behest of his brother and sister; while Absolom was killed by David's army while in revolt against his father. The David and Absolom motif was particularly popular, being used, for example, to describe the reaction of Henry II to the news of his son Henry the Young King's death. In this instance, it was more fitting, as the young Henry was indeed in rebellion against his father, unlike Henry I's sons.

Orderic has the grief of the people mirroring that of their king.

> As so great a ruler lamented, all the people of the realm could give rein to their tears, and this mourning lasted for many days. All in common still lament the sudden loss of Prince William, whom they considered the lawful heir of the English realm, with the flower of the highest nobility.[45]

The public grief of the people is an interesting counterpoint to the private grief of Henry as a father, the process of grieving reflecting the dual role of the king as both a private man and a public figure, the embodiment of the realm. Henry at first retires into a private room to nurse his grief as a man and a father. Only then can the process of grieving pass into the public sphere, and the people are able to 'give rein' to their grief, as the nation mourns the loss of the heir.

Orderic's claim that the people mourned the dead prince may be a reflection of genuine sentiment, or a conventional motif of the mourning of the loss of a young prince. The sense of loss attached to the death of a young man who would have grown up to be king was profound, and could create great outpourings of sentiment, regardless of the prince's actual capacities. As we shall see, the death of the Young King in 1183 created a putative saint's cult, despite the fact that the young man had never done anything obviously to deserve such a following. The loss of even such an unpromising and politically troublesome young heir seems to have unleashed great emotions, as youth and potential cruelly lost was in itself a tragedy.

There may be a specific political context for this sense of loss. The wreck of the White Ship had a profound impact on the political development of Henry's reign. Deprived of a legitimate male heir (but with illegitimate offspring in plenty), the succession to Henry was thrown into dispute, and eventually led to the civil war between Matilda, Henry's daughter, and his nephew, Stephen of Blois, a situation made more complex by the claims of William Clito, the son of Henry's elder brother Robert Curthose. As a direct result of the disaster, Henry was forced to reconsider his dynastic plans. In 1127 Henry persuaded the reluctant Anglo-Norman barons to recognise his daughter Matilda as his heiress. Orderic, writing in about 1135, did so knowing the potentially baleful political effects the death of William would have on the realm. The stress in his account on the sense of loss of he 'whom they considered the lawful heir' seems to reflect this.

Orderic ends his account with a churchman's homily, as if to emphasise the conventional nature of the passage. Unlike, say, the death of Rufus, the prince's drowning had been all the more shocking for being apparently inexplicable. If it was the judgement of God, then His purposes were obscure. However,

> sinners in their blindness cannot see or understand the things which the heavenly king rightly ordains for His creation, until sinful man is captured like a fish on a hook or a bird in a net and entangled in sufferings beyond hope of escape. Indeed when he hopes for long life, happiness and honour, he suddenly experiences death, wretchedness and ruin; of this we may see clear examples in daily events from the beginning of the world to the present day, both in modern and ancient records.[46]

This conclusion of Orderic's can serve as a summary of the whole medieval ecclesiastical approach to historical writing, the belief that the will of God could be discerned in the affairs of man.

For William of Malmesbury, whose *Gesta regum Anglorum* was a more secular work than Orderic's *Ecclesiastical History*,[47] the White Ship disaster represented the dashing of Henry I's dynastic ambitions. Like Orderic, he placed it in the context of one of the sons' betrothal, and implied divine disfavour. In this case, the betrothal was that of William to a daughter of Count Fulk of Anjou, so young that she 'was scarcely of a marriageable age' when the two were betrothed in 1113.[48] By this marriage Henry gained Maine as the girl's dower, and control of that territory while Count Fulk was absent on a pilgrimage to Jerusalem, when it had been consigned to Henry's safe-keeping. William of Malmesbury's account unsurprisingly shares many features with that of Orderic, principally the youth and rashness of the young men, and the drunkenness of the crew, and the desire of the younger men to outpace the king's ship. Malmesbury stresses the speed of the vessel, which was new and made of fine materials, and 'sped swifter than a feathered arrow'.[49] The survival only of a humble man, described here as a 'country fellow', also appears,[50] but the emphasis of the passage is rather different, playing down the religious imagery, rather locating the story in its political context. In so far as there is a didactic or moralistic purpose to William's version of the wreck, it is in exposing the vanity of human ambition, as Henry's best-laid plans are swept aside in a single disastrous incident. William's account is full of classical allusions, notably to the shipwreck in Vergil's *Aeneid*.

The section describing the disaster follows a description of Henry I's first wife, Matilda (or Edith) of Scotland. Matilda was a descendant of the old Wessex ruling house, through her mother St Margaret, who had married Malcolm III of Scotland. Matilda was also the patron of William of Malmesbury, to whom she wrote a letter encouraging him to write his *Gesta regum Anglorum*.[51] William was himself of mixed Anglo-Norman blood (as was Orderic). Through Matilda and her son, Henry I was able to present his rule as uniting the Norman and Saxon elements of the kingdom. Although in no way an Englishman, Henry could be made to appear more 'English' than his father and brothers; England has been the first realm which he ruled, and his seizure of

Normandy from his brother Robert Curthose could even be presented by William of Malmesbury as a reversal of the verdict of 1066, occurring as it did forty years to the day after the battle of Hastings.⁵² His marriage to Matilda-Edith, and the birth of William, was widely held to be a fulfilment of the prophecy of the Green Tree, which was recorded in the late eleventh-century *Life of St Edward* (the Confessor).⁵³ This prophecy stated that England would be restored when a green tree that had been separated, and a section carried a distance of three furlongs, grew back together, which was later taken to refer to the marriage of Saxon and Norman dynasties, the three furlongs representing the reigns of the three Norman kings (William I, William II and Henry I). Prince William was therefore the linchpin of Henry's programme to portray himself as a truly English king. To emphasise this, William of Malmesbury refers to the Green Tree prophecy not, as might be expected, in the context of a description of Henry's marriage to Matilda, but in the passage leading up to the White Ship disaster, where he describes the marriage of William to the daughter of Fulk of Anjou, and the ambitious dynastic programme that Henry hoped would result from this match. 'It was supposed King Edward's prophecy was to be fulfilled: the hope of England, it was thought, once cut down like a tree, was in the person of that young prince again to blossom and bear fruit ...'

Malmesbury then describes how this structure came crashing down as a result of the disaster.

> But God had other plans; these expectations went down the wind, for the day was already at hand when he [William] must fulfil his fate ... And now peace dawned, the bright fruit of so much labour, the hopes of all men were lifted as to a tower's top, when all was thrown into confusion by the mutability of human things.⁵⁴

The chronicler then goes on, not to moralise further on the passing of earthly glory as might be expected from a monk, but to list the political changes that were wrought by this disaster. He lists the most notable of the dead, who included William's natural brother Richard and sister Matilda, countess of Perche, and Henry's niece, the countess of Chester. The political results were that Henry, in the hope of begetting a new legitimate male heir, married Adela of Louvain, and that Fulk of Anjou, angered by Henry's refusal to return the dower land of Maine, in 1122, on his return from the Holy Land, allied himself with William Clito. These were current political affairs in 1125, when William wrote the first version of his *Gesta regum Anglorum*.

Another intriguing dynastic twist was added by Orderic Vitalis. In his passage describing how the more sensible passengers left the ship before it set sail, he added that Stephen of Blois disembarked, suffering an attack of diarrhoea. Had he drowned along with his cousin, it is possible to imagine that England could have avoided the troubles that were to beset his reign (1135–54), leading a biographer of Henry I to comment that this bout of sickness changed history.[55] As no other author refers to Stephen's timely departure, it is of course possible that Orderic is commenting ironically, with the benefit of hindsight, on the caprice of fortune.

There is one personal touch in William of Malmesbury's portrait of the drowned William which is absent from other versions. He claims that the prince had boarded the ship's lifeboat, and was heading for safety, but turned back in an attempt to rescue his half-sister Matilda, countess of Perche, whose screams for help he heard. By returning to the ship he sealed his own fate, as the boat became overloaded with survivors jumping on board and sank. This incident, if true, gives an insight into family affections, as William did not disdain to attempt to rescue his illegitimate sister. It may reflect a desire of William of Malmesbury to please his patron, the Empress Matilda, by presenting a chivalrous image of her dead brother, emphasising the familial solidarity among Henry I's offspring. After all, Matilda's illegitimate half-brother Robert of Gloucester was to prove her key partisan in the civil war of Stephen's reign.[56]

In contrast to this 'political' account of the disaster, Henry of Huntingdon gave a highly moralistic gloss to the story. He referred to it both in his *Historia Anglorum* and his letter *De contemptu mundi*. The latter work and a set of epigrams reflect his moral concerns as a writer. In the *Historia*, he (uniquely among chroniclers) saw the wreck as a judgement of God for a specific sin, rather improbably stating that 'All of them, or nearly all, were said to be tainted with sodomy …',[57] an accusation that is not repeated in other accounts. This need not refer to homosexuality, but rather to sexual sin in general. In order to emphasise the wreck as an act of divine intervention, he ignores the drunkenness of the crew, and instead claims that the ship struck a rock despite conditions being calm, after God made a thick fog descend. 'And death suddenly devoured those who had deserved it …' For Henry, Prince William was not the seed of a restored Anglo-Saxon monarchy, but instead represented 'the Normans' who 'sought the English kingdoms' before 'God himself obstructed them'. Henry gives a far more sympathetic treatment of the death of William Clito, the son of Robert of Normandy, in 1128, mourning him as a 'young Mars'.[58] This may explain his hostility to Henry I and his progeny, although it is hard to see how Clito could be presented as less Norman than his dead namesake Prince William.

In the *De contemptu mundi*, Henry unsurprisingly uses the White Ship disaster as an opportunity to moralise on the passing of worldly glory. He portrays William as young and arrogant, puffed up with pride as a result of receiving too much reverence too young. He expects to inherit the throne, but God says 'Not so the wicked, not so'. As a result of the disaster,

> instead of wearing a crown of gold, his head was broken open by the rocks of the sea; instead of being dressed in gilded apparel, he was tossed about naked in the waves; instead of gaining the loftiness of kingly rule, he was buried in the bellies of fishes at the bottom of the ocean. This was the change in the right hand of the Most High![59]

This passage, with its rhetorical use of opposites, is typical of Henry, and reminiscent of his reflections on the death of Henry I, where he uses similar images of gems and fine cloth. A similar theme is taken up by Orderic, who ends his account of the disaster with a poem, reflecting that 'Purple robes and home-spun rot in the deep together …'.[60]

The fear of drowning must have been a common one in the middle ages, especially among the Anglo-Norman and Angevin kings, who needed to cross the Channel frequently on affairs of state. It is probable that William Atheling's death compounded Henry's own fears; in 1131, after experiencing a rough crossing from Normandy to England, Henry expressed his gratitude to God for his delivery by swearing not to collect the Danegeld tax for seven years, and to make a pilgrimage to Bury St Edmund's.[61] The chronicle of John of Worcester which records this event illustrates it with a picture of an alarmed-looking

Henry in a ship on a high sea, complete with fish, ready perhaps to feast again on royal flesh. Henry's gesture of thanks for surviving the perils of the sea was a typical one for a medieval king. Later Edward I founded the abbey of Vale Royal in Cheshire in thanks for delivery from shipwreck, and Edward III similarly founded the abbey of St Mary Graces. Henry's own fears would have been exacerbated by a fear that the dynastic disaster of 1120 might repeat itself, as he was accompanied by his wife, Adela of Louvain, and his daughter and remaining legitimate heir, Matilda the Empress. Had the royal vessel gone down, Henry's entire dynasty would have perished, although arguably England might have avoided civil war had Stephen of Blois been able to ascend an uncontested throne. John of Worcester (whose chronicle contains many stories of omens) went on to record how Henry's own death was portended by the sea. In 1133, when Henry sailed for Normandy, the fact that he was leaving England for the last time was indicated by many signs, including the fact that ships came loose at their anchorage in an otherwise calm sea.[62]

The White Ship disaster should therefore be read not only as a personal tragedy for Henry but as a dynastic disaster, and an illustration of how precarious any policy built on the expectations of a single male heir was. The troubles of Stephen's reign only made the disaster more poignant for those writers who enjoyed the benefit of hindsight. On a spiritual level, the dramatic and terrible nature of William's death provided fodder for the moralising commentaries of ecclesiastical chroniclers, who dwelt on the passing of worldly glory. With the exception of Henry of Huntingdon, the chroniclers struggled to identify a specific sin for which William and his companions might have deserved punishment. The disaster cannot comfortably be placed in category of 'deserved deaths'.

The death of Henry, the 'Young King', illustrates two themes that run through this book: the use of royal death by ecclesiastical writers to make moral points, and the putative cults of sanctity (more characteristic of later medieval kings) that developed around the dead ruler.

Henry, the Young King, was the eldest son of Henry II, and was – uniquely in England – crowned in his father's own lifetime (in 1170) in order to guarantee his succession. This process was far from unusual on the Continent – in France, the early Capetians had carried out anticipatory coronations of their sons, while in Germany, where the elective element of succession was reasserting itself over the hereditary, it was virtually standard practice for the emperor to have his son crowned as king of the Romans (in effect, king of Germany and emperor-elect) in his own lifetime. In the more settled and centralised kingdom of England, such a practice was highly unusual. Henry may have been influenced by the uncertain succession that had clouded the end of his predecessors' reigns. Henry I's death had, of course, precipitated the civil war between the rival claimants Matilda and Stephen, while the settlement that ended that war led to Stephen's own sons being passed over in favour of Henry of Anjou. As King Henry II, the latter was keen to ensure that this did not prove a precedent. By having the younger Henry crowned, he was hoping to establish firmly the principle of dynastic succession.

In addition, it seems that Henry was seeking to establish a 'federal' settlement of his domains, with the constituent parts of the Angevin Empire assigned to his various sons. The younger Henry, as the eldest surviving son, was to receive his father's lands of England, Normandy and Anjou; the second son, Richard, the maternal inheritance of Aquitaine; and Geoffrey, the third son, Brittany (by marriage to its heiress). Whatever the elder Henry's intentions, the land settlement for his sons was to prove traumatic, as his sons jockeyed for power with their father and with one another.

Despite being granted the royal title, the younger Henry was given little in the way of real authority. Frustrated by this lack of power, and angered by his father's plans to provide land for the fourth son, John, from his own lands, Henry rebelled in 1173, supported by his mother, Eleanor of Aquitaine, and by various members of the English ruling elite who had their own grievances against Henry's rule.[63] The rebellion lacked any coherent power-base and was defeated fairly easily.

The Young King died in the course of a second revolt against his royal father, on 11 June 1183 at Martel in Périgord. He and Geoffrey had sided with rebels in Aquitaine against Richard, and against their father.[64] Rather than reconsider the political events leading up to his death, let us examine the phenomena reported around the scene of his death, and how these represent important, and recurrent, elements in medieval portrayals of royal death. There are two remarkable elements of the

Young King's death, as represented by contemporary writers: the moving and highly coloured accounts of his death itself; and the subsequent claims that the dead prince was a saint, with miracles occurring as his bier progressed from the south to its eventual burial at Rouen.

The younger Henry, having been pillaging the south west, including attacking monasteries, was seized with a fever (or dysentery) at Martel. There, after being forgiven by his father Henry II, he died after a period of penance. His body was eviscerated, the brain and intestines being buried at the abbey of Grandmont – which, ironically, he had pillaged only a few weeks previously. On the way to Rouen, there were reports of miracles being performed at the sites where his bier rested. At Le Mans, the cortège was seized by the clergy and people of the city, and the body buried in the cathedral. The corpse was later reclaimed by the dean of Rouen cathedral, and taken there for the intended burial.

Accounts of the Young King's death embody many familiar elements of chroniclers' descriptions of royal death: a *contemptus mundi* motif, of death coming to all no matter how exalted; the father's (Henry II's) mourning for his wayward son; an element of divine judgement on the dead man; and a moving death-bed scene.

The scene of the Young King's death was presented as one of great humility. Thomas de Agnellis (possibly the archdeacon of Wells),[65] whose sermon sought to represent Henry as a saint, claims that he had been in a state of penance for 'many days' before his death.[66] Geoffrey, prior of Vigeois, has him dying in humble surroundings, in the house of 'Stephen, surnamed the Smith'. [67] Geoffrey emphasises the poverty of the Young King's followers; stopping at his own house of Vigeois on its journey northwards, the party was unable to pay for a mass for the dead king, so a collection was organised that raised 12*d*. for the purpose.[68] Ralph de Diceto emphasises that Henry died when he was 'in the flower of youth', aged only twenty-eight, and far from home in Gascony, among 'barbarous' people.[69] His youth is significant, given the medieval literary tradition that saw young men as rash, and re-quiring the counsel of their elders, as here is a young man who died in rebelling against his father.

This 'how are the mighty fallen' motif was popular among monastic chroniclers when referring to deaths of kings. We may refer, for example, to Orderic Vitalis's account of William the Conqueror, abandoned on

his death-bed by all but the least of his servants, or to Henry of
Huntingdon's horrible account of the putrefying remains of Henry I,
which he used to tell the reader to 'learn to hold in contempt' the affairs
of the world and of the flesh.[70] In the *Gesta Regis Henrici* account of
the Young King's death, Henry II is given a long speech in which he
mourns his son, and expresses the sentiment that death comes to rich
and poor alike.[71] The author of the *Histoire de Guillaume le Maréchal*
opts for a more secular treatment of a similar theme; fortune has struck
down the Young King:

> Mais Fortune qui tost se change
> E tost est devenue estrange
> Fu vers els molt tost estrangiée
> E en petit d'ore changiée.[72]

All accounts of the death agree that Henry II was heart-broken, and
grieved upon hearing the news of his son's death. Most sources report
that Henry II, only a few miles away at Limoges, wished to visit his son,
but feared that reports of his being on his death-bed were a trap. Hearing
news of his son's death, the king was inconsolable and wept bitterly.[73]

What Henry's personal feelings really were it is impossible to say. The
monastic writers were probably more concerned with the conventional
representation of grief than with its actual occurrence; they were tapping
into a long tradition of the royal father grief-stricken on hearing the
news that his beloved but rebel son is dead. The example of David and
Absolom was the archetype for this motif. The courtier Walter Map,
who was unsympathetic to the prince, wrote that 'you might liken him
to Absolom'.[74] Like David, Henry II was not present at his son's death,
and had to hear the news from a messenger. Far from being glad to
hear that the rebel leader has died, David lamented the death of his son
and 'that day victory was turned to mourning for the whole army ...'
(2 Samuel 19: 2). In Map's eyes, the Young King's death was a relief,
releasing Henry, in the role of David, from his troubles. This David and
Absolom motif was employed explicitly by the Emperor Frederick II
when mourning the suicide of his rebellious son King Henry in
1242,[75] a tragedy that was presented as an unavoidable sacrifice for the
greater good of the empire.[76]

The younger Henry for his part played the role of penitent son seeking

1. The death of Harold at Hastings, 14 October 1066, from the Bayeux Tapestry.

2. King John's funeral effigy in Worcester Cathedral. In Purbeck marble, *c.* 1225–30.

3. Eleanor of Castile, the wife of Edward I, Westminster Abbey, 1291–93.

4. The tomb of Edward II in Gloucester Cathedral, *c.* 1330–35. (*National Monuments Record*)

5. The Wilton Diptych. Richard II kneeling in front of two royal saints, Edmund the Martyr and Edward the Confessor, and St John the Baptist. (*National Gallery*)

6. Richard II in captivity. From Froissart, *Chroniques de France et d'Angleterre*, British Library, MS Harley 4380, fol. 181. (*British Library*)

7. Henry VI, sixteenth-century copy of lost original. (*National Portrait Gallery*)

8. Richard III and his wife, Anne Neville, the daughter of Warwick the Kingmaker. Miniature from copy of Salisbury Roll, late fifteenth century.

the forgiveness of his father. We are told by Geoffrey de Vigeois that he received the letter and accompanying ring that the king sent him as a token of his forgiveness, and wrote back asking, in the words of the twenty-fifth Psalm (verse 7) 'do not remember the sins and offences of my youth, but remember me in thy unfailing love', a fitting request by a young and wayward prince.

There were those who thought the Young King a saint and promoted his cult. This was a man who, in the weeks before his death, had taken to plundering shrines and monasteries to fund his mercenaries. Walter Map saw the Young Henry as a rebel and a perjurer, and claimed that, although he died penitent, he had vowed to continue the struggle against his father if he lived.[77] He saw his death as divine punishment for swearing an oath against his father, and punningly states, in reference to his death at Martel, that he was 'smitten with the hammer (*martellum*) of death by the all-righteous avenging hand . . .'.[78] The motif of untimely death as the punishment of God was a common one in clerical writers' descriptions of the deaths of kings, especially if they were held to be oppressors of the church. The chroniclers saw the death of William Rufus by arrow wound as a suitably dramatic death for the great anticlerical ruler. The death was so sudden that he was unable to receive the sacraments and was damned. In a closer parallel with the Young King's involvement in pillaging shrines, Eustace, son of King Stephen, died soon after robbing the shrine of St Edmund; the martyred King Edmund had exacted revenge beyond the grave by striking down the later king's son.[79] William of Newburgh observed that Eustace thereby 'suffered the early death which God willed' and that his death was doubly timely in that it paved the way for the peace agreement between Stephen and Henry of Anjou.[80]

Does the death of the Young King fit this pattern? His death was not sudden in the sense that Rufus's was. It was untimely, as he was struck down in 'the flower of youth', but he had ample time to make arrangements to meet his maker, and the more favourable accounts, such as that of William Marshal's biographer, make much of his careful preparations to die 'a good death'. We are told that 'Fortune' struck him down, but at least allowed him the opportunity to make a *bone repentance.*[81]

A death by dysentery could provide fuel for the moralists, as it was a dirty, unpleasant death. When the Young King's brother John died in this way in 1216, Roger of Wendover cast it in terms of the king's self-indulgence and therefore unfitness to rule: 'His sickness was increased by his pernicious gluttony, for that night he surfeited himself with peaches and drinking new cider, which greatly increased and aggravated the fever in him.'[82] No chronicler seems to have drawn the same conclusions when describing the Young King's death, but this is not to say that they missed the opportunity to moralise on the timing and manner of his passing. According to Howden, he contracted dysentery out of anger with his father, the health of his body being upset by an imbalance in his temperament.[83] Diceto pointed out to his readers that, while Henry I's name lived on, that of his son would soon be forgotten, as he had died without issue.[84] Had he been loyal, it is implied, he would have lived to inherit his father's lands and titles, but his rebellion had doomed him to death and oblivion.

In his account of the Young King's death, the writer of the *Histoire de Guillaume le Maréchal* portrayed a moving death-bed scene in which Henry, having rather light-heartedly taken the cross, conveys his crusader's cloak, and the mission of going to the Holy Land to fight for the faith, to his friend and tutor in chivalry, William Marshal.[85] William takes the cloak, emblazoned with the red cross of the crusader, and promises to take it with him to the Holy Land. Thus the author of the *Histoire* presents Henry as dying a pious crusader, who asks the Marshal to commend him to God, 'a Deu m'en aquiterez'.[86]

In less secular versions of the story, particularly that of Geoffrey de Vigeois, the Young Henry goes to extremes of self-abasement and penitence. Henry is said to have prostrated himself before the crucifix, and to have asked to be taken from his bed and placed upon one of ashes, with a stone for a pillow and a halter around his neck.[87] All these actions imply not merely penance but exaggerated, almost extravagant, humility, supporting the chroniclers' aim to draw the readers' attention away from the affairs of this world to those of the next. It is doubtful whether Vigeois's accounts of Henry's penance and poverty are entirely complimentary to the Young King's piety; on the contrary, following as they do descriptions of the depredations of Henry's *routiers*, and his rejection by the people of Limoges, his description may equally be categorised as one of divine judgement.

The idea that the Young King died in a pious manner is supported in other accounts of his death, although the *Histoire* author, who sought to portray his hero, William Marshal, and his lord, Henry, in a chivalrous light, makes great play of the crusading motif. Most sources agree that he died surrounded by churchmen. Geoffrey, prior of Vigeois, mentions the presence of Bernard, bishop of Agen, who administered the last rites, and many other men of religion.[88]

Death-bed scenes were highly significant in their use by chroniclers to make an edifying comment on the passing of the dead king. Henry's death presents him in a good light, in contrast to accounts of earlier kings, such as William the Conqueror, who was supposed to have been abandoned by his faithless servants, or Rufus, dying almost alone and unshriven on the forest floor.

What are we to make of the claims about the Young King's sanctity? Thomas de Agnellis was his greatest advocate. He wrote a sermon on Henry's death, in which he is presented in suitably saintly terms; for example, Henry is referred to throughout as *sanctus vir*. His bier, as it processes through the land, becomes the focus for many miracles. A leprous man and a woman afflicted by haemorrhages are cured by touching his bier, while a man suffering from fainting is cured simply by seeing his relics.[89] These miracles are reminiscent, to the point of being directly based upon, those performed by Christ in the synoptic gospels (Matthew, 8: 1–4; 9: 20–22). Like the woman suffering from haemorrhages, who was cured by merely touching the hem of Christ's robe, they are cured for their faith alone.

Further on, the dead prince's progress was greeted with displays of celestial pyrotechnics. At the monastery of St-Savin, lights appeared in the sky above the church when his body rested there. Four miles out of the city of Le Mans, as the procession approached, a light is seen in the sky in the shape of a cross, and a beam of light shone down upon the bier. It was hardly surprising, given such a fanfare, that the people of Le Mans should wish to seize the relics of this saint.[90] The revelation of the body of a saint by a divine light was a motif that appears in the saints' lives of several Anglo-Saxon royal martyrs, such as St Kenelm and St Ælfwald.[91] Temporary burial at Le Mans did nothing to reduce the body's efficacy. At Sées, on the way to Rouen, it cured two children, one of whom suffered from dropsy, and another who was blind from birth and unable to move his arms and legs.[92] Thomas returns here to his biblical theme, comparing these miracles to those that Christ performed on the sabbath, to the disgust of the Pharisees.[93]

Finally, on reaching Rouen, the Young King's body was examined to make sure that the people of Le Mans had not kept any parts of it as relics (a not-unknown phenomenon – St Hugh of Lincoln had once bitten off the nose of Mary Magdalene in order to take the relic home with him). Here the attendants received one of the most efficacious proofs of sanctity: the body was incorrupt, despite having travelled for forty days in the heat of a French midsummer. The motif of the incorrupt saint's body is such a common one that examples would fill a book. To use but one example in the context of English kings, the body of St Edmund was reported still incorrupt in about 1100, and again in 1198. [94]

On the face of it, the Young King was an unlikely candidate for sainthood. He had been pillaging shrines, including that of St Martial at Rocamadour, in the weeks before his death, and he died a rebel, albeit one who had sought and gained his father's forgiveness in his last hours. Nor was his life characterised by any charitable deeds. His crusader's vow seems to have been taken lightly, and he was never to fulfil it. His adult life was characterised by that most secular of twelfth-century pursuits, chivalry, and the author of the *Histoire de Guillaume le Marechal* treats his life as one long round of tournaments.[95]

Thomas de Agnellis's motives in promoting the Young King's cult may have been directly political: he was an associate and advocate of Eleanor of Aquitaine, at that time held as a virtual prisoner by Henry II. He has the dead king appear to his mother in a vision, wearing two crowns (that of a king and that of a saint). Could the 'Pharisees' be those who doubted the younger Henry's sanctity? William of Newburgh, who dismissed the sanctity of the Young King, may have had the associates of Eleanor in mind when he criticised 'certain people' who had promoted the cult.[96] More pithily, William comments that the affair tells us only that 'stultorum infinitus est numerus (the number of fools is infinite)'.[97] Clearly there was a political struggle being fought over the Young King's memory.

Those involved in the funeral procession, and the events surrounding it, were themselves not above political infighting, and this may have influenced their actions. Robert de Neubourg, the dean of Rouen, insisted on the removal of the body from Le Mans to its intended resting-place in the Norman city. Robert was a central figure in political changes some months later, following the death of his uncle, Archbishop Rotrou in November 1183.[98] The canons of Rouen elected Robert as their new archbishop but were overruled by Henry II, who placed Walter of Coutances on the archiepiscopal throne. Walter, who had recently been elected bishop of Lincoln, was very much the king's man; he was a close associate of the royal chancellor Raoul de Varneville.[99] Robert's role on acquiring the Young King's remains – a potentially valuable relic – for Rouen may have been part of a campaign to further his own influence with the cathedral chapter, and may even have been (or have been interpreted by the royal party as being) a hostile move against the elder Henry and his supporters.

At a more fundamental level, what we may be seeing is the association of sanctity with the dead king, on account of his being anointed. In the later middle ages, even kings with such dubious claims to sanctity as Edward II and Henry VI were greeted as saints in some quarters, as they were kings who had met a violent end. Admittedly, the Young King did not die violently, but his death may still have been a blow to those who hoped he might represent a better prospect than the Old King, Henry II. Sudden or untimely deaths could in themselves be taken as proofs of sanctity. In the fourteenth century, Ranulf Higden complained that Edward II was being revered simply for the violence of his death, observing however that that 'kepynge in prison, vilenes and obprobrious dethe cause not a martir ...'.[100] As we have seen in our own time, dead members of the royal family are able to attract veneration no matter how vain and foolish they were in life, if they are seen as an alternative to the existing order. There was, despite the attempts of church reformers to desacralise kingship, still an aura of holiness surrounding a king. Just as the *Histoire* author stressed Henry's pious desire to ensure that William Marshal fulfilled his crusading vow, so Ralph de Diceto tells us that, after death, Henry was wrapped in a linen cloth consecrated with the chrism from his coronation thirteen years previously.[101]

Finally, the religious situation in south-west France may have lent itself to the development of popular cults. In an attempt to limit the depredations of *routiers*, such as those mercenaries in the Young King's employ, the twenty-seventh canon of the third Lateran Council in 1178 anathematised mercenaries (as well as those more important enemies, heretics) and authorised indulgences for those who resisted them.[102] Geoffrey de Vigeois tells us that, at the time of the Young King's death, two peace movements arose in the region: the knightly *paciferi* and the popular movement of Durand de Orto.[103]

This may have provided the right religious climate for a burgeoning saint's cult, but Henry, who was himself responsible for so many of the *routiers'* abuses, hardly seems a fit subject for veneration by the men of peace. The enthusiasm of the people of Le Mans to possess his relics, and the reports of miracles at Sées and St-Savin, may suggest a cult that was stronger in the Plantagenet dynasty's Norman-Angevin-Poitevin heartland than in the south west. Maybe the people of Henry's ancestral lands were more inclined to see him as a saint than those who had seen him plunder their churches so soon before his death; according to Geoffrey of Vigeois, the people of Limoges, denying Henry re-entry to their city, declared that 'we will not have this man to rule over us'.[104]

The descriptions of Henry's death have parallels with the death narratives of other Anglo-Norman or Angevin kings, albeit often in negative ways; namely, that the same themes are introduced, but are often treated in an opposite manner to that with which we are more familiar. For example, the theme of the state of the dead body is used to make Henry saintly, whereas in other royal deaths it is the body's corruption that is described, to emphasise the king's mortality. Henry enjoyed a surprisingly 'good death' in the accounts of the chroniclers; the worst that can be said about his manner of his death (as opposed to its timing) is that he died in humble, straitened circumstances, but this was not entirely a bad thing for a would-be saint.

It is the question of Henry's supposed sanctity that must dominate any consideration of his death. How are we to explain the attempts to sanctify a man who had been plundering churches shortly before his death? While the allure of sacral kingship must have played its part, politics may have been a more immediate cause, as the cult seems to have appeared in the northern areas of France, which would have been Henry's territories had he lived (Aquitaine being intended for Richard, then count of Poitou). Furthermore, Thomas de Agnellis favoured

Eleanor of Aquitaine, and the imprisoned queen may have had a political motive for promoting her son's cult. In later medieval England, popular cults around dead kings or nobles had a political nature. It is difficult, nonetheless, to discern any great personal qualities that the younger Henry possessed that fitted him for sainthood. His appeal is probably better explained in terms of disappointed expectation: the Young King who was never to come into his own. In short, the main factor working in his favour may simply have been that he was not Henry II.

Henry II's own death, in 1189, occurred in the context of his troubled relations with his sons. His attempt to arrive at an inheritance settlement that pleased all four of his legitimate male offspring had always been a potential cause of conflict, both between Henry and his sons, and among those sons. These conflicts were stoked and exploited by the French kings, Louis VII and (after his succession in 1180) Philip II. Henry's refusal to assign any real measure of power to his son had been the cause of the Young King's revolt. Likewise, shortly before death, Henry II faced another rebellion by his eldest surviving son, Richard, count of Poitou, the future king Richard I, protesting at his father's refusal to recognise him unequivocally as his sole heir.

The chroniclers use the events of Henry II's death to reflect credit upon either the old king himself or his eldest son and successor Richard, depending upon their own prejudices and political sympathies. Roger of Howden has the old king dying a good death, taking communion and making confession in his last hours.[105] In contrast, when the faithless Richard arrived at Chinon to pay his respects to his dead father, blood flowed forth from Henry's body, a posthumous sign of displeasure at his son's conduct. Roger seems to imply in this episode that Henry's power lived on beyond his death, as he describes how the king was laid out in state, girded with a sword, wearing spurs, and arrayed with the regalia of crown, sceptre and gold ring.[106] In contrast, Richard of Devizes was more sympathetic to Richard, presenting him as a caring and solicitous son. When describing Richard's deeds on the Third Crusade, Richard of Devizes places a speech into the mouth of Safadin (Al-Adil Saif ad-Din), Saladin's brother, in which the Muslim sultan praises the English king. He claims that Richard was his father's favoured son, 'loved ... above all his brothers', and that Henry had been brought low not by the loyal Richard but by the treachery of his other sons (an odd idea, given that there was only one other brother, John, alive at this time).[107]

These three histories illustrate some of the tensions surrounding the relations between kings and their offspring, and how these problems manifested themselves in the event of death. In the drowning of William Atheling, we see the political problems associated with the death of an heir. A king who through fate or choice had left himself with only a single legitimate male heir was placing all his dynastic eggs in one basket, as the death of William demonstrated vividly. It led not only to the collapse of Henry's diplomacy in northern France, but in the longer term to the succession falling upon a daughter who was far from universally recognised or respected by the nobility. The result was the seizure of the throne by Stephen in 1135, and the subsequent civil war.

William Atheling's death, and the later death of Henry the Young King, also represented a dashing of hopes for the future at a more emotional level. The chroniclers address not only the political implications of the death of the prince but also the emotional implications for the ruler. The private man and the public figure of the king overlap uncomfortably, as does the grief of the man at the loss of a son, and the grief (or possibly relief, in the case of Henry II and the Young King) of a king at a blow to his dynastic ambitions. The tension between the role of the king as a man and his role as the embodiment of power is exposed in these circumstances. For Henry I, on hearing the news of his son's drowning, personal grief and political disappointment complement one another. In contrast, personal and political emotions are in conflict in the mourning of Henry II for his son.

A third player is present in this drama; besides the king and the prince, there is also the people – a vague, amorphous figure. Chroniclers' generalisations about the people mourning for their loss do little to tell us who these people were or why they mourned. The loss of a young prince of great promise does, however, seem to have made an emotional and political impact on wider sections of the population. In the disturbed circumstances of the Angevin domains in France in 1183, this led to a putative saint's cult developing around the Young King. No such cult developed around William Atheling, but the chroniclers' reflections on the cruelty of fate and the ineffable actions of God reflect a profound sense of loss.

The case of Henry I and his daughter Juliana raises rather different issues. As a woman, and as an illegitimate daughter, Juliana's relationship (both personal and political) with her father was clearly rather different from that between a king and a legitimate male heir. Her attempted killing of her father attracted the opprobrium of the chronicler, as she was committing an unnatural act, raising a weapon against both her father and a king. Again, Henry's role as a father overlaps with that of a king, and Juliana, despite the wrongs done to her, is doubly condemned for transgressing against his authority.

5

Killing the King

The fourteenth and fifteenth centuries were a dangerous time to be king of England. Of the nine kings who reigned between 1307 and 1485, four (Edward II, Richard II, Henry VI and Edward V) were deposed and subsequently (almost certainly) murdered, while a fifth (Henry IV) survived numerous assassination attempts, and a sixth (Richard III) died on the battlefield. If we are to include royal dukes, the period becomes a veritable bloodbath. Not only did the possession of royal blood become highly dangerous in this period,[1] but many of the stories which began to circulate about the manner of some of these numerous killings were themselves remarkable. The Wars of the Roses were, arguably, little more than a vendetta among a section of the aristocracy, as local rivalries between great households and blood-feuds between families were acted out on the battlefield. This goes some way toward explaining the high mortality rate in battle among the royal dukes and the great families, as sons revenged slain fathers. For example, Edmund Beaufort, duke of Somerset, was killed at the first battle of St Albans in 1455; his son Henry continued the struggle for the Lancastrian party, and defeated the Yorkists at Wakefield in 1460, where Richard, duke of York, and one of his sons were killed, and where the earl of Salisbury, father of Somerset's other chief enemy Warwick, was captured and subsequently lynched. The younger Somerset was in turn attainted and executed by the triumphant Yorkist Edward IV, son of the dead duke of York.[2]

The comparative frequency of royal murder was also a product of the disturbed political circumstances of the times, and the end result may have been much the same as in death by battle; after all, many of the deaths following battles were in effect murder dignified by battle. The moral overtones of death in battle and death by murder were so different as to represent almost opposite poles of the late medieval moral spectrum. War, and civil war especially, was not to be welcomed or encouraged, but the battlefield did provide a suitable opportunity for God to give his verdict. Battle contained within it an element of the earlier idea of trial by combat, where God would grant victory to the combatant who had justice on his side. The idea of death as divine justice, already discussed with reference to the Anglo-Norman and Angevin kings, is apparent in accounts of events such as Richard III's death at Bosworth. The Crowland Continuator, for example, gave an account of Richard dreaming of 'a multitude of demons apparently surrounding him ...' in scenes reminiscent of accounts of Rufus's death written more than three centuries previously. He concluded that Henry Tudor's success was 'a glorious victory granted by heaven ...'.[3]

The associations of murder and usurpation were very different. In the medieval period, not only was murder of course a crime and a grave sin, the murder of a king increasingly came to be viewed as a crime against nature and against the divine moral order. The Old Testament story of David and the Amalekite set out the idea that it was a grave crime to raise one's hand against the Lord's anointed. David heard the news of King Saul's death in the disastrous battle of Gilboa from an Amalekite who had escaped alive from the remnants of the Israelite army. Learning that the soldier himself had killed Saul, David had him executed, despite the fact that it was a mercy-killing at Saul's own request.[4] St Paul stated that 'the powers that be are ordained by God' and that Christians should uncomplainingly submit to authority,[5] so the overthrow and murder of a ruler was a sin, no matter how justified the circumstances might appear. Sedition was widely identified with heresy. Conversely, heretical practices such as necromancy were identified with sedition in the later middle ages.[6] Tyrannicide was declared a form of heresy by the council of Constance in 1415, and the parlement of Paris similarly condemned tyrannicide in 1416, probably as a reaction against the pretensions of Henry V of England to the French throne.[7] By reminding political opinion that Henry was the son of Henry IV (the usurper and murderer of Richard II), the house of Valois could reinforce its claim to the French crown against that of the Lancastrians.

The concept of treason, which developed in the later middle ages, was closely tied to the idea of killing the king. Treason was a crime so serious that it carried the terrible penalty of hanging, drawing and quartering.

Under English law, 'encompassing' (plotting or even speculating upon) the death of the king was treasonous. This made the definition of treason conveniently vague, and encompassing the king's death became a convenient catch-all clause for kings or their counsellors to use to remove political opponents. It was often linked to the accusation of necromancy, the charge that the accused had employed a magician to divine the date of the king's demise. Regicide and treason were also associated with heresy. The charge was levelled against the wives or associates of notable political figures in the fifteenth century, including against the household of George, duke of Clarence, the wife of Humphrey, duke of Gloucester, and Joan of Navarre, the widow of Henry IV. Women were often the accused, as the female sex was viewed as less rational and therefore more prone to be misled by the devil, but the aim was often to attack a powerful male figure by association. In Clarence's case, it led to his fall and execution in 1478. Charges of witchcraft or necromancy were notoriously difficult for the accused to disprove, as anyone suspected of consorting with the devil was taken by definition to be a liar and deceiver. Such accusations were increasingly popular in the fourteenth and fifteenth centuries as a means of destroying political opponents, most notably in Philip IV of France's campaign against the Knights Templar in 1307–14.[8]

Given this background of horror at crimes of treason and regicide, usurpation was not taken lightly, and the killing of a king was not an act that could be carried out openly. Not until 1649 was an English king executed after a judicial process, and never again after that. This left only the furtive act of murder as a way to dispose of a king. The secretive nature of such murders inevitably created problems of legitimacy for the succeeding ruler, as doubts over the fate of the dead king (or a cult of martyrdom) began to gather around him.

There were, however, a number of circumstances to which a would-be usurper could appeal in order to justify the overthrow of a king. Edward II and Richard II may have ended their days by violence, but both were overthrown with at least a show of constitutional process. The articles of accusation raised against Edward condemned him as a *rex inutilis* (literally, a 'useless king'), expressing a belief that, if a king spectacularly failed to live up the expectations placed upon him, it was in the interests of the realm for him to step aside. The articles listed a number of charges which are essentially elaborations of this theme, but item 5 also accused him of having violated his coronation oath 'to do justice to all', making Edward's deposition in effect the result of a breach of contract between him and his subjects. As he was 'incorrigible without hope of amendment', there was no option (so the argument ran) but to remove him.[9] A contemporary chronicle account further emphasised the idea that the abdication was the result of a mandate from the realm, with the archbishop of Canterbury preaching on the theme *vox populi vox dei* (the voice of the people is the voice of God).[10]

The legal fiction was maintained that Edward had not been overthrown, but had abdicated his throne 'of his free will and by the common counsel and assent' of the realm, and was to live a private life of repentance for his sins as 'the Lord Edward, formerly King of England'.[11] The fact that Mortimer and Queen Isabella, leaders of the coup against Edward II, claimed to rule in the name of Edward's young son Edward III also helped create a veneer of legitimacy, as the direct line of succession had not been broken.

The overthrow of Richard II in 1399 was arguably a more blatant act of usurpation. In purely dynastic terms, the end result of the overthrow of Edward II was merely that his son became king earlier than he might otherwise have done. The deposition of Richard in favour of Henry of Bolingbroke, however, was a more dramatic break, in favour of a man (Henry IV) who was by no means the obvious heir (Richard's heir presumptive was in fact his young cousin Edmund Mortimer), and one who claimed that he had taken up arms merely to regain his paternal inheritance, which Richard had confiscated. Henry appealed to a number of precedents to justify his seizure of the throne. One of these was the right of conquest, a dangerous precedent as it might encourage possible future usurpers, but one with obvious historical resonance, harking back to 1066, the date from which all English kings had begun to number their reigns. (The conventional numbers given to kings derive from this late medieval formulation, Henry IV, for example, being 'King Henry, the Fourth since the Conquest'). Henry was quick to reassure the aristocracy that he had no intention of using his right of conquest illegally to disinherit any of them.[12] His idea also reflects the concept of battle as a form of judicial combat, and that God had shown his favour to Henry by allowing him to conquer the realm.

More prosaically, Henry appealed to his dynastic claim, promoting an apocryphal story that his ancestor, Edmund 'Crouchback', the younger son of Henry III, had in fact been born before his brother, Edward I, but had been passed over on account of a physical deformity. (The name 'Crouchback' probably means not 'hunchback' but 'cross-back', a crusader.) This unlikely story smacks of desperation on Henry's part. His more realistic dynastic claim came from his being, like Richard II, a grandson of Edward III, but even this claim was clouded by his father John of Gaunt being only the fourth son.

Like Edward II, whose deposition of course provided a precedent, Richard was supposed to abdicate his crown and retire into private life. Of course this did not happen. Henry's regime was at pains to propagate the idea that Richard had voluntarily resigned his kingly authority, and the French chronicler Jean Creton, a probable eyewitness to Richard's capture at Conway, suggests that he was tricked into surrendering his crown by the earl of Northumberland.[13] Richard was prevailed upon before parliament to absolve his subjects of their oaths of allegiance to him. Like Edward II, he was condemned as a *rex inutilis*: 'I confess [to] have been and [that I] am wholly insufficient and useless and ... am not unworthy to be deposed.'[14] Henry, before a parliament gathered around a dramatically empty royal throne, laid claim to the royal title, on the grounds of inheritance, 'that ryght that God of his grace has sent me, with the helpe of my kyn and my frendes, to recover it', and the fact that the realm under Richard had been nearly 'undone for defaut of governance and undoyng of the gode lawes'.[15]

The new regime in each case went to great lengths to maintain the semblance of a legal handover of power. This is an indication of the unwillingness to kill a king, or at least to be seen to do so. Even in the troubled circumstances of the late fifteenth century, this remained the case. The conflicts known to history as the Wars of the Roses began in earnest with the first battle of St Albans in 1455, yet it was not until 1460 that Richard, duke of York, laid claim to the kingship, only to be rebuffed by parliament, and only in 1461 did his son claim the throne as Edward IV. Despite capturing Henry VI in 1465, and incarcerating him in the Tower, he did not kill the Lancastrian king until 1471, and only after his brief restoration had demonstrated that Henry, albeit as an unwitting focus for conspiracies, posed a serious threat to Edward's rule.

These proceedings – the legal or semi-legal means by which kings were deposed – were carried out in public, and deaths in battle of course took place in public, allowing us a reasonable chance of ascertaining something like the truth through the chronicle accounts or rolls of parliament. Royal murder, in contrast, was a secret and private affair. As we shall see, the lack of hard information about the circumstances of these deaths allowed colourful stories to flourish.

Of all the memorable and unpleasant deaths suffered by the medieval kings of England, surely none was more memorable or less pleasant than that of Edward II at Berkeley Castle in 1327. It was described in the following way by Sellar and Yeatman in *1066 and All That*:

> HORRIBLE SCREAMS were heard issuing from the Berkeley where Edward II was imprisoned and the next day he was horribly dead. But since not even the Barons would confess to having horribly murdered him, it is just possible that he had merely been dying of a surfeit in the ordinary way.[16]

Given the authors' declared aim to record only the parts of history that are memorable, they are curiously coy about the exact method by which Edward was supposedly despatched; namely, the insertion of a red-hot spit through his anus. This curious form of death clearly needs more comment than even more serious historians than Sellar and Yeatman have given it. The death of Edward II is paralleled by another celebrated royal death, that of Humphrey, duke of Gloucester, over a century later. Why should this particularly hideous mode of killing be ascribed to them? A certain amount of mystery surrounds both deaths, but it is interesting not only to consider whether they were killed in this way, but also why people believed they were, and how the stories arose.

Edward II was deposed by his wife, Isabella of France, and her lover Mortimer in 1326, and confined in Berkeley Castle, Gloucestershire. There were apparently a number of unsuccessful attempts to rescue him, which effectively sealed his fate by forcing his captors to hasten his end. Isabella and Mortimer subsequently ruled in the name of the young Edward III, Isabella's son by the dead king. In 1330 Edward III came to power through a coup in which Mortimer was killed and Isabella stripped of power and sent into dishonourable but comfortable retirement.

The death of Humphrey, duke of Gloucester, in 1447 also occurred in circumstances of extreme political conflict. Humphrey, the uncle of King Henry VI, had been Protector of the Realm during the king's minority, but had always faced competition from more favoured councillors, principally the Beaufort family and William de la Pole, duke of Suffolk. In February 1447, Suffolk engineered Gloucester's downfall. Gloucester was arraigned for treason before a parliament at Bury St Edmunds, in the heartland of Suffolk's power and stuffed with the latter's supporters, and died shortly after his arrest upon his arrival at Bury. There were no signs of violence done to his body, which was publicly exposed to the parliament to prove as much. There seem to have been no allegations of foul play at the time, and it seems not unlikely that Duke Humphrey died of exhaustion after a long journey in midwinter and of shock and despair at his imprisonment.[17]

This did not stop rumours circulating. Suffolk was himself impeached in 1450 (and certainly murdered shortly afterwards), and the personal reputation of 'Good Duke Humphrey' soared in proportion to Suffolk's unpopularity. In short, the situation was ideal for the circulation of allegations that Humphrey had not died of natural causes. For example, in June 1447, the yeoman keeper of Gloucester Castle was indicted for treason on the grounds that he had claimed that the duke had been killed by King Henry, and that it would have been better had the king and queen been killed instead, as Humphrey would have made a better king.[18] The Kentish rebels of 1450 sang an invective against the 'traitors' who 'drownyd ye Duke of Gloucester'.[19]

In the case of Duke Humphrey, three versions exist of the story of death by red-hot spit. A *Chronicle of London* contains the following account:

> Some seid he died for sorowe, some seid he was murdred bitwene ij ffedir-beddes; And some seid he was throst into the bowell with an hote brennyng spitte. And when he was founded deed he was laide opyn, that all men myght behold hym ... but no wounde nor tokyn of wounde cowde be persaived upon hym.[20]

Another London account, the so-called *Great Chronicle*, tells the same story, reporting the common belief that he was 'stuffid atwene ij ffethyr beddis' or was killed 'by meane of an hoot brennyng spytt threst into the nethyr part of his body', adding that 'soom said he was drownyd in wyne ...'.[21]

The Burgundian writer Georges Chastellain, in his *Temple de Bocace* of 1463, wrote that Duke Humphrey was tied naked to a bed, placed on his knees, and a red hot iron spit thrust into him through a cow horn with a hole in the end that had been placed in his anus. He was then placed naked between two sheets, to make it appear as if he had died of natural causes in his sleep:

> [he was] laid out stark naked on a bed, tied with cords ... Making cries and
> groans as if to pierce the heavens, and, laid on his knees and elbows, he had
> a cow's horn, pierced at the end, placed in his fundament, through which
> was passed a burning-hot iron spit, passing as far as the heart, so as to appear
> that his death had come naturally, for he was placed naked on a bed between
> two sheets to give that impression..[22]

The *London Chronicle* is actually one of three, consecutive, chronicles in the same manuscript. It takes the history through from 1440 to 1496, so the account of Humphrey's death was probably written up to half a century after the event.[23] Chastellain's account was written in 1463, and was part of a work effectively updating Boccaccio's *Fall of Princes*, a popular late medieval theme.[24] This was particularly appropriate for Chastellain, as the work was dedicated to Margaret of Anjou, the wife of the deposed Henry VI of England, who was then in exile in her father's county of Bar. The reference to the murder of Gloucester, given Margaret's former close association with the supposed perpetrator Suffolk, is curious, to say the least. The account bears striking similarities to that in the *London Chronicle*, and the reference to his being 'mis au lit entre deux draps' echoes the 'ffedirbeddes' of the English account. These similarities suggest that, although written considerably later, the *London Chronicle* version records a story in circulation by 1463, and that it and Chastellain may share a common source. The qualifying 'some seid' suggests that the English account is drawn from popular rumour, not taken from Chastellain, whose account is presented as fact, albeit in the context of moralising literature.

Let us now compare the accounts of Duke Humphrey's death with some accounts of that of Edward II. Perhaps the most famous, and certainly the most vivid, of these is found in the chronicle of Geoffrey le Baker. He describes how Edward's captors attempted to kill him first by ill-treatment, depriving him of proper clothes and food, and imprisoning him above a charnel-house, then attempting to suffocate him with heavy pillows, and finally

> they passed a red-hot soldering iron through a trumpet-like instrument (*cum ferro plumbarii incense ignito trans tubam ductilem*) (so that no visible mark would be left to be seen by any friend of justice) into his anus, through the intestines and into his wind-pipe. And so died this great soldier, with a terrible scream. [Those who heard it] prayed with compassion for the departed soul. Thus he whom the world hated, as previously it had hated his master Jesus, was received into heaven.[25]

Baker's account is the first in which the red-hot-spit story appears. As in the London chronicle account of Gloucester's death, the murderers attempt to smother him before applying the *coup de grâce*. The terrible screams in Chastellain's account occur here, and just as Humphrey's were such as to pierce heaven ('percer les cieux'), so those of Edward mark his soul's passage to heaven, and are greeted with reverence by those who hear them. Even in the details, Baker's account resembles that of Chastellain, as in both a horn or trumpet is used to guide the passage of the hot iron.

A further similarity between the two reported deaths is the story, related by Adam Murimuth, that Edward II's body was publicly displayed, but that no marks of violence were found upon it.[26] This echoes the account in the late fifteenth-century Fabyan's chronicle of Humphrey's body being exhibited before parliament to demonstrate that he had not apparently died by violence.[27]

The political context is all-important in understanding the death stories of Edward II and Humphrey, duke of Gloucester. Geoffrey le Baker collected and synthesised his sources for the death of Edward some twenty years after the event. In the words of a modern commentator:

> to what extent [Baker's accounts] belong to English history as well as to English literature is hard to say ... At the time [of writing], the cult of Edward II was flourishing, and the legend was eroding historical accuracy, but, on the other hand, men wanted to disassociate the ruling king, Edward III, from the savage murder of his father for which his mother and her lover, both by then disgraced and the latter dead, were responsible.[28]

Edward III needed disassociating from these events, and may well have felt ambivalent about them. One of the supposed killers, John

Mautravers, having offered to expurgate himself in 1345, was received back into Edward's service.[29]

Similarly, there were political reasons for Gloucester's death to be portrayed as a grisly murder. Although he died in disgrace, the coup of 1450, which saw his nemesis Suffolk murdered, led to the rapid rehabilitation of Gloucester. The new Yorkist government was keen to create a myth of 'Good Duke Humphrey', even if the real Duke Humphrey had been largely motivated by a desire for quasi-regal power and personal aggrandisement. Richard, duke of York, could be viewed as Gloucester's political heir, opposed to conciliation with France and to rule by the Beaufort clan, and indeed, he replaced Gloucester as heir presumptive until the birth of a son to Henry VI in 1453.[30] Humphrey's rehabilitation was completed in 1455, when he was declared innocent of the treason charges brought against him by Suffolk. The chroniclers who recorded his death were sympathetic to the Yorkist government and its version of events; the red-hot spit story thus appears in a chronicle of the City of London, which was firmly Yorkist in its sympathies. The City's trading connections with Flanders ensured that the merchants would support that faction which favoured the alliance with Burgundy and war with France.[31] Allegations that Gloucester was murdered were also made by the St Albans chronicler Whethamsted,[32] who was in general sympathetic to the Yorkists,[33] was a friend of Gloucester's, and had reason to be grateful to him for his patronage of the abbey of St Albans, where the duke was buried.[34] Whethamsted puts a speech into Gloucester's mouth in which he compares his relationship to Henry VI with that of David to Saul.[35] This comparison seems to make Humphrey into a regal figure and, like that made by the keeper of Gloucester Castle, to suggest that he would have made a better king than Henry.

The political situation helps to explain the background to the death stories, but it does not explain why such a peculiar method of killing was believed to have been employed. Let us examine a number of possible explanations. One is that death through extreme suffering might confer sanctity on the victim. Edward II is presented as a royal saint, killed in a horrible manner that echoes the martyrdoms of the saints. Geoffrey le Baker compares him to Job, patient in suffering, and, as we have seen, to Christ, betrayed by his own people. Like Christ,

Edward is mocked by his tormentors, being forced to wear a crown of straw and to shave with cold river water.[36]

Both Edward and Humphrey are known to have enjoyed posthumous unofficial cults of sainthood. Edward's tomb, like that of his dead opponent Thomas of Lancaster before him, became the focus for this cult, and attracted many pilgrims, especially from among the common people.[37] In the sixteenth century, the people of London, in particular the poor and unemployed, similarly venerated what they mistakenly believed to be Duke Humphrey's tomb in St Paul's.[38] Edward II, duke Humphrey, Thomas of Lancaster and Simon de Montfort, who had likewise been treated as popular saints, were all royal or quasi-royal figures (de Montfort being Henry III's brother-in-law) who were held to have stood for the people and fallen foul of tyranny. Although their political careers in life were far from blameless, in death they became martyrs, and their sanctified souls accused the tyrants who had destroyed them. Perhaps the contradiction in popular consciousness between a veneration for royalty and a hatred of tyrannical rule could only be resolved in figures who were simultaneously royal yet victims of tyranny.

Not everyone shared the view that Edward II was a saint. Ranulf Higden in the *Polychronicon*, written at roughly the same time as le Baker's account, also refers to his having been – to quote an English translation – 'sleyne with a hoote broche putte thro the secrete place posterielle'. But he goes on to remark that 'kepynge in prison, vilenes and obprobrious dethe cause not a martir ...'.[39] Furthermore, while the unofficial canonisation of Edward or Humphrey may account for stories of their violent death, the actual method does not seem very holy. Collections of saints' lives such as Jacobus de Voragine's *Golden Legend* record many stories of appalling tortures, including some by hot iron, and many involving the threat of rape or penetration, but none by the exact method supposedly used on Edward and Humphrey.

On the contrary, this means of death seems humiliating, and even blackly comical. Bottom-poking with a hot iron as a means of violent comedy occurs in Chaucer's *Miller's Tale*, in which in an elaborate piece of trickery the clerk Absolon attacks his fellow Nicholas, who has stuck his naked backside out of a window, in the following way:

And he was redy with his iren hoot,
And Nicholas amydde the ers he smoot,
Of gooth the skyn an hande-brede aboute,
The hoote kultour brende so his toute,
And for the smert he wende for to dye.⁴⁰

The incident is a typical *fabliau* scenario, involving elements of trickery and sexual innuendo. The tone is coarse and scatological throughout. Nicholas had 'risen for to pisse' and upon appearing at the window 'leete fle a fart',⁴¹ while in an earlier piece of trickery Absolon had been compelled to kiss their hostess Alisoun's 'naked ers Ful savourly'.⁴²

Could the two death stories have their origins in this type of humour? It seems unlikely, given the otherwise reverential tome of the accounts. Baker sought to portray Edward as a saint; Higden did not, but his account was aimed at moral improvement, reminding his readers that, if Edward was no saint, his sufferings may have helped 'diminishe his peynes' in the next life.⁴³ Chastellain's account of the death of Gloucester also pointed a moral. Could there be a sexual element to the humour? It has frequently been suggested that the means of death visited upon Edward II might be a comment on his supposed homosexuality. This may be the case, although it begs the question as to how far Edward's misrule was attributed to his sexuality, as opposed to his excessive favouritism. In any case, there were no such accusations against Duke Humphrey. It is also not easy to interpret the means of death as a comment on a more general passivity of character. Again this may apply to the unmartial Edward, but Humphrey had fought with distinction in France, and his fall from grace in 1440 was a result of his storming out of court in protest at the government's attempts to pursue peace with France.⁴⁴

A later accusation against Richard II suggests that 'sodomy' (whether we define this as homosexuality or as sexual sin in general) was seen as rendering a king unfit to rule. Gluttony was also seen as incompatible with being a good ruler, as a lack of self-control implied an inability to govern others, and the sin of gluttony was viewed as being related to (and a cause of) sexual overindulgence. According to Adam of Usk, the 'doctors' and bishops who were assembled by Henry IV to find grounds for the deposition of Richard 'decided that perjuries, sacrileges, sodomitical acts, dispossession of his subjects, the reduction of his people to servitude, lack of reason, and incapacity to rule, to all of which King Richard was notoriously prone, were sufficient reasons ... for deposing him'.[45] As Adam's modern editor points out, these charges were based on the deposition of the Emperor Frederick II by Pope Innocent IV at the council of Lyon in 1245, with one interesting exception: the reference to sodomy has been added, in place of the charge of heresy against Frederick. It may be that the theologians (or Adam) added the reference to 'sodomitical acts' in a deliberate allusion to Edward II. Richard was often compared to Edward, whose deposition provided an obvious precedent.

The use of the red-hot poker story, at least in the case of Duke Humphrey, is grounded in practical rather than symbolic reasons. The story does not occur in the most contemporaneous accounts of the deaths of either Edward or Humphrey. Adam Murimuth, who was a contemporary of the events that he described, did not mention it, writing only that it was 'commonly said' that Edward had been murdered;[46] admittedly, having received patronage from Mortimer and Isabella, he may have been saying less than he knew. Most accounts of Duke Humphrey's demise do not suggest death by violence; a continuation of a London chronicle covering the years 1446–50 says only that 'he died in his bedde atte Bury ...',[47] while a later version of the London *Brut* says only that he died of 'sorou', although the author alludes darkly that 'the certainte of his deth is not yit openly knowe, but ther is no thynge so prive, as the gospel saith, but atte last it shal be openne'.[48] These, it must be remembered, were chronicles likely to be sympathetic to Gloucester, yet they were unable to set forth any accusation of murder apart from innuendo.

We have two situations in which a king or prince of the blood is dead, an unpopular government has been overthrown, and the new regime has an interest in blackening the name of its predecessor. Yet in neither case is there much material evidence for murder. Edward was probably murdered, but we have no conclusive evidence about the circumstances, and there was even a story that he escaped, which one modern historian warns us not to dismiss entirely.[49] Humphrey was almost certainly not murdered. Having set up a packed parliament at which to try him, Suffolk was hardly likely to kill him before proceedings began. Hence there was a need for the new regime to promote a murder story involving means that would leave no outward mark. The same applies to the claim of the Kentish rebels that the duke was drowned, another form of death that would leave no signs of violence. In the cases of both Edward and Humphrey it is worth noting that the examination of the body is stressed, although this too may itself be part of the legend.[50] In Humphrey's case it was only reported in Fabyan's Chronicle up to half a century after the event, so it might be yet another element borrowed from Edward's story.

Why was the use of a red-hot spit specified, rather than smothering or poisoning, which could equally have left no obvious signs of violence? It is not easy to find precedents for this method of death in saints' lives and histories. It seems likely, however, that there are certain archetypal death-stories that recur in different settings. In the case of Duke Humphrey, the motif of death by impalement may have been current in the late fifteenth century. This was the era of Vlad the Impaler, prince of Wallachia, whose use of impalement often took the form of penetrating the victim through the anus or vagina. In one instance, according to legend, 'he had a red-hot iron stake shoved into a woman's vagina, making the instrument penetrate her entrails and emerge from her mouth'.[51] Vlad's notoriety was reaching the west toward the end of the century, with stories of his cruelty circulating in Germany in the early 1460s.[52] At around the same time Edward IV's constable John Tiptoft was using similar methods in England, which seem to have been inspired by the impaling of Turkish prisoners by the Hospitallers in Rhodes, which he had witnessed while returning from a pilgrimage to Jerusalem in 1458.[53] His victims' bodies were, however, impaled only after they had been executed. They were 'hanged uppe by the leggys, and a stake made scharpe at bothe endes, whereof one ende was putt in att bottokys, and the other ende there heddes were putte uppe one ...'[54]

The motif of impalement in such a way as to 'spit' the victim from anus to mouth has older origins. Two twelfth-century examples, one from an English chronicler, demonstrate this. According to Henry of Huntingdon, Robert of Bellême, a Norman lord, 'drove stakes through people of both sexes, from anus to mouth (*ab ano usque in ora*)'.[55] Similarly, Guibert of Nogent tells of how the French lord Thomas of Marle would thrust his lance into a victim's mouth, and it would emerge through their anus – an interesting variation.[56] In both cases, a local tyrant is portrayed as using this particularly cruel form of death, but is later dealt with by a just king (Henry I and Louis VI respectively). Such a cruel and unusual punishment is associated with tyranny; that is, with illegitimate authority. The idea that it is a literary topos for tyranny is reinforced when we consider how impractical it would actually be to impale a body so perfectly that a spike entering one orifice would emerge exactly through another at the opposite end of the body.

Smothering is offered by the London Chronicle as another possible cause of the death of Duke Humphrey, and le Baker tells us that Edward II's murderers at first attempted to kill him in this way. The motif of smothering with a pillow or similar item of bedding is a common one in royal murder accusations, dating back to Caligula supposedly disposing in this way of Tiberius.[57] The stories of two celebrated late medieval murders employed this motif, using language very similar to the 'ffedirbeddes' account of Duke Humphrey's death. The death of Thomas of Woodstock, who like Humphrey was duke of Gloucester and a younger son of a deceased king (Edward III), occurred in mysterious, and politically expedient, circumstances in 1397. During the reign of Henry IV, a confession was obtained that the murderers

> sesoient li dit Duc de Gloucester coucher sur un Lyt, & les ditz William Serle & ... Fraunceys misterent sur luy un fetherbed; & [ils] coucherent dessuz le bouche de dit Duc de Gloucestre tan qu'il fuist morte.[58]

The similarities between this account and later versions of Duke Humphrey's death suggest a possible confusion between the deaths of the two dukes of Gloucester. The motif occurs again in Thomas More's version of the death of the 'Princes in the Tower', whose murderers

> among the [bed]clothes so bewrapped them and entangled them, keeping down by force the featherbed and pillows hard unto their mouths, that within a while, smored and stifled, their breath failing, they gave up to God their innocent souls ...[59]

These murders (or supposed murders) are linked by their furtive nature, and the fact that in none of the cases did contemporaries know exactly what had occurred. The motif of smothering seems appropriate as a metaphor for the smothering of the truth, and the occurrence of the deaths in the privacy of the bedchamber reflects their secretive nature.

Chastellain provides an alternative account of Duke Humphrey's death in another work, which prefigures another famous royal killing. In his chronicle, he relates that Humphrey was killed by drowning in wine, in preference to strangling, so that no signs of his violent death would appear:

> En vin plain une cuve,
> Failloit qu'estranglé fust
> Cuidant par elle estuve
> Que la morte n'y parust ... [60]

Chastellain is believed to have died in 1475, three years *before* the celebrated death of the duke of Clarence, drowned in a butt of malmsey wine.[61] Chastellain's alternative account – chosen, like the red-hot spit or smothering stories to suggest a death that left no outward marks – could very well be the source for the Clarence story, which did not appear until 1483, and all versions of which, according to Clarence's biographer, 'lack foundation'.[62]

Unless earlier precedents for the red-hot poker story are found, it may be that in the case of Edward II it was a genuinely new story, modelled to fit his supposed homosexuality and passivity. In the case of Humphrey, duke of Gloucester, the story was probably 'borrowed', either intentionally or via popular rumour, from the death of Edward II, and moulded to fit the circumstances. Whichever was the case, there was an older tradition of impaling as a punishment employed by tyrants on which the author could draw.

The circumstances of the death of Richard II in 1400 were remarkably similar to those of Edward II, with one key difference: unlike Edward, or Humphrey, duke of Gloucester, Richard did not enjoy a rapid rehabilitation following his death. The Lancastrian dynasty was not overthrown in a matter of two or three years, but continued for six decades. Although Richard enjoyed something of a rehabilitation in the reign of Henry V (1413–22), it was inconceivable that the Lancastrian regime would allow any light to be shed upon the circumstances of his death. Therefore we do not see the proliferation of stories about his mode of death that arose for those of Edward II or Duke Humphrey. Instead, rumour took the form of many claims that Richard still lived.

Some chroniclers seemed happy to accept the comforting 'official' version that Richard had died in prison in Pontefract Castle. According to Adam of Usk, he had been ill-treated, 'tormented, bound with chains, and starved of food' by his gaoler, 'N. Swynford' (probably Sir Thomas Swinford), who 'tormented [him] with starving fare ...'. Adam stopped short, however, of saying that he was murdered, claiming that he 'pined away even unto death' upon hearing of the defeat of his partisans in the rebellion of 1400.[63] The pattern of confinement, followed by ill-treatment stopping short of actual murder, repeated that attributed to the last days of Edward II. The *Historia Ricardi Secundi* echoes Adam of Usk in claiming that Richard sank into despair on hearing of the defeat of the rebels, and thereafter refused food and was slain by 'the sword of hunger'.[64] Other accounts state that he was deliberately starved, or that he starved himself, to death.[65] As with Edward II, Richard's body was exposed to demonstrate that he had died, but not in such a way as to allow inspection for wounds; Usk says that it lay 'with the face uncovered so that all could see it'.[66]

One account gives an intriguingly different cause of death. According to the chronicle known as the *Traison et mort de Richard II*, which was sympathetic to Richard, he was hacked to death.[67] This explanation is highly implausible, given the fact that Richard's body was later displayed,[68] but is interesting in its symbolism. The late medieval and early modern idea of the king's two bodies linked the concept of his mortal, carnal body with his immortal body, the body politic, that lived on even when individual monarchs died. By presenting the murder of Richard as a violent, dismembering attack on his body, the author of the *Traison* emphasises the unnatural nature of regicide, which was an attack not just on the king but on the body politic. A similar use of body symbolism was employed by Adam of Usk, who related how, at his coronation, Richard had lost a shoe, a spur and finally his crown, which was rather improbably said to have been blown off his head by a gust of wind. This was interpreted as a prophecy of how first the commons and later the nobles would rebel against him, and he would finally be deposed. The prophecy vividly maps out the body politic on Richard's corporeal body.

Later tradition made the deposition and murder of Richard a major turning-point in English history. Tudor historians, writing in the aftermath of the conflict that we call the Wars of the Roses, and keen to praise the stability and unity brought to the nation by Henry VII, interpreted the wars as God's punishment of the nation for the murder of Richard.[69] Following the *Traison* version, Shakespeare has Richard being killed with an axe.[70] He was strongly influenced by the Tudor historian Edward Hall, who saw Henry IV as 'first author of this division' for his deposition of Richard.[71] The horror with which deposition was viewed in Shakepeare's day is shown by the fact that his play, *Richard II*, was originally performed with the abdication scene (Act 4, Scene 1) excised. When the earl of Essex's supporters had the play performed with that scene restored, it was in effect a declaration of his rebellion against Elizabeth I.[72]

The next great royal murder was carried out by Humphrey, duke of Gloucester's political heirs, the Yorkist dynasty. This was the death of Henry VI in 1471. As noted above, it took the regime of Edward IV a long time finally to make the decision to remove the Lancastrian monarch. The 'readeption' of Henry (his restoration by an unlikely alliance of his queen, Margaret of Anjou, and her former enemy the Earl of Warwick) in 1470–71, and the subsequent restoration of Edward IV, sealed his fate. Margaret and Warwick's bid for power rendered Henry not merely an inconvenient hangover from the previous dynasty, but a focus (albeit unwitting) for faction and conspiracies against Edward. Like Mary, Queen of Scots, Charles I, and Louis XVI and Marie-Antoinette in later centuries, his mere existence made him dangerous (although these other monarchs all contributed to some extent to their own ends by engaging in intrigue).

The *Arrivall of Edward IV*, the 'official' Yorkist account of Edward IV's restoration, has it that Henry died of 'pure displeasure, and melencoly' upon hearing the news of the battle of Tewkesbury, where his wife was defeated and his only son killed.[73] We need not take this seriously as an explanation for his all too convenient expiry, but, interestingly, something similar had previously been used to account for the equally politically convenient 'pining away' of Richard II and the death by 'sorrow' of Humphrey, duke of Gloucester.[74] A more sceptical hand later added the words 'or was mordered' in the margin, in response to the *Arrivall's* claim that he had 'dyed'.[75] Henry enjoyed a posthumous career as a royal martyr. Details of the manner of his death were few; John Warkworth merely stated that he 'was putt to dethe'. He records the timing with some exactitude, 'betwyx xj. and xij. of the cloke' on the night of the 21 May 1471, the very day that Edward IV arrived back in London, and implies that Richard of Gloucester (the future King Richard III) was responsible for implementing the murder, as he was in the Tower at the time, but sheds no light on the method of killing.[76]

Fabyan's chronicle reported that 'Of the death of this Prynce dyuerse tales were tolde: but the most common fame wente, that he was stykked with a dagger by the handes of the Duke of Gloucester'.[77] We see yet another example of a London chronicler reporting popular rumour ('the most common fame'). Writing as he was at the beginning of the sixteenth century, many years after the event and after the death of the 'Princes in the Tower', it is tempting to dismiss Fabyan's account as reflecting a later anti-Ricardian bias, but he may equally have been reporting a genuine belief among people who made the obvious link between Gloucester's presence in the Tower and Henry's convenient death. Polydore Vergil and Phillipe de Commines agree with Fabyan in blaming Gloucester for the death, the former also reflecting popular opinion, prefacing his account with the words 'ut fama est' (as the rumour is). Polydore Vergil claimed that Richard struck him down with a sword, Commines that he killed him 'by his hand' or at least that Henry was killed in his presence.[78] The Crowland Continuator, writing in about 1486, chose to remain silent on the exact cause of death, while implying very strongly that Henry had been murdered:

> I shall say nothing, at this time, about the discovery of King Henry's lifeless body in the Tower of London; may God have mercy upon and give repentance to him ... who dared to lay sacrilegious hands upon the Lord's Anointed! And so, let the doer merit the title of tyrant and the victim that of glorious martyr.[79]

Henry's burial produced ominous signs. The familiar pattern of the body lying in state, face uncovered to demonstrate the king's death, was repeated, with Henry being displayed, like Richard II, at St Paul's, and then at Blackfriars in London, where his funeral service took place. 'His

face was opyne that every manne myght see hyme'. However, 'in hys
lyinge he bledde on the pament ther [at St Paul's]; and afterward at the
Blake Fryres was brought, and ther he blede new and fresche'. [80] This
is surely intended to be read as a posthumous accusation by Henry
against his murderers, and is reminiscent of the claim some three
centuries earlier that Henry II's body had bled in protest against the
treachery of his son Richard. It is interesting to note that the account
was written in about 1473, so Warkworth cannot be accused of writing
with hindsight in the knowledge of the murderous deeds of Richard of
Gloucester. The symbolism of the bleeding corpse (if there was any
intended) must therefore be read as a reflection on past events, not a
portent of future ones. A similar story of a bleeding corpse would later
be told about Henry VIII, a reference perhaps to the blood he had shed
in the course of his reign.

Another famous death story, the supposed drowning of the duke of
Clarence in a barrel of malmsey, has equally obscure and puzzling
origins. This peculiar mode of killing appears before Clarence's death
in 1478, in some versions of the death of Duke Humphrey. If the
complaint of Cade's rebels that Gloucester had been killed by drowning
can be believed, this may put the origins of the motif back to 1450, and
the ferment of rumours surrounding the duke's death. The emergence
of similar stories about the death of Clarence in 1478 also arose in the
context of a secret, politically-motivated death where the lack of hard
facts was compensated for by rumour.[81]

Some contemporary or near-contemporary accounts refrained from
commenting on the manner of his death. The Crowland Continuator,
probably writing in 1486, stated that the execution 'whatever form it
took, was carried out secretly in the Tower of London'.[82] Others, however, reported the malmsey wine story. The Italian writer Dominic
Mancini writing in 1483 was apparently the first to record it. He wrote
that 'the mode of execution preferred in this case was that he should
die by being plunged into a jar of sweet wine'.[83] This story was repeated
by Philippe de Commines, the Great Chronicle of London and Polydore
Vergil.[84]

Again, the likeliest explanation for the origins of this story is popular
rumour. The compiler of the Great Chronicle of London, who was
probably the alderman and master draper Robert Fabyan, seems to have

been well informed, and may even have been an eyewitness of some key events described in the chronicle (although obviously not the secret death of Clarence).[85] Although writing some years after the event, possibly as late as 1501–2, he may therefore be a reliable source for public opinion at the time. He reports the death of Clarence 'as the fame ran', or as rumour had it. The meaning of the wine story (if indeed there is any) remains obscure; Mancini blamed Edward squarely for the death, and the wine motif may be a reflection of his picture of the king as corpulent and over-indulgent in food and drink.[86] A similar, but not identical, motif can be found in the *Heimskringla*, the history of the kings of Norway, where the early legendary king Fjolnir drowns in a vat of mead, while staggering drunkenly around in the dark looking for a place in which to urinate.[87] His death is a fitting end for a drunkard, but it is an accidental death, not a murder.

The most famous political murder (if such it was) of the later middle ages is that of the 'Princes in the Tower': the former Edward V and his brother Richard, duke of York. Their fate is still the subject of great, often bitter, debate in popular history, with an entire society devoted to defending the reputation of their supposed murderer, Richard III. The fact that the circumstances of their death are still capable of causing such controversy reflects just how little information was available to contemporaries. The sources present a picture of the princes slowly disappearing from public view, into the enclosed, private world of the Tower, a very real, physical enactment of their being stripped of the public, political roles of king and heir presumptive by their uncle Richard, following his usurpation of the kingship. Exactly when the public 'death' of Edward V as king was followed by the princes' actual deaths, and how those deaths occurred, was as unclear to contemporary writers as it is to us. The Crowland Continuator, for example, reported that 'a rumour arose that King Edward's sons, by some unknown manner of destruction, had met their fate'.[88]

Mancini, an exact contemporary writing in the very year of Richard's usurpation, described how they were seen less and less 'till at length they ceased to appear altogether'.[89] In these circumstances, it is no surprise to read so many writers confessing their ignorance of the manner by which they met their end, although it is interesting to note that this

contradicts the view of Ricardian apologists that all near-contemporary
sources were Tudor propaganda. The so-called Tudor propagandists
were remarkably reluctant to invent blood-curdling stories of murder.
John Rous wrote that it was 'known to very few by what manner of
death they had suffered'. The London chronicle known as Fabyan's
Chronicle says only that they were 'put unto secret death ...', a view
echoed by the pro-Tudor Polydore Vergil.[90]

Perhaps the most interesting account is that in the Great Chronicle
of London, where Fabyan – if he was indeed the compiler – allows
himself more room for speculation. Far from professing ignorance on
this occasion, he gives us three different versions of their possible mode
of death, two of which we have seen before, reinforcing the idea that
motifs of murder were reused by chroniclers. Again, Fabyan seems to
be citing popular rumour:

> But of the manner of their deaths were many opinions, for some said they
> were murdered between two feather beds, some said they were drowned in
> malmsey, and some said they were pierced with a venomous poison.[91]

The repetition of the malmsey and smothering motifs from the deaths
of Humphrey of Gloucester and Clarence is immediately obvious. The
accusation of poisoning was less common, but echoes the claim by
Polydore Vergil that Edward IV (who died of an unidentifiable illness)
may have been poisoned.[92] But is the repetition derived from the fact
that rumour drew upon the same motifs, or was it an artefact of the
chronicler's art? The extract above matches very closely the description
of the death of Humphrey in another London chronicle. 'Some seid he
died for sorowe, some seid he was murdred bitwene ij ffedirbeddes; And
some seid he was throst into the bowell with an hote brennyng spitte'.[93]
The two extracts are not identical, but the use of three different explanations, the repeating virtually verbatim of the feather bed story, and
the non-committal 'some said' all recur.

The addition of the accusation of poisoning is interesting, as this
seems to have been a less popular explanation for unexplained death,
despite its obvious usefulness as a means of killing that would leave no
external marks. The motif of poisoning through self-indulgence had
been a popular one in twelfth- and thirteenth-century accounts of royal
death, and a late tradition asserted that King John had been murdered

by poison. Perhaps murder by poison lacked the personal touch of the alleged smothering or killing by dagger (or poker) of royal-death narratives. Poison could be slow, and did not need to be administered directly to the victim by the murderer, so lacked the drama of the other methods. Furthermore, a common feature of the murder stories discussed is that, while the circumstances were not publicly known, there was still a desire to assign it retrospectively to particular henchmen. Named individuals were held to be guilty in the deaths of Edward II, Thomas of Woodstock, Richard II and the Princes in the Tower. In the desire to identify and blame individuals, a directly-inflicted death was preferable to a death at one remove such as poisoning.

An intriguing interpretation of the story of the 'Princes in the Tower' has been put forward, which locates the narrative in a tradition from folklore, that of the 'Babes in the Wood'.[94] In this type of tale, two children, following the death of their father, are given into the protection of their 'Wicked Uncle', who has two of his henchmen murder them. The henchmen then quarrel, and the uncle is later revealed to be the murderer and dies in shame. The basic framework of historical events broadly fits this, but later accounts of the princes' death seem to neatly follow the pattern. Thomas More's account introduces the two murderers, while Shakespeare's *Richard III* follows the pattern further, including a scene where the murderers of Clarence (whom Shakespeare portrays as being murdered by Richard, rather than by Edward IV), fall out. It is suggested that a sixteenth-century ballad of the 'Babes in the Wood' may even be a source for the sections of Shakespeare's play that concern the murders of Clarence and the princes. The full 'Babes in the Wood' story, however, differs from that of the Princes in the Tower in one important aspect. Whereas the Babes are led off by their murderers into the woods, the wild world outside the town and civilised society, the princes were killed in the enclosed space of the Tower, a royal palace at the very heart of society and of the political world. Their murder had more in common with that of their royal ancestors, Edward II and Richard II, and of Henry VI who had met his end in the same place. Nevertheless, there is still a sense of their being cut off from the world and society, exemplified by Mancini's poignant account that, once confined to the Tower, they were seen less and less frequently, 'till at length they ceased to appear altogether'.[95]

The 'Babes in the Wood' tale in its full form recalls an even older tradition of royal murder, dating back to Anglo-Saxon England. The children are abandoned to die in the forest, their resting places unknown, before being discovered when one of the murderers confesses. The story is remarkably similar to that of St Kenelm the (possibly unhistorical) Anglo-Saxon martyr-king of Mercia. In the eleventh-century *passio* (the term for a narrative of a saint's martyrdom) of Kenelm, he is said to have been murdered by his tutor, at the instigation of his sister, who wished to supplant him. His body was abandoned in the forest, but rediscovered by means of a miraculous ray of heavenly light.[96] The motif of a martyr-king who was murdered not directly by his enemies but by their henchmen, whose body was abandoned in the wilderness, and later miraculously rediscovered, was a common one in Anglo-Saxon saints' lives.[97]

The repetition of murder motifs by chroniclers suggests that Sellar and Yeatman may have been right after all; kings may indeed have died 'in the ordinary way', or in one of a number of such ways. In examining stories of royal deaths, it would seem that we learn less about the death itself than about political attitudes and the process of myth-making.

Some time after their deaths, murdered kings were often 'rehabilitated' following a change of regime or a cooling of factional emotions. This is demonstrated in the later reburials of Richard II and Henry VI. Richard was reburied by his usurper's son, Henry V, soon after his accession in 1413. Richard's remains were removed from their resting place at Langley and interred where he himself had intended them to lie, in his tomb in Westminster Abbey. This was an attempt to bridge the gap between Henry V and Richard II, and so legitimise the former's regime. It was customary for a new king to bury his predecessor, and Henry's reburial of Richard glossed over the fact of Henry IV's usurpation, creating the image of smooth dynastic continuity.[98] Some accounts suggest that Henry V wanted to forget his father's reign entirely, as an unfortunate interlude; the chronicler Thomas Walsingham claimed that Henry V revered Richard as his own father. By burying Richard, Henry was performing the role of a son toward a deceased father.[99] A parallel to this can be seen in Edward IV's reburial of his actual father, Richard, duke of York, and his brother, Edmund, earl of Rutland, who had been killed by the Lancastrians at the battle of Wakefield and buried obscurely in the Franciscan church at Pontefract. When he was king, Edward had them reburied in the collegiate church of Fotheringhay in 1476.[100]

Later generations interpreted Henry's action as an attempt to purge his father's sin of having overthrown and killed Richard. Edward Hall, writing in the early sixteenth century, explained that Henry V had, by honourably reburying Richard, postponed the day of reckoning for the house of Lancaster until the reign of his son, Henry VI.[101] In Shakespeare's *Henry V*, which views Henry's reign as a glorious interlude between those of his father and son, the king, on the eve of Agincourt, worries that God may choose that moment to punish him for his father's sins, and reassures himself that he has warded off such a judgement by interring Richard:

> Not to-day, O Lord,
> O, not to-day, think not upon the fault
> My father made in compassing the crown!
> I Richard's body have interred anew;
> And on it have bestow'd more contrite tears
> Than from it issued forced drops of blood.[102]

A similar service was performed by Richard III for Henry VI. Again, it was not Henry's usurper and murderer, Edward IV, who reburied the dead king, but Edward's Yorkist successor. Another similarity is the promotion in importance of the place of burial – in this case from Chertsey Abbey to St George's Chapel, Windsor. This translation mirrors that of Richard II from an honourable but obscure resting-place to a royal necropolis, which St George's was becoming under the Yorkists. In this case there was the added complication that Henry's tomb at Chertsey had become the focus for a putative saint's cult. But, as with Henry V, Richard seems to have felt the need to make an act of reconciliation and thereby legitimise his own shaky regime.

When Richard III was in turn overthrown and killed by Henry Tudor, he was, like Richard and Henry VI, buried initially in relative obscurity, in the Franciscan church in Leicester. The Crowland Continuator stated that 'many ... insults were offered' to the body, which was 'carried to Leicester with insufficient humanity (a rope being placed around the neck)'.[103] The choice of a Franciscan church echoes the resting-place of the duke of York and his son (Richard's father and brother) after their deaths at Wakefield. The Franciscan order was devoted to poverty, and their churches were, at least in theory, humble and austere, hardly suitable resting-places for royalty. Edward II's Queen Isabella was buried in the graveyard of the house of the Poor Clares at Newgate, London, but this was an exception, as she was a disgraced queen living out her last days in a suitably penitent state.[104]

Richard III was to have no posthumous rehabilitation. Richard II and Henry VI may not have been buried in royal tombs, but they were at least buried honourably. Richard II, while denied burial in his magnificent tomb in Westminster Abbey, lay in state and was given a funeral mass in St Paul's before being buried at Langley.[105] Henry VI's funeral took place in the Blackfriars' church in London, before his body was carried by boat to Chertsey,[106] where it was 'honorably enteryd'.[107] Fabyan's chronicle claimed that Henry was buried 'unreverently', but his is a lone voice.[108] Richard III, in contrast, was buried 'irreverently' after being displayed naked, in marked contrast to the funeral rites and the respectful burial given to Richard II.[109] Richard III was buried without a grave stone or an epitaph, and Henry VII later provided only £10 for a coffin. The passing of Henry VII (unlike that of Henry IV or Edward IV) did not bring any change in attitude to the dead king's remains. When the abbey was dissolved during the reign of Henry VIII, the bones were unceremoniously thrown out, and the coffin used as a horse trough.[110]

In contrast to the legitimising efforts of Henry V and Richard II, Henry VII and his Tudor successors felt no need to legitimate their dynasty by claiming continuity with Richard III. The reverse was true. Henry VII's somewhat tenuous claim to the throne was legitimated by his overthrow of the tyrannical usurper Richard, and his avenging of the presumed murder of Edward V. Tudor propaganda and iconography stressed continuity not with Richard III's rule but with that of Edward IV, whose daughter Elizabeth Henry married. The Tudor rose represented the union of the houses of Lancaster and York, while another popular Tudor image, the crown in the thorn bush, referred to the legend that Richard III's crown had been discovered in this manner on the battlefield of Bosworth. This image both called attention to the divinely-ordained Tudor victory over Richard, while conveniently glossing over the fact that Richard had been killed, making it appear as if the crown were presented by providence to Henry.[111] Richard III's reign was seen as an episode of discontinuity, with Henry restoring the natural order that his predecessor had disrupted. The Crowland Continuator, employing the devices of Richard (the boar) and the two contending dynasties, wrote poetically that 'the tusks of the boar were blunted and the red rose, the avenger of the white, shines upon us'.[112] So Henry is presented not only as a Lancastrian monarch, but as the avenger of Edward IV's murdered sons.

This tradition was further developed by the Tudor historians John Rous (whose portrayal of Richard after Bosworth was as damning as it had been sycophantic before), Edward Hall and Thomas More. This tradition led to Shakespeare's portrayal of Richard III as the ultimate in scheming evil, prepared to remove anyone who stood between him and the crown. In Shakespeare's play Richard's crime of killing his nephews is but one of many. He makes Richard responsible for the murders of Edward, prince of Wales, Henry VI, Clarence, Edward IV, and even his own wife, Queen Anne, whom he murders in order to plan an incestuous marriage to his niece Elizabeth. In a particularly macabre scene, Shakespeare has Richard woo Anne, whom he has widowed by killing the Prince of Wales, beside the corpse of her father-in-law Henry VI.[113]

The murder of a king was by its nature a secretive act. Slaying the Lord's Anointed was a heinous sin, and not one which a ruler wished to advertise. We therefore have few concrete details about the actual events; and in the shadows cast by the lack of clear fact, many rumours were able to circulate. We see the effect of rumour in the recurrence of the same motifs, and, in the case of the fifteenth-century London chronicles practically the same wording, in descriptions of murders of royalty. Some descriptions of death need to be read in the context of partisan political or moralising religious writing. The prevalence of the same striking means of death in accounts of late medieval royal murder also had a practical purpose. In the face of the public display of the dead body to demonstrate that foul play had not occurred, the dead man's partisans had to suggest a means of killing that had left no external marks, hence the recurrent stories of drowning, smothering or violent internal penetration. Motifs of murder can therefore be seen to have emerged from a complex mix of literary tradition, popular rumour and political calculation.

6

Once and Future Kings

The death of a king was an important moment of transition. It represented the closure of one reign and the beginning of another; the principle of 'le roi est mort, vive le roi' ensured the succession usually passed from father to son, at the very moment of death. But if there was any ambiguity over the death of a king, then the whole principle of succession was thrown into doubt, and a great shadow was cast over the legitimacy of his successor. The belief in the survival of a supposedly dead king could be promoted in two often overlapping spheres, those of popular sentiment and of political confusion.

The theme of kings who cheated death and promised to return is a common one in European folklore. Many nations have their own example of the motif of the sleeping king who will return in his country's hour of need: Arthur in England or Wales, Frederick Barbarossa or Frederick II in Germany and many others. The motif of the 'Emperor of the Last Days', the ruler whose appearance will usher in the Apocalypse, was often linked to legends of royal survival and return.[1] Many such stories were embroidered in post-medieval times; for instance, the legend of the sleeping Frederick II was transformed in the nineteenth century into that of Frederick Barbarossa, as the Sicilian-born Frederick II was viewed as insufficiently German to be a suitable national hero for the new Wilhelmine Reich. The idea of the king who will return is, nevertheless, an ancient one. In its medieval form, Arthur *rex quondam rexque futurus* (the once and future king) is probably the most famous example, but his alleged survival predates his 'reinvention' by Geoffrey of Monmouth, suggesting a genuine folklore tradition.

This tradition of revenant or surviving kings had an impact on the history of medieval England. On a number of occasions, rumours arose that a supposedly dead king had survived, often as a hermit. King Harold was said to have survived Hastings and to have lived out

his days as a hermit in Chester. A mysterious letter purported to tell of
the survival of Edward II, who was living as a hermit; and similar reports
circulated about other later medieval kings of England.

On a related theme, there were often impostors who were eager to
use the death or disappearance of a king in mysterious circumstances
to pursue their own dreams of glory. Such pretenders (in both senses
of the word) sprang up frequently in the fifteenth century, claiming to
be Richard II, Richard, duke of York, or Richard, duke of Warwick. The
presence of a king – or someone who at least claimed to be of royal
blood – was an important legitimating element in rebellion, something
which was by no means confined to Britain. In Russian history, there
was the appearance of a 'False Dmitri', claiming to be the son of Ivan
the Terrible, during the Time of Troubles of the seventeenth century.
The most serious eighteenth-century peasants' revolt was led by Pugachev, who claimed to be the murdered Tsar Peter. As late as 1864, an
impostor claimed to be the long-dead Tsar Alexander I.[2]

In 1113 a group of canons from the north French cathedral of Laon
were travelling in Cornwall when they encountered a man who assured
them that King Arthur was not dead. When they argued that this was
not the case, it nearly caused a riot among the locals.[3] By asserting
Arthur's immortality, the Cornishmen seemed to be acting in line with
a Celtic tradition of Arthur that predated Geoffrey of Monmouth, whose
grave would be 'concealed till Doomsday'.[4] This tradition was later
incorporated into Geoffrey's Anglo-Norman version of Arthur, whose
end is ambiguous: he is taken away to 'Avilion' to have his wounds
healed, but Geoffrey does not tell us explicitly whether or not he dies.

The sceptical Norman writer Wace, in his French romance version of
Geoffrey of Monmouth, did not commit himself to an opinion on the
truth of Arthur's survival, but his Middle English translator Layamon
introduced a supernatural element of *alven* (supernatural beings) who
support Arthur. He was the first to introduce the 'Avalon' theme in its
familiar form:

> I will travel to Avalon, to the fairest of all maidens, to Argante their queen,
> the most beautiful of the spirit-folk (*alven*), and she shall make all my wounds
> sound and make me whole with healing medicines. And then I will come to
> my kingdom and dwell with the Britons with great joy ... The Britons still
> believe that he is alive, living in Avalon with the fairest of the spirit-folk, and

they still continue to expect Arthur to come back. There is no man born, chosen by any lady, who can say for certain anything else about Arthur. But there was once a wise man, whose name was Merlin: he said in these words – and his words were true – that an Arthur should yet come to help the English.[5]

These manifestations are nevertheless ambiguous, hedged about with qualifiers such as 'The Britons still believe' and '*an* Arthur [my emphasis] should yet come . . .', which may be a contemporary political reference to Arthur of Brittany, the grandson of Henry II and enemy of King John. An effort was made literally to lay to rest the ghost of Arthur in the Angevin period with the discovery of 'Arthur's grave' at Glastonbury Abbey in 1191. It was also under the Plantagenet kings, during the reign on Henry II, that Layamon turned Arthur into a king who would help the *English* (a variant manuscript reads 'the Britons').[6] This was a source of prestige and potential profit for the monks of Glastonbury who 'found' Arthur, as their house lacked the remains of a famous saint to draw in the pilgrims.[7]

It was also politically useful for the Plantagenet dynasty to prove that Arthur was dead and buried in England, and not alive and ready to fight for the Welsh. Gerald of Wales – a loyal if far from uncritical servant of the Angevin kings – tells us of the monks' excavations that 'it was the king [Henry II] himself who put them on to this'. He was quick to point out how the find disproved his countrymen's claims that Arthur still lived:

> Many tales are told and many legends have been invented about King Arthur and his mysterious ending. In their stupidity the British [the Welsh, Breton or Cornish] people maintain that he is still alive. Now that the truth is known . . . The fairy-tales have been snuffed out, and the true and indubitable facts are made known . . .[8]

As if to emphasise the value to the English monarchy of a dead Arthur at Glastonbury, the remains were exhumed and reinterred in April 1278, to coincide with the visit by Edward I and his queen. Edward had defeated and humbled Llywelyn ap Gruffydd, prince of Wales, the previous year, and was to complete his conquest of Gwynedd in 1282.[9]

The alleged gravestone of Arthur, proclaiming that he lay 'in insula

Avalonia', seemed to prove that Avalon was Glastonbury, and that Arthur had not been healed but had died there.[10] Yet Arthur was not to be laid to rest so easily. By the end of the fifteenth century Malory had formulated the classic description of the immortal Arthur: 'many men say that there ys wrytten uppon his tumbe thys: HIC IACET ARTHURUS, REX QUONDAM REXQUE FUTURUS'.[11] It may be coincidental, but the age of Malory's popularity saw the emergence of an Anglo-Welsh king who portrayed himself as the New Arthur, and of a number of impostors who posed as royal rivals returned from the dead.

On the Continent of Europe, there were many other examples of the king who will return from the grave. The Arthur of French romance was in many ways modelled on Charlemagne, and the Arthurian cycle was seen as a 'Matter of Britain' to provide the Angevins with a rival national dynastic myth to the 'Matter of France', the cycle of Charlemagne romances that bolstered the prestige of the Capetian monarchy. The discovery of Arthur's grave in some ways illustrates another element of the legendary king, seen in the medieval picture of Charlemagne as a man of great physical stature. According to the Margam chronicler, who recorded the 'discovery' of Arthur, his bones were 'sturdy enough and large ...', while Gerald of Wales, visiting Glastonbury, saw a great thigh bone which 'when put next to the tallest man present, as the abbot showed us, and placed on the ground by his foot, reached three inches above his knee'.[12] According to Einhard, his biographer, Charlemagne 'was large and strong, and of lofty stature, though not disproportionately tall'. In tradition, he grew from this to being a giant. In much the same way, William the Conqueror was described by a monk of Caen, taking Einhard as his model, as 'great in body and strong, tall in stature but not ungainly'.[13] The Conqueror, like Arthur, had a large thigh-bone attributed to him, supposedly the one part of his skeleton that survived the Calvinist sack of his tomb in Caen in 1563. When his tomb was opened in 1522, the remains had been reported to be those of a large man with long arms and legs. A later measurement of the surviving femur suggested a man of the considerable, but by no means outstanding, stature of five feet eleven inches.[14] We can therefore see how even 'historical' kings such as Charlemagne and William could take on superhuman qualities, in the same way as the 'legendary' or pseudo-historical Arthur. Charlemagne, like Arthur, was a king who in legend was destined to return. It was widely believed that Charlemagne had never died at all but was only sleeping, either in his burial-chamber at Aachen or inside a mountain, until the time came for him to return.[15]

The 'Sleeping King' motif applied to Arthur in folklore was a very common one throughout Europe, with at least fourteen such legends.[16] Among those said to be sleeping, but to be ready to return in their people's hour of need, are to be found not only Arthur, but a number of historical kings. Charlemagne himself is said to sleep within a deep well in the castle at Nuremberg, or within a mountain (the Untersberg in Austria or the Odensberg in Hessen). Similar stories are told in Germany of Frederick Barbarossa in the Kyffhauser mountain and Henry I in the Sudemer or Rammel mountain, near Goslar. Similar legends occur in Switzerland, Scandinavia, Ireland and Man. In eastern Europe, we find a legend relating to Marko, a fourteenth-century Serbian king, who it was said was sleeping in a mountain, to return when Serbia needed him.[17]

To consider whether these legends had an influence over medieval perceptions of kingship, it is important to establish their dating. All the above stores are recorded in the collections of nineteenth-century folklorists, so the extent to which they represent a direct and unbroken tradition dating back to medieval times is debatable. To take a parallel case, it seems likely that most local associations to do with the Robin Hood legend are not necessarily ancient; most Robin Hood place-names, for example, date back no further than the eighteenth century.[18] Yet the idea of an Arthur who will return was, as we have seen, current among the Britonnic peoples as early as the eleventh century.

There were certainly versions of the 'Sleeping King' story circulating in medieval Europe. The German chronicler Ekkehard of Aura recorded a belief among the participants in the First Crusade that Charlemagne has risen from his slumber to lead them.[19] References in the German legends of the sleeping Charlemagne to his long white beard may preserve a memory of the medieval image of Charles the Great as a wise, old, white-bearded ruler: 'His beard is white and hair hoary, his stature is noble, his countenance fierce' in the words of the *Song of Roland*.[20]

The idea of the king who would return to lead his people was closely linked to that of the 'Emperor of the Last Days', who, in line with the

Sybilline prophecies, would usher in Doomsday and the reign of Antichrist by his appearance. In its earliest form, in the seventh-century Syrian work the *Pseudo-Methodius*, it was claimed that an emperor who had been assumed dead by his people would lead the Christians to victory against the Muslims, and thereby bring about the Last Days.[21] In the high middle ages, this figure came to be identified with that of the German Holy Roman Emperor, not least through the efforts of imperial propagandists. The idea that the emperor would defeat the infidel, go to Jerusalem, and so bring about the Apocalypse was first promoted in the late eleventh century by Benzo, bishop of Alba, a partisan of Henry IV in the Investiture Contest.[22] The idea was even more enthusiastically promoted in the persons of Frederick I 'Barbarossa', and Frederick II, both of whom actually went on crusade. A play from around 1160, the *Ludus de Antichristo*, expresses this idea:

> The writings of historians tell us
> That once the whole world was a Roman [imperial] fief.
> The strength of early men accomplished this,
> But the neglect of their successors squandered it.
> Though under them the imperial power fell
> The majesty of our might shall win it back.

In the play, the emperor defeats the king of France, then the Saracens, and finally goes to Jerusalem, where he gives up his crown to God. This is the cue for the appearance of Antichrist, who is then struck down by God.[23] The play therefore sets out the idealised world-view of the Hohenstaufen emperors, both of universal earthly dominion and of eschatological expectation.

This association of the German-Roman emperor with the 'Emperor of the Last Days' was most pronounced in the case of Frederick II. Barbarossa's grandson, Frederick II, both in his own lifetime and subsequently, has proved a highly controversial character. Born and brought up in the cosmopolitan environment of the Norman kingdom of Sicily, with its Muslim and Byzantine cultural influences, Frederick was not a typical north European monarch. The papacy, which felt threatened by an emperor whose southern Italian power base was uncomfortably close to Rome, was only too willing to portray Frederick's cosmopolitan outlook and use of a Muslim bodyguard as evidence of an unchristian nature.

In addition to the political tensions, Frederick's reign saw a growth in the influence of the ideas of Joachim of Fiore. Joachim's scheme of world history in the light of the Bible predicted a coming change from the present 'Age of the Son' to an 'Age of the Spirit', one of the harbingers of which was to be the appearance of a 'chastiser of the clergy'. In the eyes of some thirteenth-century Joachimites, the struggle between Frederick and the popes was a sign of this imminent change, with Frederick and his heirs identified with Antichrist.[24] Others, while agreeing with this general framework, saw Frederick literally on the side of the angels, as the Emperor of the Last Days.[25] Frederick's decision to take the cross in 1215 added to these expectations. In the course of the Fifth Crusade, in which Frederick's intervention was awaited in vain, the papal legate Cardinal Pelagius circulated the spurious book of *Prophecies of Hannan.* This portrayed a figure not unlike the legate himself as leader of the Christians, and predicted the coming of two kings to their aid, one of whom was identified as Frederick.[26]

Frederick did go to Jerusalem eventually, in 1228–29, and he died in 1250, a year with a pleasingly round number, although not the year 1260 that some Joachimites believed would see the dawning of the Age of the Spirit. Much to the disappointment of many, both pro- and anti-Frederician, his death did not bring about momentous changes. His return, like that of Arthur, seems to have been expected by many, leading some impostors to claim to be Frederick, and even to gain a measure of popular support. The emperor was rumoured to have gone into exile or to have become a hermit; or to have disappeared into Mount Etna, in another version of the 'Sleeping King in a Mountain' motif. Etna was considered a resting-place of heroes, including King Arthur.[27]

In many versions of the legend, the Sleeping King is guarding a treasure. In these legends, the king and his knights are often less beneficent, and they often punish a man of humble birth who tries to steal or retrieve this treasure. In some variants, the intruder's downfall comes about because he is unable to remember a word that will help him succeed in his quest. A legend associated with Craig-y-Dinas, in Snowdonia, tells of a Welshman who enters the cave in which Arthur and his knights sleep in order to steal their treasure. He awakens them by accidentally ringing a bell, and, forgetting the correct formula of

words that will make them return to their sleep, is beaten so badly that
he is crippled. He is subsequently unable to locate the cave again. A less
violent variant is the English legend of Potter Thompson. This story
comes from northern England, and tells of how the potter discovers
Arthur and his court. Beside the king he finds a garter, a sword and a
horn. He cuts the garter with the sword, awakening Arthur, but fails to
blow the horn, which would have roused the king and his knights, who
return to their slumbers.[28]

The idea of a supernatural (and often malevolent) figure guarding a
great treasure inside a hill has ancient roots, probably dating back to
pagan times. For example, Beowulf slays, but is mortally wounded by,
a dragon that is guarding a treasure inside a tumulus.[29] There was also
a Christian tradition of the sleepers legend, the Seven Sleepers of
Ephesus. These were seven Christians who, immured within a cave
during the persecution of Decius in the third century, were said to have
slept for many years, and to have awoken after the conversion of the
Roman Empire to Christianity. In an interesting association with kingship, a vision of the Seven Sleepers was among the miraculous dreams
and portents attributed to Edward the Confessor in his *Vita*. This legend,
which was first recorded in the sixth century, is itself merely a variation
on the common story of the man who falls asleep for many years, and
wakes to find the world changed, best known to us in the form of
Washington Irving's 'Rip van Winkle' and from many versions of it to
be found in folklore.[30]

How are we to apply these legends of revenant kings to the history of
English kings? The first king of England who was rumoured to have
cheated death was King Harold. If, to follow the folklorists, we classify
these survival stories according to types, the Harold legend can be said
to belong to the type of 'king become hermit'. In this instance, the last
Anglo-Saxon king was said to have survived Hastings, and to have
lived as a hermit in Chester (or, according to another version of the
legend, in Canterbury). According to the *Vita Haroldi*,[31] written in
around 1205, the king, having survived the battle of Hastings, was carried
to Winchester and was nursed back to health by a Saracen woman skilled
in medicine.[32] Going into exile, he unsuccessfully sought support in
Germany for the restoration of his power, and subsequently began a

life of constant wandering as a pilgrim.³³ After going on a pilgrimage to Jerusalem, he eventually returned to England by way of Wales, and lived out his days as a hermit in Chester.³⁴ The secret of his identity was revealed only on his death-bed to his confessor.³⁵

The idea of a king living incognito as a hermit was to be repeated in the case of Edward II, and has parallels elsewhere. In 1224, the impostor Bertrand de Ray appeared in the Low Countries in the guise of a poor hermit and penitent, claiming to be Baldwin, the emperor of Constantinople and former count of Flanders, who had in reality died in the East in 1205. Similarly, some said that Frederick II, after his death in 1250, had not died but was undergoing a period of penance as a hermit or pilgrim; in the 1280s two impostors claimed to be Frederick II in the guise of a hermit.³⁶

How is this association of kingship with the status of a hermit or a penitent to be explained? At one level, it may show the influence of folklore; for example, Bertrand de Ray is reported to have dwelt in the forest before revealing himself as the putative Emperor Baldwin. The principal source telling of the career of Bertrand de Ray is a rhymed chronicle, a genre that was particularly prone to using the conventions of the *chanson de geste*.³⁷ We may therefore be inclined to see, in the figure of the hermit-king in the greenwood, a semi-mythological figure of romance, akin to the Green Knight. The *Vita Haroldi* is full of such motifs; its structure and setting have been compared to the *Lancelot* of the Vulgate Arthurian cycle, a twelfth-century Latin translation of the Arthur romances. The creation of the Vulgate Arthur is itself an indication of the clerical, Latinate interest shown in vernacular romances around this time.³⁸ The healing Saracen woman is reminiscent of the mysterious women with healing powers to be found in Arthurian romance, such as Arthur's Argante, queen of the *alven*, or Tristan's Iseult of Ireland. In French romance, the 'good' Saracen woman, who marries the hero and converts to Christianity, is often a healer or has special knowledge of herbs or astrology. For example, in the French romance *Fierabras* the Saracen woman Florepas, who also appears in the Middle English *Sultan of Babylon*, has a special belt which can protect against age, poison and thirst.³⁹

The idea of the exiled 'dead' king as a wandering penitent pilgrim is also familiar to us from the examples of Baldwin and Frederick. More common still in romance and folklore is the king or hero in disguise, of which the king-as-pilgrim motif may be considered a sub-type. Arthur himself as a child (in later versions of the legend), before the drawing of the sword from the stone, Havelok, Tristan, King Horn and Guy of Warwick all conform to this type, as, going back further into the past, does Ulysses. Of particular relevance to the case of King Harold is Guy, earl of Warwick, who in romance lived a life of penance and pilgrimage after attaining his earldom, and returned to England incognito from the Holy Land in the guise of a pilgrim, retiring to live as a hermit. The English romance of *Guy of Warwick* was written in the fourteenth century, far too late to have influenced the *Vita Haroldi*, but the naming by William Beauchamp, earl of Warwick, of his son Guy in 1272 attests to the fact that the legend was in circulation in the thirteenth century, and it certainly derives from a common type of tale. In the *Tristan* legend, the hero appears disguised as a pilgrim at one point in order to rescue Iseult.[40] The longevity of the idea of king disguised as hermit can be seen by the appearance in Russia in 1864 of a hermit claiming to be Tsar Alexander I.[41]

The story of Edward II's flight and survival is a second example of a supposedly dead king surviving as a holy man. Following his deposition and imprisonment in 1327, Edward was said to have escaped and ended his days as a hermit on the Continent. This remarkable story was conveyed to Edward III in a letter by Manuel Fieschi, a Genoese priest and papal notary who claimed to have heard the confession of the hermit. Edward was said to have escaped from Berkeley, the body of a porter killed in the escape being substituted for that of the king by his guards, who feared the wrath of Queen Isabella should the escape become known. He made his way first to Ireland, where he took on the appearance of a hermit as a disguise, and then to France, where he was received by the pope at Avignon, before making his way to Cologne and finally to Italy, where he lived as a hermit, first in Milan and later in Pavia.[42] To add to the mystery, when Edward III was in Cologne in 1338, gathering support from the rulers of Germany and the Low Countries for his war with France, he was met by a hermit called William le Galeys, who claimed to be his father. Although some modern historians have suggested that this story may be true,[43] it fits too neatly into the folklore tradition. The fact that Edward ended up in Germany, the supposed site of Harold's exile in the *Vita Haroldi*, may suggest an influence from that earlier legend. Edward's identity, like that of Harold, was revealed only in the act of confession. In addition, the Rhineland was a classic breeding-ground for such stories of royal survival. One of the pseudo-Fredericks of the 1280s appeared in (and was driven out of) Cologne, while the other set himself up as 'emperor' in Worms, further up the Rhine valley.[44]

Another intriguing German link with the Harold story occurs in Gerald of Wales's *Journey through Wales*. Referring to Chester, Gerald repeats the story told in the *Vita* that Harold had lived there as a hermit, but adds that he was joined there by the Emperor Henry V, who (like the English king) had adopted the life of a hermit in penitence for his oppression of the pope.[45] Maybe Gerald, as a servant of Henry II, wished Harold's piety also to embrace the first husband of the Empress Matilda, Henry's mother. Gerald reproduces the story, told in the *Vita* by Harold's supposed successor as hermit, that the king's identity was revealed in his death-bed confession, but adds that the two kings confessed to one another. Only in this way did each learn of his counterpart's former royal status. He adds that both kings were buried in Chester. This story seems to tie the Harold legend in with the German tradition of emperors who lived on after their supposed deaths.

The tradition surrounding the Emperor Henry V was recorded by Gerald's contemporary, and fellow-Welshman, Walter Map. He has Henry, deciding to renounce the throne and take up a life of penance, fake his own death and even his own funeral, using a substitute body. He begins a life of wandering, but others, exploiting doubts over Henry's death, pretend to be the emperor. One such impostor reached Cluny, where he is revealed as a fake by a young man who had once served under Henry. This story includes three features of royal survival stories: the king as penitent; the burial of a substitute body; and the appearance of an impostor.[46]

An Icelandic version of the legend of Harold's life as a hermit also survives, suggesting a possible Scandinavian origin for the story.[47] This is found at the end of the *Hemingstháttr*, written down in the thirteenth century, which tells the life-story of Heming Àsláksson, a Norwegian who fought for Harold against Harald Hardrada, king of Norway, in revenge for Hardrada having attempted to kill him. After the victory at Stamford Bridge, Heming accompanied Harold south to fight at Hastings, where the king of England is wounded but not slain. The *Hemingstháttr*, like the *Vita*, has Harold rescued by a peasant family, who hide him and nurse him in their cottage. They identify him by a bright light that appears on the battlefield, signifying that he is a 'holy man'.[48] The peasants successfully conceal Harold from William's men by claiming that the trail of blood leading to their cottage is from their horse, which had been attacked by wolves, and the wife scares them away from entering by feigning madness.[49] Having recovered his health, Harold declares that he does not wish to regain his throne, as this would only cause further strife. Accompanied by Heming, he takes up the life of a hermit at Canterbury Cathedral, where he is able secretly to observe William during mass.[50] At Harold's death, William learns of the hermit's true identity and threatens to kill Heming for having assisted Harold, but relents when Heming points out that, had he wished to harm William, he could easily have done so. The king therefore spares him, and Heming spends the rest of his days as a hermit.[51]

This version is broadly similar to the *Vita* but differs in details: the Saracen healer is omitted, as are Harold's wanderings overseas, and his final choice of hermitage is moved from Chester to Canterbury. These differences do not appear substantial, however, and do not alter the main thrust of the story, which is that Harold renounces kingship in favour of the life of a hermit. It is most likely that the omission of episodes is simply because the story was pared down, as it was after all an episode in the life of Heming not a 'Life' of Harold. The *Hemingstháttr* is not merely a redaction of the Waltham *Vita*, it also refers to a Norwegian tradition of royal sanctity. We are informed that Harold chose the life of a hermit in order to emulate Olaf Tryggvason, a late tenth-century king of Norway. Olaf was said in some sagas to have renounced his kingship, to have undertaken a pilgrimage to Jerusalem, and to have ended his days there as a hermit or monk.[52]

The *Heimskringla*, the legendary history of the Norwegian kings, written by Snorri Sturluson in the thirteenth century, presents Olaf as an heroic Christian warrior, who died defending his kingdom against foreign enemies and local tyrants.[53] Olaf had converted to Christianity in 994 as part of his treaty with Æthelred, king of England, so his struggle to gain the kingship of Norway on his return to his homeland could be presented as a battle for the faith. While not giving credence to stories of Olaf's survival, Snorri does make reference to them.[54] Olaf's namesake, and one of his successors as king of Norway, Olaf Haraldsson, was later canonised, and was recognised as Norway's patron saint. St Olaf, like Olaf Tryggvason, was credited with attempting to christianise Norway, and was regarded as a martyr on account of his falling in battle in 1030. Stories of his survival as a hermit also circulated, although they did not prove long-lasting, as they contradicted the growing cult of Olaf's status as a martyr-saint. According to the *Heimskringla*, Olaf Haraldsson was contemplating following his namesake's example by abdicating his kingship and becoming a hermit, but was prevented from doing so by a vision of Olaf Tryggvason, who persuaded him to return and fight for his kingdom.[55] Snorri tells us that rumours of the king's survival after his death in battle spread, as his body had been taken to a hovel to hide it from his enemies.[56] It is possible that the two Olafs were conflated in legend (just as Charlemagne and Charles V, and Frederick I and Frederick II, were later conflated in German 'sleeper' legends), and that Snorri straightened out this confusion by giving them different but complementary deaths, both of which in their different ways reflected the sanctity of the king.

It may well be that the Harold survival legend was of Scandinavian origin, or at least was influenced by Scandinavian sources. As we have seen, the figure of the hermit-king occurs in the person of Olaf Tryggvason, and there are many other similarities between Harold and the two Olafs, including the decision to go on pilgrimage to Jerusalem. For example, Olaf Haraldsson's body was retrieved by loyal peasants and kept in a hovel, in much the same way as the living Harold is saved in the *Hemingstháttr*.[57] The *Vita Haroldi* author may even have had Scandinavian influences, as at the beginning of the work he relates a story about Harold's father, Godwin, surviving an assassination attempt by altering orders for his execution contained in a letter he is carrying to the king of Denmark. This is an exact copy (except with the direction of the journey reversed) of an incident in Saxo Grammaticus' *History of the Danes*, where Amleth (Shakespeare's Hamlet) cheats death in the same way.[58]

Another possibility is that there was something appropriate about a king who was no longer a king taking on the garb of a hermit or pilgrim.

Medieval kingship had a strong sacral element to it. It may have therefore been considered natural that, once stripped of the office, if not the aura of kingship, the exiled ruler should become a holy man; after all, by virtue of his receipt of the unction of anointing, he was already a 'holy man'. Deposed kings also posed a problem for their successors, as they occupied an ambiguous liminal status, as they were no longer kings but still possessed something of the aura of kingship. To quote the well-worn, but appropriate, phrase from Shakespeare's *Richard II*:

> Not all the water in the rough rude sea
> Can wash the balm off from an anointed king;
> The breath of worldly men cannot depose
> The deputy elected by the Lord ... [59]

It could be argued therefore, that, by becoming a hermit or pilgrim, the king was retaining this sacral element; a usurper might be able to strip him of his temporal office but never of the special status that had been imparted by God.

In some instances, the deposed king might be allowed to live out his life in the cloister; this was the fate of Childeric III, the last Merovingian king of the Franks, who in 751 was quietly moved aside by Pepin the Short, his mayor of the palace and the first Carolingian king. This non-violent end was unusual in such cases, but the Carolingian mayors were already the effective rulers of the kingdom, so Pepin's replacement of Childeric was a formal change of monarch rather than a change in power; the new king felt sufficiently secure to allow his predecessor to live. The despatch of Childeric III to a monastery – effectively an act of incarceration – had obvious practical benefits in placing him politically *hors de combat*, but it may also reflect a continued respect for an anointed king. After all, the practice of anointing the king with holy oil, modelled on the biblical anointment of Saul and David, was a practice that had been pioneered by the Merovingians.[60] At the coronation of Clovis, traditionally regarded as the first Christian king of the Franks, a dove was said to have descended from heaven bearing an *ampulla* of holy oil, conveying divine legitimacy on the dynasty.

An earlier Frankish royal precedent was less happy for those concerned, but illustrates neatly the symbolism of the tonsure as a negation of kingship, but still a symbol of sanctity. Following the death of Clovis, the founder of the Merovingian kingdom in Gaul, his inheritance was divided between his four sons. After the death of one of these, Chlodomer, in 524 the remaining brothers decided radically to simplify the family tree by killing Chlodomer's sons, who were under the protection of their grandmother Queen Clotild, Clovis's widow. Tricked into handing them over to their would-be murderers, Clotild was offered a choice of scissors (with which to cut off their hair) or a sword (with which they would be slain). For the Merovingians, this was an important piece of symbolism, as long hair was the sign of their kingship. Clotild chose the sword: 'If they are not to ascend the throne, I would rather see them dead than with their hair cut short.'[61] One son, Chlodovald, escaped, and cut off his own hair, as he 'had no wish for earthly dominion, but devoted himself to God',[62] becoming a monk and later being canonised as St Cloud.[63] Clovis himself had used a similar tactic on a rival Frankish king, Chararic, and his son. After capturing them in battle, he forced Chararic to become a priest and his son a deacon, and cut off their hair. Upon hearing that the two men planned to regrow their royal manes, Clovis gave them a more severe trim: he cut off their heads.

There is one notable post-medieval example of a king who retired to live a religious life. The Holy Roman Emperor Charles V abdicated his throne in 1556 and retreated to the monastery of Yuste in Spain for the last two years of his life. In his lifetime, Charles had been viewed by some as a new Frederick II,[64] while, after his death, he took on the 'Sleeping Emperor in a Mountain' role associated with Frederick, supposedly sleeping within the Odenberg in Germany or the Untersberg in Austria.[65] In both these instances, he seems to have been confused in the popular imagination with Charlemagne.

Finally, in medieval tradition there was something of a special relationship between hermits and kings. Hermits often appear as one of the few groups of people who were able to upbraid kings. In 1195 Richard I was warned by a hermit, 'Be thou mindful of the destruction of Sodom and abstain for what is unlawful; for, if thou dost not, God's vengeance shall overtake thee.'[66] We need not concern ourselves here with the controversy over what this suggests about Richard's sexuality; the point is that it is an example of the special ability of hermits to admonish kings. This tradition was an ancient one, dating back at least to Alexander's legendary encounter with Diogenes, when the barrel-dwelling

Cynic philosopher complained that the all-conquering Macedonian king was blocking the light. Ascetics with their contempt of the world were unlikely to be impressed by kings, while holy men, possessing a direct link with God, were the natural medium by which God could convey His disapproval of earthly pride.

We may see in stories of kings becoming pilgrims or hermits two elements: that of the sacral nature of the king; and the tradition of the hero in disguise. These may explain the form in which stories of royal survival often appeared, but it does not explain the reason why such stories circulated. To answer this we need to look at general ideas of kingship, and at more particular questions of political circumstances, and those in which death occurred.

The stories associated with King Harold appear to have arisen in an unusual way. Although there are conflicting stories about his final resting place, Harold was probably buried in the abbey of Waltham, of which he was an important patron. The cults of putative royal martyrs were often a source of income for the religious houses in which they lay. The single manuscript in which the *Vita* is found contains the Waltham chronicle,[67] actually a tract on the discovery of the Holy Cross, a stone cross with miraculous powers, to contain which the abbey (then a house of canons) had been founded in about 1030. It also contains a list of relics given to the abbey by Harold; and a list of miracles performed before the abbey's shrine of the Holy Cross.[68] The chronicle predates the *Vita*, having been written after 1177, and seems to have been known to the *Vita* author. It contains the earliest full version of the story that Harold's body was identified by Edith Swanneshals and buried at Waltham.[69]

The *Vita* follows the pattern of a saint's life associated with an account of the saint's relics and miracles. This typically consisted of a *Vita* describing the events of saint's life, a *Passio* relating his or her death, a *Translatio*, on the subject's burial, and a *Miracula*, relating the miracles he or she performed in life and posthumously.[70] If the manuscript context suggests that the *Vita Haroldi* is a saint's life, so too does much of the content. The author says that Harold 'obtained first a legal crown and afterwards one of eternal glory'.[71] In this case the relics and miracles associated with the 'saint' are not his, but those of the Holy Cross itself.

The possibility of a saint's cult developing, after the Conquest, around Harold was potentially embarrassing to Waltham Abbey. In 1120 the king's body was moved to a less prominent position, and around the same time the canons rebuilt the church, promoting the cult of the Holy Cross. The Waltham chronicle, although maintaining the claim that Harold was buried at Waltham rather than in Sussex, sought to promote the veneration of the Holy Cross at the expense of Harold, thereby suppressing a potentially embarrassing cult while still maintaining the traffic of pilgrims to the house.[72] By the time of the composition of the *Vita*, however, the conflict between Norman colonists and an Anglo-Saxon population had long become a thing of the past. By about 1205, when the *Vita* was composed, members of the Anglo-Norman nobility were probably speaking English as their first language. The cult of Edward the Confessor was part of this process of Anglicisation, and Aelred of Rievaulx's *Life of St Edward* promoted the Plantagenet dynasty of Henry II as the inheritors of Edward's Anglo-Saxon realm and as the conciliators between the English and Normans. Henry II, as the grandson of Henry I's Anglo-Scottish wife Matilda, was a descendant of the royal house of Wessex, and this is alluded to by Aelred in Edward's prophecy of the green tree, which was separated but would grow back together.[73] In this Harold was a usurper and interloper (as too, for that matter, were the Anglo-Norman kings). Aelred, whose *Life of St Edward* was read by the *Vita Haroldi* author, wrote that 'Harold himself, having despoiled himself of the realm of the English, either died wretchedly or as some people think, fled to live in penitence.'[74] The *Vita* therefore was distant enough in time from the Conquest for a glorification of an Anglo-Saxon king to be politically acceptable, but in a context where Harold was still viewed as a usurper and perjurer. While at pains to defend him against these accusations, the author nevertheless renders Harold politically safe by emphasising his renunciation of worldly ambitions and his adoption of the life of a penitent.

The *Vita Haroldi* can be viewed as that peculiar document, a 'Life' not written with the intention of promoting the cult of one of a monastery's distinguished dead, but of proving that he was in fact buried somewhere else entirely. It becomes the life of a saintly patron, not that of a patron saint. There is a *Vita*, but Harold is portrayed therein not only as a worker of miracles but as a recipient of a miracle of the

Holy Cross, by the power of which he was cured of the effects of a stroke.[75] In gratitude for this cure, Harold set about endowing and rebuilding the abbey.[76] As one authority has remarked, Harold in the *Vita* does not perform miracles, rather miracles and supernatural happenings occur around him.[77] There is no *Passio* of Harold, who the *Vita* tells us did not, as was popularly believed, die a violent death.[78] The place of the *Translatio* is taken by an account of the discovery of the Holy Cross, while the *Vita* itself insists that Harold's relics are not contained at Waltham, and that the body is that of a substitute.[79] There is a short and incomplete *Miracula* at the end of the *Vita*, in the form of an account supposedly written by Harold's successor as hermit in Chester, which the *Vita* author used as a source.[80] Whether by accident or by design the compiler breaks off before describing any miracles, while the manuscript as a whole contains a list of the miracles of the Holy Cross. The manuscript should therefore be seen not as a 'Life of St Harold' but as a celebration of the cult of the Holy Cross, following the pattern of a saint's life, but with an inanimate object as the subject. If this is the case, then the *Vita*'s reference to Harold's failure to gain support for a political comeback, and his subsequent life as a penitent, can be seen as a way of depoliticising any cult of Harold.[81] It may be objected that, as the *Vita* was written some time over a century after the Conquest, it seems unlikely that a cult of Harold would still have had a political resonance. If the *Vita* was intended to discredit Harold's cult, then its author would scarcely have written 'it was evident from his miracles that he had gone to heaven' or have appended a list of the miracles performed by 'that most saintly king'.[82] The author also pointedly refers to Harold as 'a most famous and lawful king – rightfully and lawfully crowned',[83] at a time when the full rehabilitation of the Anglo-Saxon kings and saints in the thirteenth century, represented by Henry III naming his two sons after the Anglo-Saxon royal saints Edward and Edmund, was still in the future.

The *Vita* is an example of a survival story recorded long after the events described, and which had been effectively depoliticised by time and changed circumstances. More immediate political concerns during periods of political disturbance and transition leant themselves toward a belief in revenant kings. Such periods could throw up some or all of

the following: uncertainty over the actual fate of a deposed king; opposition to the new regime; and messianic expectations of the appearance
of a deliverer from conditions of political oppression or of social and
economic distress. The movement around Bertrand de Ray, the impostor
who claimed to be Count Baldwin of Flanders, may have embodied
social and political demands, as the townspeople of Flanders and Hainault rallied around him as a symbol of opposition to comital authority,
represented by the real count's daughter Joanna and by the French
crown. It was said that after the exposure and death of Bertrand his
return was nevertheless awaited by his followers. 'At Valenciennes people
await him as the Bretons await Arthur.'[84] While acting as a means of
expressing political discontent, he also therefore seems to have been
viewed in a mystical sense. It has been argued that Bertrand and
others like him should be viewed as eschatological figures, although the
nature of the sources should again alert us to the use of topoi from
romance – hence the reference to Arthur.

There was a traditional unwillingness to depose or indeed harm a
king, so deposition, and the problems that it created as to how to dispose
of the previous ruler, was rife with the possibility for rumour and
counter-rumour. A usurper was placed in a dilemma: in order to secure
his position, the king whom he had displaced needed to be dead, and
to be seen to be dead; however, the guilt of having slain an anointed
king was not a stain that any ruler wished to bear. To take the deposed
Richard II as an example: alive he could be the focus for rebellions such
as that of the *ducketti* against Henry IV in January 1400; dead, his murder
was used a piece of anti-Henrician propaganda by the rebels of 1403.[85]
In these circumstances, perhaps the best course of action was for the
deposed king to be 'helped' on the way to death. Edward II, Richard
II, Henry VI and Edward V (not to mention several royal dukes in the
later middle ages) all died in this manner, almost certainly murdered
in captivity, and in obscure circumstances. The secrecy of their deaths,
however, left open the possibility in people's minds that the dead king
had in fact survived, and the public display of his body, which occurred
in a number of such cases, did little to dispel these rumours. A historian
of Richard II's deposition refers to the philosopher Jacques Lacan's idea
of the king 'between two deaths', in an ambiguous, even phantasmal,
state of having 'died' as a king, and in effect of having been condemned

to death by his deposition, and later dying in mysterious circumstances, but without having gone through the usual process of death and public royal burial that marked the transition from the old reign to the new.[86] Any ambiguity over the circumstances of royal death could create a loophole of doubt that allowed survival stories to flourish.[87]

The pattern of an ambiguous death leading to rumours of survival was not restricted to the fourteenth and fifteenth centuries. The legend of Olaf Tryggvason's survival, which, as we have seen, may have been the model for that of Harold, was able to grow out of ambiguity over his death. Snorri Sturlusson in the *Heimskringla* claims that, at the final sea-battle against his foes, the defeated Olaf leapt into the water, and held his shield over his head as he sank into the depths, so that his enemies could not capture him.[88] This end, like that of Arthur in Geoffrey of Monmouth and Wace, is ambivalent, in that the audience is not told for certain that he died, and there is no body to prove his death. One might assume that Olaf drowned, but the Germanic heroic tradition did not preclude heroes from fighting even when in or under the water, as Beowulf had 'carried thirty corselets over his arm when he plunged alone into the sea'.[89]

Both chronicle accounts and legends of Harold Godwinson's death at Hastings (and the much-debated images of the Bayeux Tapestry) give conflicting versions of his death and of the fate of his body. In most versions, Harold's body is supposed to have been so badly mutilated or even dismembered as to be unrecognisable, which could obviously help give rise to rumours that the body was not in fact his. The first variant, which seems to be the earliest, has it that Harold was buried by William by the seashore in Sussex. The English king's mother, Gytha, offered William the body's weight in gold if he would release it for burial, but the Norman duke refused. This refusal is usually, but not invariably, depicted as contemptuous. William of Poitiers relates that Harold's body was identified, with difficulty, by undisclosed 'signs'. Gytha's offer is refused as 'not seemly', and the body mockingly buried by the sea in Sussex (where Harold held lands) so that he might be 'guardian of the shore and sea'.[90] The *Carmen de Hastingae Proelio* of Guy of Amiens uses the same 'guardian' formula, but more admiringly, without the tone of irony,[91] as if the dead Harold's body, like the head of Bran the Blessed in Welsh legend, will watch over Britain.

By the time that William of Malmesbury was writing his *Historia regum Anglorum* in about 1125, the idea that Harold was buried at Waltham had become current. In Malmesbury's account, William turns down Gytha's offer of money for the body, not in order to deny her the body but rather as an act of magnanimity. He releases the body to her without payment, and she buries him at Harold's church of Waltham.[92] The version of the story in the Waltham Abbey chronicle, written between 1177 and 1189, says that his body was so badly hacked by Norman horsemen that it was unrecognisable until his mistress, Edith Swanneshals, identified it from a birthmark known only to her (another romance or folklore element of the unknown king identified by a secret sign). In this version it was not Gytha but a group of canons from Waltham who offered money to William for the body.[93]

Given a combination of political crisis and rebellion following William's seizure of power, the possible development of a cult around Harold, and some ambiguity over whether his body had been identified and buried, we can see how the English population might have hoped for Harold's return and have circulated stories of his survival. The *Vita Haroldi*, in contrast to the earlier Waltham version, maintained that the remains in Waltham Abbey were not those of Harold, but that Edith Swanneshals, confronted with a series of bodies mangled beyond recognition, was unable to make an identification and 'seized upon and carried away with her the mutilated corpse of another man for the sake of appearance', knowing that it was not Harold.[94] The *Vita* author seems deliberately to set out to refute the earlier versions, including those of William of Malmesbury, whom he mentions by name, and the Waltham chronicler. Incidents from the latter are included, but given a different interpretation. For example, when Harold visits Waltham on his way to Hastings, the stone statue of Christ (the Holy Cross which was the house's most sacred relic) bows to the king. The Waltham chronicle views this as an ill omen, indicating England's imminent abasement,[95] while the *Vita* author argues that it was a recognition of Harold's piety. Gyrth, a brother of Harold, supposedly told Walter, abbot of Waltham, years later that 'Perhaps you've got some peasant ... but you haven't got Harold'.[96] We need not take the details of the story too literally; the *Vita* author maintains that this took place during the reign of Henry II, an improbably long time after Hastings for Gyrth to still be alive.

Besides which Gyrth, too, was supposed to have fallen at Hastings.[97] But the theme of substitution of a king's body by that of a lesser mortal is interesting.

Looking at later medieval kings, there is again the question of ambiguity. After his death in Berkeley Castle, Edward II's body was exposed, and was later viewed at his funeral in Gloucester Abbey. The exposure of the body was designed to demonstrate that he had no wounds, in an attempt to quash rumours of his murder, but it also had the important political purpose of demonstrating that Edward was indeed dead, clearing away remaining doubts over the new regime. This did not prevent stories of his survival circulating. There is no unambiguous evidence for his body being examined after death, while at his funeral the crowds were kept at bay by solid oak barriers so that his body was viewed publicly only at a distance.[98] The later story of his living as a hermit was plausible because of these earlier rumours about his survival. In the Fieschi letter, the substitution of the body of the porter for that of Edward explained away the fact that a funeral had taken place for a supposedly living king. The story seems psychologically and politically implausible: if Edward had escaped, why did he disappear, to resurface years later as a hermit in Germany, rather than making an attempt to rally support? The story is again similar to the *Vita Haroldi* in the use of a story of substitution of another body for that of the king. Nevertheless, the fact that such stories became current illustrates the problems for a regime brought about as a result of carrying out the murder of a king: such an act was so shocking that details of it must not be made known; yet in the absence of such details others could begin to imagine that the king was not dead. Such rumours were probably reinforced by the fact that a number of attempts were made to liberate the king. One such attempt, by his confessor Thomas Dunheved (a possible link with Fieschi, who was also said to have been Edward's confessor), seems to have succeeded for a time, and there is no specific evidence for his recapture.[99] In 1330–31, when parliament held an enquiry into Edward's murder, Thomas Berkeley, the lord of the castle in which Edward had been murdered, not only claimed innocence of any involvement in his death, but maintained that he had been unaware that the former king was dead until the time when parliament had summoned him. Parliament evidently believed his claims, as he was acquitted.[100]

Much the same can be said of Richard II, who died in similarly obscure circumstances in Pontefract. There was no public announcement of his death; the council issued ambivalent instructions in February 1400 that if he was alive he should be kept under close guard, but that if he was dead then he should be shown to the people to demonstrate as much. The council expressed its supposed belief that he was still alive but, to issue such orders, was presumably aware that he was not. His body was taken to London, where it was displayed with the face uncovered on a number of occasions. The dead king was given a public funeral procession through London, and (as specified in his will) religious observance was made at his tomb in Westminster, but Henry had him buried in the relative obscurity of Langley.[101]

Despite the display of his body, rumours of Richard's survival in Scotland were circulating soon afterwards, aided no doubt by the ambiguity of his empty tomb in Westminster, which gave an adventurer the opportunity for his imposture.[102] The most obvious parallel in England to that of Bertrand de Ray and the false Fredericks is to be seen in the figure of Thomas Ward of Trumpington, the impostor who claimed to be Richard II. He had the backing of the king of Scotland and of Richard's former chancellor, William Serle. In this sense, Ward's bid was clearly political and was supported by partisans of Richard. In the eyes of some of the peasantry, however, the expectation of Richard's imminent return may have gone beyond the purely political and have represented the desire for a messianic deliverer.

A last footnote to the tradition of royal survival can be seen in the impostor-pretenders Lambert Simnel and Perkin Warbeck, who challenged Henry VII, although their impostures owed more to the immediate political circumstances of the time than to any mystical or religious beliefs. Historical hindsight, owing more than a little to Henry's own propaganda, sees the Tudors as restorers of peace and unity after the disturbances of the Wars of the Roses. To use the Tudors' own ideological imagery, Henry's reign, and in particular his marriage to a daughter of the Yorkist Edward IV, represented the marriage of the red rose and the white, or in the title of the work of Tudor historian Edward Hall, *The Union of the Two Illustrious Houses of Lancaster and York*. This impression is reinforced by the simplified genealogies to be found in many history books, where the Yorkist line seems to die out with

Richard III, with the exception of Henry Tudor's queen, Elizabeth of York. The reality was rather different.

Henry's assumption of to the throne rested more on the successful outcome of the battle of Bosworth than on his hereditary claim, which was tenuous and clouded by illegitimacy. It came via the Beauforts, the children of John of Gaunt by his mistress and later wife, Katherine Swynford, who were retrospectively legitimised by act of parliament, with the caveat that they were not to be in line for the throne. In addition to this, far from having died out, the Yorkist line remained stubbornly alive. There were the surviving children of George, duke of Clarence (the murdered brother of Edward IV and Richard III), notably Edward, earl of Warwick, whose claim to the throne inspired the imposture of Lambert Simnel. The marriage between John de la Pole, earl of Suffolk, and Edward IV's sister Elizabeth produced seven sons, the eldest of whom, John, earl of Lincoln, was the instigator of the Simnel rebellion. Apart from Henry's queen, Elizabeth of York, three of Edward's daughters remained, two of whom had or would have children. In addition, the fate of the 'Princes in the Tower' (Edward V and his brother Richard, duke of York) was uncertain. Richard III's apologists argue that Henry's failure to end doubts over their fate by publicly displaying their bodies points to Richard's innocence of their murder and Henry's guilt. If they had survived Richard's reign, and Henry had ordered their murders, he would probably have displayed their bodies and given them a proper funeral, as Mortimer and Isabella, Henry IV and Edward IV had done with their murdered predecessors. It is worth noting that, after Bosworth, Henry had ensured that there could be no doubts as to the death of Richard III. The Great Chronicle of London described how Richard's body was stripped, 'naught being left about him so much as would cover his privy member', and placed on display in the Franciscan church of Leicester, 'for all men to wonder at, and there irreverently buried'.[103] Fabyan's Chronicle tells the same story, that he lay 'that all men myght behold hym ...'[104] Whatever the truth, the possibility, however remote, that Edward V and his brother might be alive cast a further cloud over Henry VII's legitimacy as king. A great deal of unfinished dynastic business from the House of York remained to threaten Henry's position.

If the uncertainty over the fate of the 'Princes in the Tower' created problems for Henry VII, the lack of a credible Yorkist heir who was unambiguously alive and at liberty posed difficulties for any would-be opponent. Not only had the sons of Edward IV vanished, but the earl of Warwick, Clarence's son, was held under close confinement by Henry in the Tower. The solution was the creation of proxies for the inconveniently missing pretenders. This phenomenon appears to be unique in English history, with the exception of Thomas Ward, the pseudo-Richard II, although, as we have seen, the case of the false Baldwin in twelfth-century Flanders presents a continental parallel. No eschatological expectations or signs of popular excitement, however, were associated with the impostures of Lambert Simnel and Perkin Warbeck. Neither man seems to have enjoyed popular support in England. Lambert Simnel's rebellion was based on the backing of Yorkist lords in Ireland, who had enjoyed a large measure of autonomy during the civil wars and the Yorkist period, and was supported on the battlefield of Stoke by the use of German mercenaries. Perkin Warbeck relied on the support of the kings of France and Scotland, at least when it was diplomatically useful for them to provide it, and of Margaret of York, the duchess of Burgundy (and sister of Edward IV), who claimed to recognise in Warbeck her long-lost nephew. The Yorkshire rebellion of 1489, which Polydore Vergil claimed had some Yorkist overtones, seems however to have been essentially a protest against royal taxation and encroachment on the rights of the church.[105] The Cornish rising of 1497, which coincided with Warbeck's planned invasion, seems to have been unconnected in terms of political demands, although it was inspired by opposition to the taxes that were being raised for the threatened war. In time-honoured fashion, the rebel leaders expressed their loyalty to the king, claiming only to be opposed to his 'evil advisers'.[106]

Did anyone really believe in these impostures? The lack of popular support for the rebels suggests that the impostures were the result of political calculation among the elite, rather than wishful thinking among the people. Lambert Simnel seems to have been quite deliberately and cynically promoted by John, earl of Lincoln, and his allies, who knew full well that the real earl of Warwick was in the Tower. Henry VII paraded the real Warwick through the streets of London to prove the falsehood of Simnel's pretence.[107] The pathetic scene of the prisoner riding under close guard through the city is reminiscent of the readeption of Henry VI, when the king was led through the streets tied to the back of a donkey.

Margaret of Burgundy claimed that Warbeck was her nephew, in marked contrast to the countess of Flanders who had failed to recognise the hermit Bertrand de Ray as her 'father'. It is difficult to believe that there was not an element of calculation in this. Margaret's court was a centre for pro-Yorkist intrigue, and it is likely that the duchess was happy to seize upon any opportunity to discomfit the Tudor regime. It is just possible that James IV of Scotland believed Warbeck to be who he claimed, as he granted him the hand of his kinswoman Katherine Gordon in marriage.[108]

Lambert Simnel, as *1066 and All That* notes, ended his days 'as a blot on the king's skitchen'. According to Polydore Vergil, writing some thirty years after the event, Henry, either as a punishment for the baker's son's pretensions or as an act of mercy to the young man, set him to work in the royal kitchens, and later as his falconer.[109] This story bears a strong folklore element. In the story of Havelock, the hero spends his youth as a kitchen boy, his true identity unknown, while the motif of the king transformed into a menial can be found in Icelandic folklore.[110] In folklore, the substitution of the king by another, or his relegation to a humble role, was a means of the king learning humility. There is, for example, the legend of Alfred the Great being chided by a peasant for burning the cakes while in disguise, or of Robert Guiscard of Sicily, who, legend has it, was replaced by an angel, while he himself was condemned as an impostor, and was only allowed to regain his position after he had learned to repent of his former arrogant conduct.[111] An interesting story of a similar disguise dating from Henry Tudor's own lifetime has George, duke of Clarence, trying to prevent his brother Richard from marrying Anne Neville (a marriage that would threaten Clarence's own claim to the Neville estates), disguising Anne as a kitchen maid in an attempt to hide her from his brother.[112]

There are many different elements in the idea of the king who cheats death, from mundane political motives to semi-messianic hope, set against a background of common ideas in folklore about sleeping kings. There is also a close relation between some of these stories and the themes of royal sanctity discussed in the previous chapter. Whereas most late-medieval survival stories were grounded in political ambition, the story of Harold's survival appears to be non-political, in that the king was rendered safe by abandoning his hopes of restoration and becoming a hermit. For a survival story to take off required a combination of wishful thinking and genuine doubt over a king's fate. We see this in the uncertainty about the deaths of many medieval kings, that, in politically disturbed conditions, could give rise to rumours of survival and encourage the schemes of impostors. The nature of deposition also encouraged such stories by creating an element of doubt; a usurper was presented with the paradox that he needed to kill his predecessor to ensure his safety, yet was unable publicly to advertise the fact that he had done so. The nature of kingship made this a particularly sensitive issue, as no ruler wished to be branded a regicide, the slayer of the Lord's Anointed.

7

Royal Saints and Martyrs

Martyrs are not long in the making. The very day that Diana, Princess of Wales died, a floral tribute appeared outside Kensington Palace bearing the inscription, 'Born a lady, became a princess, died a saint'. Camille Paglia called her a '*mater dolorosa*', while William Rees-Mogg, writing the day after her death, referred to the 'lava of sanctity' that, if allowed to 'harden', would prevent a rational assessment of her life.

The saint also had an immediate cult-centre, the road tunnel in Paris where she died. 'I just felt I had to come here myself,' said one mourner. There were also suggestions from the very beginning that this death was a martyrdom: onlooker Bernard Bidow told the press that 'my idea, from the very beginning, is that maybe there were figures in perfidious Albion who thought her an embarrassment'.[1] The princess was therefore a martyr at the hands of an uncaring establishment, and so became a repository for anti-establishment feelings. Royalists could regret her passing; establishment figures could use her death as a means to criticise the establishment, with even *The Times* editorialising against the royal family's decision to remain, apparently aloof, at Balmoral.[2] The liberal media, only four months into a Labour government, turned her into a martyr for a politics which was radical sounding but conservative in practice. She became the 'People's Princess' for the people's party, praised by the *Guardian*'s Jonathan Freedland for her 'revolutionary doctrine' of 'hugs and warmth and confession'.[3] All these quotations, it should be added, come from the immediate aftermath of Diana's death, so were more or less spontaneous reactions, and cannot simply be dismissed as part of the popular hysteria that accompanied her funeral six days later.

One point that was apparently missed by the media was how medieval the reaction to Diana's demise was. Talk of a 'doctrine of hugs and warmth' may have been characteristic of the end of the twentieth century, but the concept of a royal martyr, venerated by the people as a victim of tyranny, a simultaneously establishment yet anti-establishment figure, can be seen on several occasions in late medieval England.

The role of the medieval king crossed the divide between the ecclesiastical and secular spheres. He stood above the classic division of medieval society into three orders of workers, fighters and those who prayed, as his function required him to defend his people, but also to possess a quasi-priestly nature. The king was God's anointed, as demonstrated in the use of holy oil, crown, orb and sceptre in the coronation ceremony. This practice was modelled on Saul's anointing by Samuel, and was developed by the Capetian kings of France. It increasingly became the standard form of coronation ceremony in the West, superseding older forms, such as the Scottish practice of simply seating the king on the Stone of Destiny. He was not merely a leader of the *bellatores*, the fighting class. Given the priestly aura surrounding kingship, it should come as no surprise that, from the thirteenth century, something of a cult of royal saints developed. The impetus for this was largely dynastic, as rulers sought to have a pious ancestor canonised, to reflect sanctity upon their own rule. To name but a few, the French royal house made use of St Louis (and, of greater antiquity, Charlemagne), the German emperors also had Charlemagne, while England had Edward the Confessor and a number of earlier Anglo-Saxon royal saints, most notably St Edmund, the martyr-king of East Anglia. Some of these figures were of considerable antiquity, but others were figures from relatively recent history, such as St Louis, Louis of Toulouse (from the Angevin ruling house of Naples) and Alfonso of Aragon. The sacral nature of kingship was increasingly emphasised in later medieval England, manifesting itself, for example, in the belief that the king could cure skin disease by his touch. The importance of anointing was increasingly stressed, to the extent that Henry VII was unwilling to execute the pretender Lambert Simnel because, although an impostor and usurper, he had undergone a coronation ceremony at Dublin.

The later medieval English monarchy was also aware of an old tradition of Anglo-Saxon royal martyrs. The East Anglian king Edmund, who was martyred by the Danes in 870, was represented with Richard II on the Wilton Diptych, alongside Edward the Confessor and St John the Baptist. On Henry V's triumphal entry to London following the victory at Agincourt, the decorations included representations of 'twelve kings of the English succession, martyrs and confessors ... and the emblems of their sanctity plain for all to see', alongside the arms of St George, St Edward the Confessor, St Edmund, and England.[4] Henry held St Edward the Confessor, one of those Anglo-Saxons saints, to be among his 'special protectors'.[5] Likewise, a song to celebrate Henry VI's coronation as king of France in 1430, 'Speed our King in his Journey', invoked a number of saints, including specifically English saints, one of whom was the Anglo-Saxon royal martyr St Oswald.[6] Although virtually every kingdom of Europe had its own royal saint or saints, Anglo-Saxon England seems to have been unique in producing so many royal martyrs.[7]

Oswald was one of the earliest Anglo-Saxon martyr-kings. A Christian king of Northumbria, he was killed in 642 in battle against the pagan King Penda of Mercia. Most of these martyr-kings, like Oswald and St Edmund of East Anglia, died defending their kingdoms against pagans. Oswald's predecessor Edwin, the first Christian king of Deira, had also died in battle against Penda (and, less conveniently for the hagiographers, against Cadwallon, the Christian king of Gwynedd) in 633. To these royal martyrs we could add many more ecclesiastical martyrs, such as St Boniface (Wynfrith), who was martyred by Frisian pagans while engaged in missionary activity in 754, and St Alphege, the archbishop of Canterbury who was murdered in 1012 by Danes who pelted him with meat bones after getting drunk at dinner. As in the case of Edwin, the exact circumstances did not fit the image of a Christian martyred by pagans neatly, as the Danish kings were by then Christian, and Alphege was a hostage who was killed when a ransom was not paid, so the image of his being brutally killed by mindless heathens on account of his faith is hardly a true reflection of the events.

Not all were killed by the heathen. There was a long tradition of the sanctification of kings or princes who were killed by their fellow-Christians, and usually by political opponents including other kings and rival family-members. The earliest of these was Oswine, king of Deira (the southern half of Northumbria), murdered in 651 on the orders of Oswiu, king of Bernicia (northern Northumbria). Two seventh-century Kentish princes, Æthelred and Æthelbert, were supposedly murdered by their cousin King Egbert and therefore sanctified as martyrs. Ælfwald, king of Northumbria, was murdered in 788, and Ealhmund, a Northumbrian prince, was also murdered in the late eight century by King Eardwulf of Northumbria. Both were venerated as saints. King Æthelbert of East Anglia was martyred by being executed at the hands his fellow-Christian Offa, king of Mercia, in 794. Kenelm, the boy-king of Mercia, was said to have been murdered by his sister Gwendreda (or Cynethryth) in 821, and was revered as a martyr. In a story reminiscent of the finding of St Edmund's severed head in the forest, he was taken deep into the woods to be killed, and his head struck off, but the whereabouts of his remains were revealed by a heavenly light. Another Mercian prince of the ninth century, Wigstan, was said to have abdicated his claim to the throne in order to pursue a religious life, but was nevertheless murdered in 849 by his kinsman Beorhtfrith, who sought to marry Wigstan's mother. Edward the Martyr, king of England 975–79, was murdered at Corfe on the orders of Queen Ælfthryth, an archetypal 'wicked-step-mother'. The beneficiary of this murder was her son (Edward's half-brother) Æthelred, who ironically was to be the father of Edward the Confessor, Edward the Martyr's saintly namesake.[8]

These saints' martyrdoms, whether suffered at the hands of pagans or of Christian enemies, can be characterised as being inflicted by figures of illegitimate authority. Pagans by their nature were illegitimate in their authority from the point of view of Christian writers, and there was a long tradition dating back to the stories of the martyrs of the early church of saints being killed by anti-Christian emperors, kings or governors. In the cases of Kenelm and Edward the Martyr, although they were killed by fellow Christians, their slayers were again illegitimate authority figures, who killed the true king or heir in order to gain what was not rightfully theirs. Although not heathens, they might as well have been, as they subverted divinely-ordained authority.

Another precedent for the cults of royal sanctity of the high and later middle ages can be seen in the circumstances of the martyr-kings' deaths. With the exception of the saints slain by foreign or pagan armies, most of the Anglo-Saxon royal martyrs were killed at the instigation of their own relatives, or even by the ruling king, although the killing itself was carried out by henchmen. These were precisely the circumstances (or, in the absence of firm information, rumoured circumstances) in which many of their later counterparts were to die, two of whom, Edward II and Henry VI, were subjects of cults of sanctity.

The most popular English saint-king, however, was arguably Edward the Confessor, who was not a martyr. A look at Edward's cult helps illustrate something of the nature and problems of royal sanctity in the middle ages. Along with St Edmund, Edward proved the most popular of the Anglo-Saxon canonised kings. Not until the mid fourteenth century did St George begin to be recognised as a patron saint of England, and only later still did he displace the two royal saints as *the* patron.[9] His cult was promoted by the post-conquest kings, especially those who had an exalted view of the role of the monarchy. Henry III rebuilt Edward's foundation and burial-place of Westminster Abbey in a style to rival Louis IX's Sainte-Chapelle in Paris, and with the intention of making it the necropolis of the English kings.[10] Henry was the first English king to promote the idea that the monarch could touch for the King's Evil, that is cure scrofula by touch, an idea borrowed from the Capetian kings of France. His model for this, apart from his French rivals, was possibly Edward, among whose miracles was the cure of a woman with scrofula by his touch.[11] Guibert of Nogent in 1124 had explicitly stated that the French kings possessed this ability, but that their English counterparts did not, so it was clearly of great propaganda value for Henry III to assert a claim to a power that had previously only attached itself to his Capetian rivals.[12] The Confessor appears with Edmund in the Wilton Diptych, a celebration of another king's exalted view of royalty, this time Richard II's.

These two royal saints represent two different aspects of sanctity, the virgin and the martyr, which were often combined in the type of the virgin martyr, a type especially common among women, and among the martyrs of the early church. There were obvious advantages for a ruling dynasty in counting saints in its lineage, and most royal houses of Europe by the fourteenth century had acquired a saint in the family. The virgin or martyr saint was, however, in some ways a problematic role for a king, as he must have failed the test of successful kingship on one or both of two counts. A virgin king must count a failure as a dynast, while a martyr king must be considered a failure in the role of defender of his country and people. Some royal saints, notably Charlemagne and Saint Louis, were able to attain sanctity by being Christian warriors, who were seen as having successfully combined military success with a pious life. (We are, of course, speaking here of the ideal, not reality; Charlemagne christianised the Saxons by terror, while the holy warrior Louis IX was a hopeless crusader.) A martyr-king such as Edmund was valuable in retrospect in demonstrating the commitment of the English kings to the defence of Christendom against the pagans, and as such could be classed alongside the many Anglo-Saxon royal martyrs, such as the Northumbrian kingly saints Oswald and Edwin. What use, however, was Edward the Confessor, whose key claim to sanctity, his virginity, ensured that his death created a succession crisis that plunged England into war and alien conquest?

It would be wrong to see Edward simply as a 'weak king'. He was beset with problems: different claimants to the throne; an overmighty nobility (especially the Godwin family); and the threat of foreign invasion. Some modern historians present him not as an effete otherworldly virgin-king, but as a vigorous man and ruler, healthy, active, a shrewd ruler who exploited his childlessness as a diplomatic asset to play potential enemies and successors off against one another.[13] In this guise, he becomes not a weak asexual ruler but an eleventh-century Elizabeth I, a strong virgin king. Some later images of the saint depict him in a martial form. The representation of him in stained glass at the church of Heydour (Lincolnshire), dating from around 1360, depicts him alongside the other two patrons of England, SS. Edmund and George, and all three of them are shown wearing armour.[14]

So much for the 'real' Edward, but hagiography was not concerned with realistic political, still less personal, motivation. The usual formula for saints' lives at this time was a *Vita, Translatio* and *Miracula,* which represented the three main requirements for sanctity: a good life, an uncorrupt body, and signs, preferably after death as well as during life, of miraculous powers.[15] The translation of the dead sainted King Edward revealed an uncorrupt body, a traditional token of sanctity.[16] But there was also plenty of fuel for the first and third elements of hagiography, the *Vita* and the miracles, leading to the posthumous development of a cult.

Whatever the truth, the hagiographers seem to have been confronted with the problem of Edward's perceived 'weakness' as a king. He could certainly never be portrayed as a warrior saint-king, in the way that

St Louis would be. The mid twelfth-century *Vita* by Aelred of Rievaulx makes a virtue of his 'weakness'. In one story, his 'meek' behaviour in allowing a thief to rob his treasury under his royal eyes is shown as a saintly virtue, as Edward felt sorry for the man, who was young and poor, allowing him to escape the clutches of his chamberlain, to whom he reflected that 'perhaps the one who took it [the treasure] needed it more than we'.[17] The one success over armed foes that is recorded in Aelred's *Vita* was achieved by the grace of God, without Edward lifting a weapon in anger. When the King of Denmark organised an invasion of England, his fleet was sunk, and the king drowned, by divine intervention. The knowledge of this was vouchsafed to Edward by a miraculous vision, causing him to laugh in the middle of high mass.[18]

The 'weakness' (which, dynastically speaking, it was) of Edward's chastity was also seen differently by contemporaries and later hagiographers. There is no firm evidence to suggest that Edward's childlessness was due to his having committed himself to chastity, nor of any contemporary perception that this was the case. There were possibly rumours in the king's old age that his marriage had not been consummated, but nothing more.[19] The anonymous *Vita* may imply that the marriage was chaste in its references to Edward and his queen Edith as 'father' and 'daughter', although this may be merely a spiritual metaphor.[20] It was not until the twelfth-century accounts of Osbert and Aelred that Edward – as it were – became a virgin. The problematic issue of why an avowedly chaste king should take a wife was addressed by Aelred, who argued that Edward was caught between his desire to live chastely and the political need to take a wife. He presents Edith as a willing collaborator, waiving her right to the 'marriage debt'. Interestingly, Aelred saw fit to deny that Edward's chastity was due to a desire not to bring another 'traitor' (i.e. a grandson of the troublesome Earl Godwin, Queen Edith's father) into the world.[21] This may possibly reflect a contemporary rumour that Edward had no wish to produce an heir beholden to the Godwin clan. Aelred, it has to be said, was very hostile to Godwin, who is painted as the villain of the story, although he pointed out that Edith was unlike her terrible kinsmen. This stands in marked contrast to the anonymous *Vita*, which was dedicated to Edith and praises the Godwins.

We can see the mechanisms by which Edward came to be seen as a saint; but why should such a 'good man, but a bad king' be venerated?

The answer may be that his reign was viewed as a golden age by those looking back from after the Conquest, and from the troubled reign of Stephen, when the *Vitae* by Osbert and Aelred were written. The earliest, anonymous *Vita*, written probably around or soon after the Conquest, uses this very term: 'A golden age shone for his English race.' 22 Various accounts relate prophecies made by Edward toward the end of his life, foreseeing terrible events for England. The anonymous *Vita* author and Aelred of Rievaulx both relate Edward's vision of the green tree.23 Aelred states that the nobles and prelates of the kingdom are 'servants of the devil' and that as punishment God will hand the kingdom over to 'the hands of the enemy' within a year of Edward's death; an obvious reference to the Norman Conquest.24 This oppression will only end when a green tree, which has been cut in half and a half carried three furlongs away, will have its parts reunited without the aid of man.25 It has been suggested that this prophecy originally had no significance, except as an impossible event; in other words, the oppression would never end.26 Aelred of Rievaulx, however, with the benefit of nearly an extra century's hindsight, was able to interpret it as a favourable reference to the reigning monarch, Henry II, whose actions helped bring about Edward's canonisation. In this version, the three furlongs represent the reigns of the first three Norman kings, the reunion of the tree is the marriage of Henry I to Matilda of Scotland, a descendant of the Anglo-Saxon ruling house, and their daughter the Empress Matilda, and grandson Henry of Anjou are the blossom and the fruit of the tree.27

Edward the Confessor's cult was promoted by Henry III perhaps more than any other person, but he had been canonised in the previous century, in 1161, and his cult was developing long before that. If we accept the dating of the anonymous *Vita Regis Aedwardi* to the years immediately after his death in 1066, we can see that his cult developed extremely quickly. Even a more conservative dating allows for the fact that Edward's miracles were being recorded in the early twelfth century.28 This earliest *Vita* both recorded miracles performed in Edward's own life, and miracles occurring at his tomb. In his lifetime, Edward cured the blind, as well as curing a scrofulous woman.29 At his tomb, 'the blind receive their sight, the lame are made to walk, the sick are healed ...'.30

Edward's body exhibited the conventional signs of sanctity, which were manifested before his canonisation, testifying to the fact that a cult was developing. The anonymous *Vita* recorded Edward's death and funeral. For obvious reasons, the author did not record the body's lack of corruption, which could not be revealed until the tomb was reopened in 1102. Nevertheless, the manner of Edward's death implied his sanctity. The death itself is presented in idealised terms, with the king dying peacefully and piously, setting the affairs of both this world and the next in order. After death, the king's body displayed the 'glory of a soul departing to God. For the flesh of the face blushed like a rose, the adjacent beard like a lily, his hands, laid out straight, whitened, and were a sign that his whole body was given not to death but to auspicious sleep.' These signs anticipated the incorruptibility of the king's body and indicated his sanctity. [31] According to Osbert of Clare, who was later the prior of Westminster, at the opening of the tomb in 1102 the body was found to be uncorrupt, and gave off the characteristic sweet odour of sanctity. The bishop of Rochester, who was in attendance, was rebuked for attempting to pull out hairs from the king's beard, a sign that his relics were already sought after, as the bishop defended his actions by maintaining that they were motivated by devotion not by presumption.[32] While Aelred made this translation an occasion of the proof of Edward's sanctity, Osbert also says that some attended the opening out of a desire to see the king's face again, suggesting personal loyalty to the dead king as a motive, rather than a belief in his sainthood.

In many ways, the cult of Edward the Confessor resembles that of the unofficial cults of royal martyrs in the later middle ages, which will be discussed below. These characteristics include the reporting of miracles at the tomb very quickly after death and a popular following for the early cult. The Confessor's cult is usually seen as not being a popular one, in that the canonisation was the result of lobbying by the abbey of Westminster and Henry II.[33] A reference in Aelred of Rievaulx's *Life* of the Confessor indicates that, before his canonisation, Edward enjoyed an unofficial popular cult. In one of the miracle stories, the countess of Gloucester, when being told by her seamstress that the day was the festival of King Edward the Martyr, mistakenly thinks that she refers to Edward the Confessor, whose cult, she observes scornfully, is celebrated by the common people (*rustica multitudo*).[34] These 'spontaneous' popular cults tended to die out rapidly without political support, and there is no evidence to suggest that the Confessor's remained 'popular' by the time of his canonisation. This came about due to pressure from the abbey of Westminster, and in particular the prior Osbert of Clare, who wrote one of Edward's early biographies in 1138. Westminster, a royal foundation that was increasing in importance, wanted a saint of its own to lend it prestige; it was dedicated to St Peter, a saint of great significance, but one with no local resonance. The advocacy of Henry II, at a time when Pope Alexander III desperately needed support against an imperial-sponsored anti-pope, helped clinch the canonisation in 1161, and the new saint's body was formally translated to a magnificent new tomb in 1163.

What appeal did Edward's cult hold for the *rustica multitudo*, and why did this appeal not last? It is probable that the popular cult influenced the development of the official one, as Osbert of Clare, prior of Westminster and Edward's main advocate within the chapter of the abbey, was himself cured by a miracle of the Confessor, according to Aelred of Rievaulx. So personal gratitude as well as the interests of his house may have influenced Osbert, who may have been one of the agents for the transfer of the putative cult from the populace to the high ecclesiastics who were the only ones with the power to press for canonisation. The anonymous *Vita* appears to be associated with Edward's court, particularly Queen Edith his widow, and his former courtiers were the first to promote the cult.

The sanctification of kings may appear a contradiction, given that chronicle accounts of the deaths of kings often present them as the opposite of saints, their glory passing, their bodies corruptible. There was another aspect of kingship that made it not unlike sanctity, namely the king's position as God's anointed. The holy chrism made the king in some ways akin to a saint, one who was God's anointed; fragrant oils were often associated with saints, some of whom demonstrated their superiority to the corrupt state of humanity by being able to secrete such oils. In many dynastic myths, such as that of the kings of France, the coronation chrism had descended directly from heaven, demonstrating the divine mandate of the king. Some writers pointed to the parallel between Christ the King, and the king anointed with chrism (*christus*).[35] The king's power to cure scrofula by touch was a unique example of a miracle performed by a non-saint, and put the king on a par with saints.

The earliest biography of Edward the Confessor combines a secular biography with a putative hagiography, listing his miracles and reflecting Edward's roles as both king and candidate for sainthood. The first miracle recorded was Edward's cure of a woman afflicted by a skin disease, anticipating the power of touching for the King's Evil.[36] Osbert of Clare attributed Edward's power to perform miracles to his status as an anointed king. 'Thus Jesus Christ, the son of God, works through Edward, his anointed, and thus adds glorious miracles to miracles.'[37]

Edward's cult was enthusiastically promoted by Henry III in the thirteenth century, and Henry's translation of Edward's remains to a new tomb became associated with his own burial in Westminster Abbey. In turn a cult of sanctity (ultimately unsuccessful) briefly developed around Henry's own resting-place, with reports of miracles being performed at his tomb. Before being placed in his own tomb in 1290, Henry was initially buried in 1272 in the place formerly occupied by Edward before the latter's translation, and it was during this time that the cult of Henry developed, apparently with official encouragement, not least from his widow Eleanor of Provence.[38] The decision in 1290 to remove Henry to a new tomb in a less central position may reflect the failure of attempts to promote his cult.[39]

With this tradition of royal sanctity in existence, it is perhaps not surprising that later kings attracted veneration as martyrs after their deaths. In 1183 the death of Henry, the Young King (the son of Henry II) led to a brief veneration of him by some as a saint. Edward II was presented by some as a royal saint, killed in a horrible manner that echoed the martyrdoms of the saints. Geoffrey le Baker compared him to Job, patient in suffering, and to Christ, betrayed and sent to his death by his own people. Edward, Thomas of Lancaster, Simon de Montfort, and Humphrey, duke of Gloucester, all enjoyed unofficial cults of sainthood. Their tombs became foci for their cults, and attracted many pilgrims, especially from among the common people. These were all royal or quasi-royal figures who were held to have stood for the liberties of England, and to have fallen foul of tyranny. (Simon de Montfort was the brother-in-law of Henry III. Thomas of Lancaster was the cousin of Edward II. Humphrey of Gloucester was the son of Henry IV, and therefore the uncle of Henry VI, the reigning king at the time of his death.) Although their lives may have been far from saintly, in death they became martyrs. To examine the unofficial cults of these figures, it is necessary to ask why they were deemed saints, and by whom. The cult of royal martyrs was often an embodiment of opposition to the established regime, which, because it was articulated through the veneration of a royal or semi-royal figure, did not threaten the established order. A figure who was simultaneously a prince and a rebel was a 'safe' person to represent the spirit of rebellion. To use a modern parallel, the 'cult' of Diana in 1997 had the appearance at the time of an anti-monarchist movement, as public grief turned into criticism of a royal family that was both physically and metaphorically distant from the mourning masses. Yet the British monarchy seems to have emerged from the episode strengthened.

There is also the question of where the impetus for the moves to canonise royal martyrs came from. It was in many senses a 'popular' movement, as represented by the appearance of pilgrims, often from the lower classes, at the tombs of the dead. Yet attempts to make these cults official by canonisation originated in the upper reaches of society, and even, in the case of Edward II, with the king, Richard II. The cults, although unofficial, were often encouraged by the religious houses that benefited materially from them, such as Evesham Abbey, the temporary resting-place of Simon de Montfort.[40] So clearly it is not possible to regard these cults as purely 'popular' and anti-establishment in nature.

Let us begin with a brief survey of the cult figures. Simon de Montfort was killed at Evesham in 1265, fighting for what remained of the baronial 'Commune of England' against the army of the future Edward I and the cause of monarchical rule. He died by violence, in battle, and his body was dismembered by his enemies after death. What remained of his body was briefly buried at Evesham Abbey, before being disinterred by the victors, but it remained there long enough to become the focus of a cult. Miracles were said to have been performed at the site of his tomb, or at the spring that appeared at the site of his death, and were recorded by the monks of the abbey.[41] De Montfort's death even seemed to be accompanied by divine portents, as a violent storm raged over the battlefield.[42] Despite official attempts to suppress it, the cult flourished in the years immediately after his death. It did not prove long-lasting, and began to wane in the 1280s.[43]

The manner of de Montfort's death was material in the creation of a cult of martyrdom. The fact that he died a violent death, in battle, for a cause that could be – and was – presented as just, made him good martyr material. De Montfort's cause had received considerable backing from the higher clergy, including such notable figures as the Cantilupe brothers, bishops of Worcester and Hereford. The presentation of his cause as a holy one was therefore not entirely a product of hindsight: crusade ideology and imagery was central to the reformers' cause, from the accusations made in 1258 that Henry III's policies were preventing the prosecution of the crusade against the Saracens, to the wearing of crosses by de Montfort's army at the battle of Lewes in 1264.[44] The crosses were distributed by Walter de Cantilupe, bishop of Worcester, who had taken the cross in 1247 and 1250, and been commissioned to preach the crusade in 1263.[45]

The shameful treatment of de Montfort's body after his death rebounded badly against his enemies. The practice of dismembering the body of a traitor following execution was developing in England in this period. During the reign of the victor of Evesham, Edward I, Dafydd ap Gruffudd of Gwynedd and William Wallace, two notable enemies of the crown, were to suffer the horror and indignity of hanging, drawing and quartering. The destruction of the traitor's body represented his utter destruction as a civil being, while the quartering of the body and the scattering of the sections across the realm communicated the fate that befell traitors to the populace, while denying the dead man a burial place that could act as a focus for those wishing to honour him.

De Montfort's death, occurring as it did on the battlefield, was not of course a judicial execution, but the treatment of his body seems to have been carried out for a deliberate political purpose. If so, it backfired badly against the government. The dismemberment of de Montfort's body shocked even royalist chroniclers.[46] Those who promoted his cult used the dismemberment to add to the sense of martyrdom; a prayer in his honour includes the line 'Manus pedes amputari, caput corpus vulnerari (hands and feet cut off, head and body wounded)'.[47] Evesham, where de Montfort had died and where his trunk had briefly rested, became the focus for his cult, while the pieces of his dismembered corpse themselves became foci for local cults. (There is, sadly, no evidence of a cult based on his genitals, which, along with his head, were dispatched to Lady Mortimer of Wigmore, the wife of one of the earl's

Marcher enemies.) [48] Some of his limbs, however, were recovered by sympathisers, and 'quickly, by terrible signs shown through them, were held in veneration'.[49] One foot found a resting place as far away as Alnwick in Northumberland, where it became the focus of a cult.[50] The government took measures to suppress the cult. Article eight of the Dictum of Kenilworth of 1266 condemned anyone who maintained that de Montfort was a saint or who spread stories of his miracles. This indicates the speed with which the cult developed, as well as the seriousness with which the regime took the threat that such a cult posed to its authority.[51]

De Montfort was not, of course, a king, but quasi-kingly qualities can be perceived in his cult. He was close to royalty, being married to Henry III's sister Eleanor. He was effective ruler of England at the time of his death, and to his supporters he had taken on the kingly role of protecting his country and people, a role that was evident in his cult. A prayer in his honour that appears in the list of his miracles, described him as 'Protector gentis Angliae' ('Protector of the People of England').[52]

Studies of de Montfort's cult have thrown light on the status of his followers, with contradictory results. There is ample evidence to suggest that his cult was a 'popular' one, drawing its support from the poor. Sixty per cent of the beneficiaries of his recorded miracles were from the lower classes, while the prior of Waltham dreamed 'that he saw Earl Simon among a crowd of poor people'.[53] It has been argued that peasant support was an important element in de Montfort's cause.[54] Such support for the cult may indicate knowledge and approval of de Montfort's character and aims on the part of those peasants who participated in the revolt.[55]

Conversely, de Montfort's cult was far from being exclusively plebeian in character. One of his relics – the foot that was not taken to Alnwick (by a nobleman, John de Vescy), came into the possession of his ally Llywelyn ap Gruffudd, prince of Wales. Visitors to his shrine in Evesham, and beneficiaries of his miracles, included people of high status as well as the poor. Indeed, his cult was disproportionately popular among higher status members of society.[56]

Thomas of Lancaster died in similar circumstances to de Montfort, fighting for a 'baronial' opposition movement against a 'tyrannical' king, at Boroughbridge in 1322. Unlike de Montfort, he did not die on the battlefield but was captured and executed as a traitor at Pontefract. He was originally condemned to the cruel traitor's death of hanging, drawing and quartering, but this was commuted to beheading on account of his royal blood.[57] Unlike de Montfort, and unlike others who were executed for treason, his body was not dismembered after death, as such a fate would have been unseemly for the cousin of the king. Despite his ignominious end, his resting-place also became the focus of a cult, and stories of miracles occurring at his tomb were circulating only six weeks after his death.[58] As in the case of de Montfort, the government attempted to suppress the cult, but its development was aided by the overthrow of Edward II in 1327, in which year the new regime began moves to have Thomas canonised.[59] The Douce Hours, a book produced around 1325–30, includes an image of Thomas of Lancaster and St George, both armed, perhaps suggesting that Lancaster shared some of the warrior-saint's qualities.[60] The rule of Mortimer and Isabella only lasted until 1330, when Edward III gained power in his own right; he was naturally unwilling to promote a cult of opposition to royal authority. Earl Thomas's cult, unlike that of de Monfort, survived to become a long-term feature of the sacral landscape, as it was promoted by the house of Lancaster, especially after Henry IV's seizure of power.[61] It suited the Lancastrians to have a dynastic saint, while promoting the cult of one who had fought against a tyrannical king had obvious uses for Henry in helping justify his usurpation of Richard II.

Ranulf Higden offered the following assessment of Thomas of Lancaster, as translated into Middle English by John Trevisa (some spellings have been modernised):

> Of this erle and of his dedes is ofte greet stryf among comoun peple (in vulgo disceptatio est), whether he schulde be acounted for seyntes other none. Some seyn yis, for he dede many almes dedes, and worschipped [respected] men of religion, and maynteyned a trewe querel, as it semed, to his lyves ende; also his enemyes durede afterward but a while, and deyde in schentful [shameful] deeth. Other seyne the contrarie, and telleth that he was an housbonde man, and rought nought of his wyf, and defouled a greet multitude of gentil wommen and of gentil wenches; yif eny man offended him a lite, he lete slee hym anon. And apostates and evel doers he favored strongliche, for he schulde nought be i-punisched by the lawe. Also wolde he comytte all his doynges to oon of his sectretaries to doo with as he wolde. Also that he

foloweth schamefulliche in tyme of fyghting for the right anon to the dethe, and suche on schulde nought de accounted a saynt, nameliche whan he was I-take and I-slaye maugre his teeth. But offrynges and likenes of myracles that now beeth done in the place there he was byheded what issue they take, it schal be knowe after this tyme.[62]

Higden neatly summarises the arguments for and against his sanctity, and so provides us with a guide to what attributes a saint was expected to possess. In favour of his sanctity were that he had lived a pious life, fought and died for justice, and that his enemies perished soon after. Against, that he was an adulterer, that he favoured evil-doers, was cowardly in battle, and died on the scaffold not on the battlefield.

Similarities between the careers of Simon de Montfort and Thomas of Lancaster were obvious, and were commented on by Thomas's contemporaries. The author of the *Vita Edwardi Secundi* remarked that the example of the civil war in which de Montfort 'laid down his life in the cause of justice' persuaded the king's counsellors to accept the Ordinances, the rebels' programme of reforms.[63] He goes on to remark that, had he resisted, the king would probably have been taken captive by the Ordainers, for 'did not Earl Simon de Montfort thus bridle King Henry and consign his son Edward to prison?', but concludes, citing the example of de Montfort's death at Evesham, that 'it is not safe to set oneself up against the king, because the issue of it is wont to be unfortunate'.[64]

A homily for Thomas of Lancaster also contains elements that owe much to the cult of Simon de Montfort. Thomas is linked with the prototype anti-royal saint, Thomas Becket:

> Gaude Thoma, ducum decus, lucerna Lancastriae,
> Qui per necem imitaris Thomam Cantuariae;
> Cujus caput conculcatur pacem ob ecclesiae,
> Atque tuum detruncatur causa pacis Angliae ...[65]

The shared Christian name Thomas of course helped identify Lancaster with the earlier martyr, as the homily continues: 'Deus, qui, pro pace et tranquillitate regnicolarum Angliae, beatum Thomam martyrem tuum atque comitem gladio persecutoris occumbere voluisti ...'.[66] Only the word *comitem* [earl] makes it clear that the writer is referring to Thomas of Lancaster, not Thomas of Canterbury, who equally fell 'by the sword of the persecutor'. The comparison with Becket was also a feature of some of the literature surrounding the cult of Simon de Montfort. A lament for the dead earl declared that

> ... par sa mort, le cuens Mountfort conquist la victorie,
> Come le martyr de Caunterbyr, finist sa vie
> Ne voleit pas li bon Thomas qe perist seinte Eglise,
> Ly cuens auxi se combati, e morust sauntz feyntise.[67]

This song occurs in an early fourteenth-century manuscript, so may itself be associated with Thomas of Lancaster, rather than with the cult of Simon per se. Furthermore, the office for Thomas of Lancaster borrows from the similar office for 'saint' Simon de Montfort: Earl Simon was described as 'Totius flos militiae' ('flower of all knighthood'), Earl Thomas as 'flos militum regalis' ('royal flower of knights'), while his office regrets the spilling of the blood of 'Thomae floris militum' ('Thomas, flower of knights').[68]

As this description demonstrates, Thomas's royal blood was stressed. It has already been argued that Simon de Montfort was treated as a pseudo-king in the literature of his cult. This was all the more true of Thomas, who was a cousin of the king. The office quoted above also describes him as 'the royal vessel ... beheaded for the cure of the kingdom' and stresses that he is 'of an illustrious race ... born of a royal bed'. We are reminded that his father, the Lord Edmund, was son of a king, while his mother was from the royal house of Navarre.[69]

Thomas of Lancaster seems to have enjoyed a popular following. It has been argued that the opposition to Edward II was popular as well as baronial in its base. Ordinary people were aware of the rights which the Ordinances had given them, and naturally supported Lancaster, the most prominent defender of reforming principles.[70] Within weeks of his death, miracles were reported at Thomas's tomb in Pontefract, and a guard was dispatched to prevent pilgrims visiting it. In 1323, a mob of two thousand was reported to have attacked this guard, and killed two of its members, when it attempted to prevent offerings from being left.[71] Even if two thousand is an exaggeration, this is testimony to the popularity of his cult.

The case of the cult of Edward II had similarities to that of his adversary Lancaster, in the sense that he too benefited from a reversal of political fortunes after his death. He was deposed in 1327 and died, almost certainly by being murdered, soon afterwards. His tormentors, Queen Isabella and Roger Mortimer, were themselves overthrown by Edward III in 1330. Unlike de Montfort and Thomas of Lancaster, Edward II did not die in or after a battle, but he was nonetheless said to have died by violence, thereby promoting the feeling that he could be considered a martyr.[72] Likewise, although it would be hard to portray him as a fighter for justice and liberty, he could certainly be seen as a victim of tyranny in the shape of Mortimer and Isabella. Edward's tomb at Gloucester Abbey became a focus for pilgrimage. The chronicle of Gloucester Abbey claimed that the offerings of the multitude of people visiting the tomb 'ex diversis civitatibus Angliae' ensured that within six years the abbey's aisle of Saint Andrew could be completed.[73] It was not, however, Edward's son but his great-grandson, Richard II, who moved to have him canonised, commissioning a book of Edward's miracles in 1390, to be sent to the pope.[74]

As with Thomas of Lancaster, Ranulf Higden summarised the opinions he had heard on the question of Edward's sanctity, to the effect that some held him to be a saint, on account of his violent death, but concluded that 'kepynge in prison, vilenes and obprobrious dethe cause not a martir'. It was not enough for a man to die a violent death for him to be a saint:

> For nother prisonment ne persecucioun and greves preveth a man a seynt, for evel doer suffreth suche peynes; neyther offrynges ne liknes of miracles proveth a man a seynete, but the holynes of the rather lyf accorde therto, ffor suche beeth indifferent to gode and to yvel.[75]

There is certainly evidence from chronicles (if we count the *Miracles of Simon de Montfort* as such) that these cults were popular, in the sense of being promoted, or at least supported, by the 'people'. The lower classes supported, and benefited from, the cult of Simon de Montfort. The 'common people' were said by Higden to be those who debated the claims of Thomas of Lancaster to sanctity. The people flocked to the tomb of Edward II at Gloucester, and their offerings enriched the abbey. So why did the 'people' promote these cults of royal or aristocratic martyrs, whose status in society was the opposite to their followers'?

Clues may be found in a later event, the great revolt of 1381. The events of the revolt demonstrated the allure which royalty still held for the peasantry (and their urban allies) even when these groups were in revolt. In the so called 'Peasants' Revolt', the rebels who had up to that point shown no awe of authority were pacified in part through the personal intervention of the young Richard II. Following the killing of the rebel leader Wat Tyler, the fourteen-year-old king, according to some accounts, offered to 'lead' the rebels, declaring, according to the Westminster Chronicler, 'I am your king, your leader, your captain.'[76] By this action, he was able successfully to undermine the revolt, as well as by appearing to concede one of their key demands, the end of serfdom. Manumissions (later ignored by authorities, as they had been issued under the threat of coercion) were drawn up by thirty clerks, and the rebels began to drift away.[77]

The ease with which the rebellion was defused by Richard can appear startling. Was there more to it than the portrayal by the chroniclers of the rebels as an ignorant mass, who pleaded for mercy from the king as soon their leader was killed?[78] Far from being an ignorant rabble, they possessed a remarkable degree of political sophistication, as shown by the execution of individual unpopular ministers, the targeting (possibly by the Londoners) of sites associated with the hated John of Gaunt, duke of Lancaster, the relative restraint of their actions while within the City of London, and sets of demands that looked beyond immediate social and economic grievances. A sense of loyalty to the crown seems also to have been part of the political outlook of the rebels, who, according to the Westminster chronicler, maintained that they did not stand against the king, but rather 'that they were protecting the king and the welfare of the realm against traitors to him'.[79] The Anonimalle Chronicler attributed to them a question-and-response 'wache word' of 'With whom haldes yow?' to which the reply was 'Wyth kynge Richarde and wyth the trew communes'.[80] 'True' (trew in Middle English) means not only 'real' or 'genuine' but 'loyal', as seen in Chaucer's statement that the Knight of the Canterbury Tales 'loved chivalrie, trouthe and honour ...'.[81] The last, and most radical, set of rebel demands called for the abolition of all lordship, but still envisaged a society governed by the king (with a prelate to govern the church): they demanded that 'no lord should have lordship in future, but it should be divided among all men, except for the king's own lordship'.[82] The extent to which peasant ideology envisaged a king of sorts even within a subverted society is shown by Walsingham's report that, in Norfolk, the rebel leader Geoffrey Litster set himself up as a 'King of the Commons', who made 'noble knights' serve him at table.[83]

The rebels' illusions of kingship can be seen to arise not from the ignorance of a rabble that must have a leader, but from some kind of consistent ideology, albeit one betraying a great deal of 'false consciousness'. But why should the ideology of the labouring classes place such hopes in a figure at the very pinnacle of the ruling classes? The failure of the revolt, and its failure to develop a coherent ideology, has been blamed on its lack of allies in the political classes, and the absence of any attempt by the rebels to woo such allies. Such criticisms, however, seem to miss the point; namely, that the 'political class' represented by John of Gaunt, Archbishop Simon Sudbury, Hales, Legge and the other unpopular ministers at a national level, and the landlords, tax commissioners and justices at a local level, *was* the enemy. The king, as divinely-appointed ruler, was viewed (wrongly, as the rebels were to learn to their cost) as above social divisions, as the exemplar of justice, an honest broker who would ensure that the 'trew communes' would receive the justice denied them by the lords and the king's tyrannical counsellors. In the 'three orders' system of medieval social theory, the king did not fit entirely into any of the orders or estates but stood outside and above them.

In the twentieth century, such an idea could be seen at work in the demonstrations that led to 'Bloody Sunday', the massacre that sparked off the 1905 revolution in Russia. Workers demonstrating for improved conditions and political reform were fired upon by the troops of Tsar Nicholas II, despite the fact that they were carrying icons and pictures of the tsar himself, in the belief that their 'Little Father' would help them if only they were able to appeal to him directly. They had initially petitioned the tsar in the most humble terms, expressing the belief that he was merely being misled by evil counsellors: 'Sire! Do not believe the ministers. They are cheating Thee in regard to the real state of affairs. The people believe in Thee.'[84] This reverence for the tsar still survives in conservative circles in post-Communist Russia, and has seen the Orthodox Church canonise Nicholas II as a martyr.[85] In the Communist era, there was also an attempt to destroy any possible 'cult centre', with the demolition of the church next to the building in which the imperial family had died, on the orders of the Sverdlovsk (Yekaterinburg) Communist Party boss, the young Boris Yeltsin.[86]

The moving speech attributed by Froissart to John Ball, although hardly reliable as a source for what the peasants believed, at least suggests what the court *thought* they might believe. Froissart has Ball, like Father Gapon, the leader of the Russian demonstration of 1905, see the king as someone to whom the peasants can appeal for justice:

> Let us go to the king, he is young, and shew him what servage we be in, and shew him how we will have it otherwise, or else we will provide us of some remedy; and if we go together, all manner of people that be now in any bondage will follow us to the intent to be made free; and when the king seeth us, we shall have some remedy . . .[87]

The idea that rebellion was aimed not against the king but against 'evil counsellors' was by no means limited to the revolts of the lower classes. Baronial revolts were similarly motivated; attacks on such bad counsellors were voiced by the Montfortian barons in the thirteenth century, who maintained Henry III on the throne as their nominal king, and in whose train the hapless king rode against his son's forces at Evesham in 1265. Likewise, Richard II's baronial and clerical opponents of the 1390s attacked his 'evil counsellors and chief fosterers of his malice', Bushy, Bagot and Green.[88] Henry of Bolingbroke's invasion in 1399 was, so it was claimed, aimed only to restore to him the lands of the duchy of Lancaster, not to depose the king, and Henry gained a great deal of support by executing the 'evil counsellors' before moving to seize the throne for himself.[89] An anonymous poem criticising Richard's kingship, written shortly after his deposition, was significantly entitled *Richard the Redeles*. The word *redeles* does not translate easily into modern English, but it means lacking in counsel or ill-advised (rather like the Old English sobriquet *Unraed* of 'Aethelred the Unready'). The modern German word *ratlos*, which has the same root, means 'helpless' or 'perplexed'. Finally, the Yorkists of 1455 and 1460 did not take up arms (or so they claimed) to depose Henry VI, but rather to rid him of evil counsellors. One account of the first battle of St Albans has Richard of York declaring that 'he had come to punish the traitors around the king'. In the course of the battle, the king himself was captured, treated with respect, and escorted to London by the Yorkist lords.[90] In 1460, the Yorkists issued a manifesto maintaining their loyalty to the king and calling for an end to misrule by his counsellors.[91] Likewise, the Cornish rebels of 1497 stressed that they were opposed not to the rule of Henry VII but to his 'evil advisers', Cardinal Morton and Sir Reginald Bray. The rebel force was fatally weakened by divisions between those who were, in the words of the London Chronicle, 'mynded to have comyn to the Kyng and to have yolded theym and put theym fully in his mercy' and those who urged open defiance.[92]

An intriguing reference in the Crowland Chronicle Continuation (written around 1486) suggests that in the fifteenth century political figures who were close to the king, but who were perceived as antagonistic in some way to the ruling elite, were revered by the populace. Commenting on the execution of the duke of Clarence on charges of treason against his brother Edward IV, the chronicler writes that the 'common folk' viewed Clarence and Richard Neville, earl of Warwick, and 'any other great men of the land who withdrew from royal circles as idols ...'.[93] Warwick the 'Kingmaker' had formerly been a close ally of Edward, but had been associated with Clarence in a previous intrigue against him, and had died on the battlefield in 1471, fighting against Edward and for the restoration of the Lancastrian Henry VI. The chronicler seems to imply it was the act of withdrawing from royal circles that created popular sympathy for such men. This suggests a latent anti-establishment sentiment among the 'common folk', but one which was only expressed through an interest in 'high' politics, not in class-conscious revolt.

The process by which rebellion could be assimilated is mirrored in the cults of political martyrs. It has been argued that these figures should not be viewed as 'oppositional' saints, as their cults, where they enjoyed any sort of longevity, did so because of royal patronage.[94] There is a great deal of truth in this; for example, there is little evidence for a genuinely popular cult of Edward II except in the years following his death, and its attempted revival in the latter part of the century was owing to its promotion by Richard II. Likewise, as we have seen, Thomas of Lancaster's cult was promoted by his Lancastrian successors, especially after they achieved power in the person of Henry IV. The exception that proves the rule is that of Simon de Montfort, whose cult was at first actively suppressed, but died out sometime in the 1280s or 1290s as it lost its political resonance. Those 'oppositional' cults that flourished did so because they were adopted by the monarchy in order to promote a sense of inclusiveness and reconciliation.

There are, however, flaws in this argument. To take one, admittedly minor, point, Edward III began moves for the canonisation of Thomas of Lancaster in 1327.[95] Edward at that time was fourteen years old, and his letters a cipher for the regime of Isabella and Mortimer, who had every political reason to wish to promote the factional cult of an opponent of the murdered Edward II, especially if the latter was attracting veneration of his own. Furthermore, the visits of pilgrims to the tomb of Edward at Gloucester are recorded during the abbacy of John Wigmore, who did not become abbot until 1329.[96] Therefore his cult cannot have been merely a spontaneous reaction to the death of Edward, and, as Mortimer and Isabella were overthrown in 1330, it is unlikely to have an oppositional character. The chronicle mentions the visits of pilgrims in the context of the building of a new aisle in the abbey church, which was funded by their offerings. The construction work occurred during John Wigmore's abbacy; it docs not necessarily follow that the pilgrims only began appearing in or after 1329. What we know of Simon de Montfort's and Thomas of Lancaster's cults is that they began very quickly. It does not follow that Edward's cult developed equally rapidly, but it is a fair assumption to make. After all, Higden was at pains to point out that it was only Edward's violent death that qualified him for sanctity, so it seems logical to suppose a cult would have developed soon after this event. Edward's death was shrouded in mystery; the means by which he was killed were a matter for speculation, and there were even rumours of his survival.[97] There was no dramatic public 'martyrdom', as there had been in the cases of Simon de Montfort or Thomas of Lancaster.

The relative failure of Edward II's cult to achieve a popular resonance can be explained by a number of factors. Politically, it was harder to construct him as a martyr for a cause, in the way that de Montfort and Thomas of Lancaster were. As Higden maintained, he had few holy deeds that could be produced as evidence for martyrdom, and the Gloucester chronicle's reference to his cult makes no reference to miracles being performed in his name. Perhaps surprisingly, his son made no effort to promote Edward's cult. It may have been politically unwise to do so, as Edward III displayed a mostly lenient attitude to his father's murderers following the execution of Mortimer. To make Edward II a martyr might have been to reopen old wounds.

The ambiguity surrounding his death may have retarded the development of a cult. The lives and deaths of Edward II and Richard II have often been compared, not least by Richard's contemporaries. The same is true of their after-lives. Richard II was repeatedly reported to have survived imprisonment by Henry IV, despite Henry's public display of the dead king's body and giving him a public funeral procession, if not a public burial. Richard was buried obscurely at Langley Abbey. These rumours were bolstered by the existence of a flesh and blood impostor, Thomas Ward of Trumpington, in Scotland, who received the backing of the Scottish king and of Richard's former chancellor, William Serle. Serle added to the realism of the imposture by continuing to issue letters in Richard's name.[98]

There seems little concrete reason for anyone outside the circle of his immediate partisans to hope for the return of Richard. Henry's rule was not notably oppressive, nor his taxes notably high. His leading aristocratic opponents, the Percys, made no attempt to promote the idea of Richard's survival, informing Welsh troops who appeared at Shrewsbury in Richard's livery that the former king was dead. There was one incident which led to a treason trial, where three Hertfordshire villagers set about collecting men and arms in preparation for Richard's imminent return. It has been argued that incidents such as this can only be explained as embodying pseudo-messianic expectations among the peasantry.[99] The idea of an impostor king as focus for resistance manifested itself in other peasant societies, for example, in the *Pugachevshina* of eighteenth-century Russia, a peasant revolt led by a man claiming to be the dead Tsar Peter, who had been murdered by Catherine the Great.

There was no cult of Richard the martyr because there was no need for one. The rumours of his survival were fed by a sense of what has been called 'loyalist opposition',[100] the same type of opposition that fed the cults of Thomas of Lancaster, possibly of Edward II, and certainly of Simon de Montfort, whose opposition was 'loyal' in the sense that he never sought to replace the king. Those who venerated Richard could pin their hopes upon his imminent return, so did not need to promote a martyr cult. Likewise, rumours of Edward II's survival, or at least an uncertainty as to the manner and timing of his death, may explain why his own cult did not gain widespread support.

One other possible reason for the lack of a Ricardian cult is that an alternative anti-Henrician martyr was available, after 1405, in the shape of Archbishop Scrope of York. He was beheaded for his part in a rebellion against Henry IV, and very rapidly attracted the type of veneration that we have seen attaching itself to Simon de Monfort, Thomas of Lancaster and Edward II. The field where he was executed, and his tomb, became places of pilgrimage for the 'vulgares', and visits to his tomb were prohibited by the authorities, as had happened in the cases of earlier political martyrs.[101] It is possible that the growth of his cult occupied the political and devotional space that might otherwise have allowed the development of a cult of Richard, not least because the latter was rumoured to still be alive.

Humphrey, duke of Gloucester, after his rumoured murder in 1447, enjoyed a measure of popular veneration, although there was never a major cult surrounding him or a move to canonise him. In the sixteenth century, the people of London, in particular the poor and unemployed, venerated what they mistakenly believed to be Duke Humphrey's tomb in St Paul's. The Elizabethan authorities sought to repress these gatherings of the London poor, ingeniously invoking the new laws against vagrancy (whereby the homeless poor were supposed to return to their home parishes, or to their masters in the case of runaway apprentices), suggesting that Humphrey's followers should return to their 'master' at St Albans.[102]

The last of the medieval royal 'martyrs' of England was Henry VI. Henry has two conflicting reputations, as England's most incompetent king and as a saintly royal martyr. He seems to have been a weak personality, ill-suited to rule, and later in his reign he suffered from a severe mental illness which rendered him incapable of governing. His reign was a period of almost continual warfare, with England fighting a losing struggle in France. This was followed by civil war – the so-called Wars of the Roses – at home. Like Edward II and Richard II, Henry died – in all likelihood he was killed – in secret and suspicious circumstances, in the process of a change of power. Henry's circumstances are

rather more complex than those in which his predecessors Edward II
and Richard II met their end, but are broadly similar. Deposed in
November 1461, and replaced by the Yorkist Edward IV, Henry was
briefly restored to the throne in October 1470. He was deposed for a
second and final time the following year, and probably murdered in the
Tower of London, in May 1471. This happened immediately after the
defeat of his wife's forces by Edward's at Tewkesbury, and the death of
his only son on the battlefield. This dual disaster ended any hope of a
Lancastrian restoration. The 'official' version in the *Arrivall of Edward
IV* has it that Henry died of 'pure displeasure and melancholy' upon
hearing the news of Tewkesbury.[103]

   After fourteen years of Yorkist rule under Edward IV, the short-lived
Edward V and Richard III, the victory of Henry Tudor at Bosworth
in 1485 led to a reversal of the political situation, in which the dead
King Henry VI could be rehabilitated. We therefore see a repeat of the
pattern of events that had taken place around the deaths of Thomas
of Lancaster, Edward II and Humphrey of Gloucester; deposition, probable murder, then the fall of the dead 'martyr's' persecutors, a
combination of events which seems to have created the optimal conditions for the development of a cult of sanctity. The veneration of
Henry as a martyr seems to have followed the pattern we have seen
in earlier examples, where a combination of the king's status as God's
Anointed, and the violence of his death, made him a martyr. The
so-called Crowland Continuator, while not naming a murderer, implied
that Edward IV was responsible, thereby rendering him a 'tyrant' as
he had 'dared to lay sacrilegious hands on the Lord's Anointed', and
his victim a 'glorious martyr'.[104] Henry's sanctity was confirmed by the
'miracles which God has performed in answer to the prayers of those
who devoutly implored his intercession ...'.[105]

   The attempted canonisation of Henry has its roots both in popular
sentiment in the years immediately following his death, and in the official
(and more obviously political) attempt by Henry VII beginning in 1494
to have him canonised. Henry Tudor, who represented himself as the
successor and avenger of the house of Lancaster, had a clear interest
in promoting the cult of Henry VI, and the work attributed to his
confessor John Blacman was instrumental in promoting the image of
the Lancastrian king as a meek, saintly, peace-loving ruler, whose

inadequacies as a monarch were due to his otherworldly nature, not madness or incompetence. The problem for this early Tudor hagiographer was that he could not present Henry, like St Louis, as a candidate for sainthood by reason of his kingship or martial exploits.[106] 'Blacman's' work might be viewed as a set of recollections, rather than a hagiography, but the chosen incidents from Henry's life were selected to emphasise his piety over his qualities as a ruler.

The portrait of Henry VI that emerges is of a pious man who was unfit to be a king.[107] In the same way, John Rous described him as 'a most holy man, shamefully expelled from his kingdom, but little given to the world and worldly affairs ...',[108] emphasising again the idea that, if he was a bad king, it was only because he was better suited to a religious life. The Crowland Continuator also stressed Henry's passivity and meekness, saying that he was a saint on account of 'the merit of a life of innocence, love of God and the church, patience in adversity ...'.[109] This idea comes down to us through Shakespeare's depiction of Henry sitting on a molehill at Towton, wishing he had been born a shepherd instead of a king.[110] Shakespeare was writing in the Tudor historiographical tradition, which sought to downplay Henry's incompetence by emphasising his saintly virtues. The Tudor tradition, in effect, argued that Henry was a poor ruler not because he was too bad to be king, but because he was too good. The canonisation process eventually died out in the course of the break from Rome by Henry Tudor's son, Henry VIII. It did, however, leave us a collection of Henry VI's reported miracles.

Before any of this took place Henry's cult was developing during the reign of Edward IV. We can therefore probably see it as a cult of political opposition, in the tradition of Simon de Montfort, Thomas of Lancaster or Archbishop Scrope. In 1479 the archbishop of York, Lawrence Booth, ordered, doubtless at the insistence of King Edward, the suppression of the veneration of an image of Henry VI that was in York Minster.[111] This may have been a spontaneous 'popular' cult, but there may also have been those among the chapter who wished to promote veneration of the dead king. The dean, Richard Andrew, had been Henry VI's private secretary.

This is an interesting example of the geographical reach of Henry's cult, but its main focus was Henry's burial-place at Chertsey Abbey in

Surrey.[112] This was a relatively humble, although by no means shameful, resting place, chosen by Edward IV in the hope that his dead predecessor would lie in obscurity – a hope that was to be frustrated by the developing cult. After the death of Edward, Henry's body was moved to the more honourable surrounds of St George's Chapel, Windsor, which ironically had been established by Edward IV as the necropolis of his own Yorkist dynasty. This move by Richard III was probably intended to accommodate a cult that had proved hard simply to suppress, and to remove the body that had become the cult's focus from its shrine at Chertsey. A precedent for such a move may be seen in Henry V's reburial of Richard II at Westminster. Although Richard II did not enjoy a martyr's cult, the political circumstances were in some ways similar: the king who had actually perpetrated the deposition (Henry IV or Edward IV) was now dead, leaving his successor (Henry V or Richard III) better placed to make a gesture of reconciliation.[113] It may also be the case that the dynasty (if not the king himself) responsible for royal murder wished to expiate the sin in some way, in the manner of those Anglo-Saxon kings who promoted the cults of those by whose deaths they had profited (as Æthelred the Unready did with Edward the Martyr).[114] A subsequent attempt by Henry Tudor in 1494 to move the remains to the even more prestigious royal burial place of Westminster Abbey was resisted by both Chertsey and Windsor, a testimony to how lucrative and significant the cult had become.[115]

An interesting contrast to this posthumous 'rehabilitation' can be seen in the treatment of Richard III's remains by the Tudor dynasty. After being ignominiously stripped, Richard's body was buried in relative obscurity in the Grey Friars' church in Leicester.[116] For all that there has been a concerted effort by his modern partisans to rehabilitate Richard, nobody then or now seems to have suggested he was a saint, so maybe the Tudors' lack of interest in Richard's resting place reflects the absence of any cult to suppress or assimilate.

An example of a miracle story at Chertsey demonstrates how the cult had a clear political aspect to it. The parents of a girl, Agnes Freman, who was afflicted with scrofula, refused to let Richard III touch her, but went instead to Henry's tomb to receive a cure.[117] Scrofula – the 'King's Evil' – had become known as a disease that an anointed king was uniquely able to cure by his touch. This miracle story is a clear indication that God was demonstrating that only the murdered Henry, not the usurper Richard, was able legitimately to lay claim to this power. We must, of course, bear in mind the context in which the miracle stories were collected, namely the canonisation process promoted by Henry VII. The Tudor king's claim to the throne was squarely built upon opposition to the usurpation of Richard, so this miracle story fits rather too neatly with the purposes of Tudor propaganda.

The seriousness with which the Yorkist regime viewed the threat of the cult of Henry VI, and the speed with which it had advanced, is demonstrated by the fact that Edward IV felt compelled in 1473 to command that no one set out on pilgrimage without royal authority. This ban was probably aimed at suppressing the cult of Henry VI. If so, its promulgation only two year's after the Lancastrian king's death illustrates how quickly the cult had appeared, like those of the earlier royal 'martyrs'.[118] The popularity of the cult is attested to by the discovery of over ninety pilgrim badges associated with it.[119]

The visual imagery of badges and most of the surviving artistic images of Henry stress his kingship. He appears crowned, holding the orb and sceptre. He is usually young in appearance, perhaps to emphasise his childhood coronation. This may convey both the idea of innocence, appropriate to a martyr, and that of legitimacy, stressing his royal birth and youthful coronation. By way of comparison, Richard II seems to have used a similar idea in the Wilton Diptych, where, although an adult at the time of its production, he had himself represented as a child. This made the political point that he had been king by right since his accession, in opposition to the baronial reformers who attempted to maintain the idea that the young king was still a child requiring their guidance. The iconography also linked Henry with many Anglo-Saxon royal martyrs, in particular the child-king St Kenelm.

Central to the Tudor propaganda drive for Henry's canonisation was the publication in 1510 of John Blacman's memoir of Henry VI. In drawing up his hagiography, Blacman stressed the very characteristics that made Henry unkingly but saintly: his excessive generosity, his simplicity (especially in dress), his piety. This illustrates the tensions between the qualities of kingship and of sanctity. Blacman records that Henry always dressed simply, like a townsman or a farmer, with a hair-shirt beneath his outer garments. This was in accord with the humble, pious life expected of a saint, but did not sit well with the expectations of a king, especially one reigning in the fifteenth century. Display had always been an important part of medieval kingship: it was important not just to be king, but to look the part. In addition to this, courtly life in the age of Henry VI was increasingly extravagant in its display and its expense, a trend that was set by the dukes of Burgundy in their spectacular court at Dijon. There is also evidence that Henry's court did indulge in its share of ceremonial, in the form of the *Liber regis capelle,* describing the ceremonial in the king's chapel.[120]

Under the influence of Blacman's memoir the iconography of Henry's cult increasingly stressed this simplicity of dress over earlier, more kingly representations, an illustration of how Henry's sanctity had become an inversion of his kingship, being based on the unroyal elements of his personality. The symbols of his sainthood in some artistic representations were his simple clothes, in particular his broad-brimmed peasant's hat (combined incongruously with his crown) and his round-toed shoes. A representation of a purse was often used as a pilgrim badge, symbolising the king's generosity.

A third element is apparent in the image of Henry, in addition to the king and the humble hermit-like saint. The symbols of humility may be associated with his martyrdom, and may even have been intended to remind the viewer or reader of Christ, who was also mocked and humiliated before His death. We have seen how descriptions of the death of Edward II include this element of Christlike suffering and humiliation, as the king was forced to shave in river water and don a crown of straw.[121] The dagger with which Henry was supposedly murdered became an object for veneration and the centre of a cult at Caversham in Oxfordshire.[122] Henry's broad-brimmed hat had an associated place among the instruments of his martyrdom, as he was said to have been mockingly forced to wear it by his captors in the Tower of London. As such, it was reminiscent of the mocking of Christ before the Crucifixion, but also of His subsequent Resurrection, where He was mistaken for a gardener by Mary Magdalen,[123] an incident that often led to Christ being represented in art wearing a gardener's broad-brimmed hat. Blacman's account presents Henry as having 'patiently endured hunger, thirst, mockings, derision, abuse, and many other hardships'. There is no independent evidence for these allegations; on the contrary, Henry appears to have been well-treated during his captivity, until he suffered a sudden, violent death. [124]

The cults of political martyrs were neither wholly popular nor aristocratic, wholly oppositional or official. Their origins lay in political circumstances where adherents of a defeated opposition could draw solace and maintain a spirit of resistance, and as such seem to have been spontaneous in origin, as they arose remarkable rapidly. Their longevity, in contrast, seems to have required official promotion. Popular backing lay in a political consciousness that accepted kingship even in rebellion, believing the king to be above class divisions. The cult of sacral kingship may have added a messianic angle to these hopes that went beyond simple political aims.

8

Queens

Long viewed as a more or less passive consort, a pawn in diplomatic marriage, or a producer of royal heirs, the queen has recently come to be seen as a more dynamic force in medieval politics.[1] Yet the death of a queen did not have the same impact as that of a king. If we exclude the Empress Matilda, who never secured effective rule of England and never took the title of queen, there were no regnant queens of England in the middle ages, only queen consorts. The death of a queen therefore never led to a handover of power to a new ruler, and so had fewer political consequences than that of a king.

It might not, however, be entirely without consequence; the king might, out of the desire for an heir (or for further sons to secure the succession), or in order to forge a new alliance, choose to remarry, thereby disrupting the delicate web of affinity and kinship which governed his relations with his nobility and with foreign powers. For example, the death in 1118 of Henry I's first wife Matilda of Scotland, followed by that of their son and heir in 1120, brought Henry's whole dynastic plans crashing down, leading to his remarriage to Adeliza of Louvain. As this marriage failed to produce any issue, it could be said that the death of Matilda ultimately led to the succession dispute and civil war that followed Henry's death.[2] The death of Anne of Bohemia, the first wife of Richard II, in 1394 without having produced an heir, led Richard to marry a seven-year-old French princess in 1396. This reflected diplomatic concerns, as Richard hoped for a rapprochement with France, and possibly an alliance to pursue the crusade against the Turks. The death of Richard's first queen therefore led to a reversal of diplomatic policy (at least in terms of marriage alliances), as the marriage to Anne had been part of an attempt to form an anti-French axis. The French marriage was greeted with hostility in some quarters, as Richard was suspected of hoping to ally himself with the king of France against his own domestic opponents.[3]

The personal impact of death on medieval people has been much debated. Behind the *ars moriendi* manuals, and the formalised ceremonial of mourning, lies the question of whether and how people felt genuine grief. The deaths of queens provide an important focus in this debate. The death of the queen tended to be greeted by chroniclers with conventional descriptions of the grief felt by the king and the people. Behind these formal accounts may lie the reality of loveless marriages, contracted for reasons of diplomacy and the continuation of the royal line, often arranged by royal parents with the betrothed having no say in the matter. The prevalence of royal mistresses, by whom kings often produced more children than by their wives, may be taken as proof that kings looked beyond the marital bed for love and sex. Most notably, Henry I, who failed from two marriages to produce a male heir who outlived him, fathered a probable seventeen children outside wedlock.

The deaths of two queens of England have been cited as examples of marital love between king and queen. The queens were Eleanor of Castile, the first wife of Edward I, who died in 1290, and Anne of Bohemia, who died in 1394. The death of Eleanor led to a spectacular public display of mourning by Edward, the erection of the Eleanor crosses in her memory. She died at Harby in Nottinghamshire in November 1290, and Edward had a memorial cross erected at every site where her bier had rested on its journey from Lincoln to Westminster, of which the most famous is Charing Cross in London. Folk etymology has it that the name Charing derives from the French *chère reine* (dear queen) in honour of Eleanor. This was the first occasion on which a queen of England had received such a lavish public funeral, indicating the extent to which queens consort had come to be viewed as 'royal', even if they did not wield actual power.[4] Eleanor received a triple burial – the first time this had been done in England – her viscera being buried in Lincoln Cathedral (conveniently close to Harby), and her heart in the house of the Dominicans in London.[5]

Edward's reaction to his wife's death has often been cited as an example of genuine personal grief, undermining the idea that medieval dynastic marriages were loveless acts of international politics. The erection of the Eleanor crosses can also, however, be seen in the context of the ongoing architectural rivalry between the Plantagenet and Capetian dynasties, as it was an imitation of the *montjoie* memorials set up along the route taken by the body of the French King Louis IX in 1270. The crosses were therefore as much a political statement as an expression of personal grief.[6] The idea that Edward's grief was without measure, and that he mourned his wife for the rest of his life, did not appear until after the accession of his and Eleanor's son, Edward II, in 1327, perhaps out of a desire by the younger Edward to promote the image of his mother.[7] The story that the crosses were set up by Edward as an expression of personal grief was first recorded three hundred years after their erection by William Camden, in his works *Britannia* (1586) and *Remaines of a Greater Worke, Concerning Britaine* (1605). The primary aim of the crosses was to solicit prayers for the dead queen's soul, a conventional piece of later medieval piety, but one which was at odds with the Protestantism of Camden's age. The idea of Edward and Eleanor enjoying a particularly close personal bond was also reinforced by the legend, which had gained currency by Camden's day, that Eleanor had saved her husband's life on crusade at Acre by sucking out the poison from a wound inflicted on Edward by an assassin.[8]

Anne of Bohemia, Richard II's first queen, died at Sheen Palace in or around June 1394. Richard was, according to the chronicler Adam of Usk, so grief-stricken that he ordered the palace to be destroyed afterwards. This is no mere legend, as a writ of privy seal issued on 9 April 1395 confirms Richard's orders.[9] He also refused to enter any chamber in which Anne had been.[10] This, unlike Edward I's building of the Eleanor crosses, does seem to reflect real personal grief, rather than fashion or politics. It has often been remarked that Richard and Anne, who were approximate contemporaries, were married relatively young (when Richard had just turned fifteen and Anne was sixteen) and in effect grew into their marriage together and may have formed a strong personal bond. They invariably travelled together on major journeys, an unusual practice at that time, which suggests their relationship was more than merely formal.[11] Richard planned to be buried in the same tomb as Anne in Westminster Abbey, the first joint-burial of an English king and queen. This wish may, however, reflect not only the personal wishes of Richard but also the changing nature of the burials of queens, which were becoming more prestigious in the later middle ages. Whereas English queens had previously often been buried apart from their husbands, the burials of Eleanor of Castile in 1290 and of Edward III's queen

Philippa of Hainault in 1369 set a pattern whereby they were interred in the choir of Westminster Abbey with their royal husbands (if in separate tombs).[12] The apparently personal touch of Anne and Richard's effigies holding hands may be merely a reflection of contemporary artistic styles, as artistic representations of people became more individual and realistic in the later middle ages. The double tomb of husband and wife first appeared in the thirteenth century in Germany.[13] Subsequently, Henry IV and his second wife Joan of Navarre, and Henry VII and Elizabeth of York, were buried in double tombs. Katherine de Valois, Henry V's queen, was buried close to him in his chantry chapel at Westminster, despite her later marriage to Owen Tudor.

The decision of Henry IV to be buried alongside Joan is an interesting example of politics dictating the geography of burial. It is significant that, although Henry's first wife Mary de Bohun was the mother of his children, and therefore was arguably both personally and dynastically the more important of his two queens, Mary was buried in relative obscurity in Leicester, hundreds of miles from her husband at Canterbury Cathedral. The marriage to Joan, a princess of royal blood, was nevertheless of great symbolic importance to Henry, a usurper who needed to reinforce his legitimacy by marrying into one of the ancient royal lines of Europe.[14] Similarly, the burial of Katherine de Valois in Westminster shows that in death her marriage to Henry V was in a sense restored, disregarding her subsequent remarriage. Her marriage to Henry was politically important, as it made her the mother of the new king, Henry VI, and the match was a result of the treaty of Troyes, which seemed to confirm the English kings in possession of the crown of France.

In the earlier middle ages queens had usually been buried in favoured religious houses, often apart from their husbands. Matilda of Flanders (William the Conqueror's queen) was buried in the nunnery of the Trinity, Caen, while her husband was buried in the equivalent male foundation in the same city. Edith-Matilda, Henry I's Scottish first wife, was buried at Westminster, while Henry was buried at Reading Abbey. It is interesting to note that Westminster Abbey was therefore a burial-place of queens long before it emerged as the royal necropolis in the late thirteenth and fourteenth centuries. Matilda's Anglo-Saxon ancestry may explain her burial in the church of Edward the Confessor. Henry's

Deaths and Burials of Queens of England, 1070–1492

Queen*	Date of Death	Age at Death	Place of Death	Place of Burial
Edith Godwin	1075	c. 55	?	Westminster Abbey
Ealdgyth (wife of Harold)	after 1070	?	?	?
Matilda of Flanders	1083	c. 52	Caen	Holy Trinity Abbey, Caen
Matilda (Edith) of Scotland	1118	c. 38	Palace of Westminster	Westminster Abbey (or Winchester Cathedral)
Adeliza of Louvain	1151	c. 46	Afflighem, Brabant	Afflighem Abbey, Brabant
Matilda of Boulogne	1152	47–49	Hedingham Castle, Essex	Faversham Abbey, Kent
Matilda the Empress	1167	63–64	Abbey of Notre-Dame des Prés, Rouen	Abbey of Bec; reburied at Rouen Cathedral, 1846
Eleanor of Aquitaine	1204	c. 82	Probably Fontevrault Abbey	Fontevrault Abbey
Berengaria of Navarre	After 1230	c. 67	L'Epau Abbey, near Le Mans	L'Epau Abbey; later moved to Le Mans Cathedral
Isabella of Gloucester	1217	41	?	Canterbury Cathedral
Isabella of Angoulême	1246	c. 58	Fontevrault Abbey	Fontevrault Abbey
Eleanor of Provence	1291	c. 74	Amesbury Abbey	Amesbury Abbey
Eleanor of Castile	1290	c. 46	Harby, Lincolnshire	Westminster Abbey
Margaret of France	1317	35 or 38	Marlborough Castle, Wiltshire	Greyfriars church, Newgate, London
Isabella of France (wife of Edward II)	1358	c. 66	Castle Rising, Norfolk	Greyfriars church, Newgate, London
Philippa of Hainault	1369	58	Windsor Castle	Westminster Abbey
Anne of Bohemia	1394	28	Sheen Palace, Surrey	Westminster Abbey

Queen*	Date of Death	Age at Death	Place of Death	Place of Burial
Isabella of France (2nd wife of Richard II)	1409	19	Blois Castle, France	St-Laumer, Blois
Joanne of Navarre	1437	c. 67	Havering, Essex	Canterbury Cathedral
Katherine de Valois	1437	35	St Saviour's Abbey, Bermondsey	Westminster Abbey
Margaret of Anjou	1482	53	Dampierre Castle, near Saumur, Anjou	Angers Cathedral
Elizabeth Woodville	1492	c. 55	St Saviour's Abbey, Bermondsey	St George's Chapel, Windsor
Anne Neville	1485	28	Palace of Westminster	Westminster Abbey

* In order of when queen, not in order of date of death.

second wife, Adeliza of Louvain, was probably buried at the Benedictine abbey of Afflighem in Brabant, a resting-place which reflected her family roots in the Low Countries rather than her period as queen of England. Matilda of Boulogne was the exception, being buried in Faversham Abbey with her husband King Stephen.[15]

In the later middle ages, when the burial of kings and queens together had become more common, separate burial might reflect an estrangement in life. Isabella of France, the wife of Edward II who was ultimately responsible for his overthrow and murder, was buried in the Franciscan church at Newgate in London, in the habit of the Poor Clares (the female order linked to the Franciscans), a suitably penitent end for one who had transgressed the bounds set for a woman, wife and queen. It has been suggested that this church became established as a burial place for 'displaced' royal women, as it also contains the tombs of Isabella's daughter, Joan of the Tower (d. 1362), who had deserted her husband David II, king of Scotland, and of her granddaughter Isabella of Bedford (d. 1379), who had been abandoned by her husband Enguerrand de Coucy.[16] It may simply be the case, however, that Queen Isabella's burial there in 1358, and that of Edward I's second wife Margaret of France before her in

1317, established a precedent for Newgate as a burial ground for royal women. It was also the site for the burial of Eleanor of Provence's heart in 1291, another important and uncontroversial royal connection.

We possess less information about the causes of the deaths of queens than we do for kings. This is partly because their deaths were less politically significant, so tended to attract less attention (and less moralising commentary) from the chroniclers. Queens tended to be treated in conventional terms by chroniclers, who present very bland portraits of them, and the same is true in death as in life. Their deaths are passed over quickly, with little reference to how they died, and the reflection on their deaths usually consisted of conventional picties on their good character and on how much they were mourned. Two twelfth-century examples illustrate this, the death of Matilda of Flanders and that of Matilda of Scotland. The death of the former, William the Conqueror's queen, in 1083, was described by Orderic Vitalis as an ideal Christian death, where the dying person was able to make confession: 'She confessed her sins with bitter tears and, after fully accomplishing all that Christian custom requires and being fortified by the saving sacrament, she died ...' Orderic goes on the describe her funeral at the abbey of the Holy Trinity in Caen, stressing how much she was mourned by the clergy and the poor, whom she had favoured, and quotes her epitaph, which describes her noble ancestry, her foundation of the abbey in which she was buried, and her charitable activities. In short, Orderic's picture is that of the archetypal good queen: pious, charitable and dying a good Christian death. Of the cause of death, he is virtually silent, saying merely that she 'fell sick'.[17] Henry of Huntingdon went to no such lengths, saying merely that in 1083 'Queen Matilda died'.[18]

Orderic was even more terse when describing the death of Matilda of Scotland, Henry I's first queen, in 1118, writing that she 'died ... and was laid to rest in the [abbey] church of St Peter at Westminster'.[19] The chronicler John of Worcester is no more loquacious on the subject, saying that 'she died at Westminster ... and was fittingly buried there'.[20] These accounts (if they can be called that) give the impression that the death of a queen was scarcely worth remarking upon. William of Malmesbury had more to say about the queen, as she was his patron, and he discusses the political implications of her death, but his description of the death itself is still conventional and uninformative. He praises her piety and generosity, while lamenting that lesser people took advantage of it, and describes how she was mourned by the people. He presents her almost in saintly terms (her mother, Margaret of Scotland, had a great reputation for piety and was later canonised): 'her body was buried at Westminster and is now at peace, while her spirit showed by tokens more than ordinary that it inhabits Heaven'.[21] Again, there are no details about the cause or nature of her death. Henry of Huntingdon may be implying that her death was swift, as she was 'cut off from the light of day', and specifies her time of death as the (admittedly vague) 'night time'. He quotes his own poem about her, which speaks of her equanimity, beauty and chastity, conventional virtues for a queen.[22]

Nevertheless, we can make some comments about deaths of queens even on the basis of this evidence. It is striking that no medieval queens of England met violent deaths. Women were – with a few notable exceptions – not war-leaders, and those who were (such as Matilda of Boulogne and Margaret of Anjou) seem not to have taken an active part in the fighting, so they did not run the risk of death in battle. Nor were any queens executed or murdered, in marked contrast to the famous executions in the sixteenth century of Lady Jane Grey, Anne Boleyn, Katherine Howard and Mary, Queen of Scots. Their role as consorts and mothers, rather than rulers, made them less likely to attract the wrath of political factions or personal enemies. As they did not wield power, they never needed to be violently removed to effect political change, in the way that Edward II, Richard II, Henry VI and Edward V were. Those who were politically controversial figures were protected by their femininity, or by their position as mother to the king. For example, Isabella of France, who shared at least some of the guilt for the murder of her husband Edward II, was hardly likely to be executed by Edward III, as she was his mother. Instead, she was allowed to live out a long retirement, and the anniversary of her death was observed by Edward with the same prayers as were offered for his more respectable wife, Philippa of Hainault.[23] In addition, there were more taboos against violence (including judicial violence) against women than against men. Joan of Navarre, the one queen accused of a capital offence (necromancy), was not executed, and was eventually pardoned.

Although women could be executed, those who were did not suffer drawn out or bloody executions, such as the hanging, drawing and quartering suffered by males convicted of treason in the later middle ages. Most medieval law codes stipulated burning or drowning as forms of execution for women, betraying a squeamishness about shedding female blood. Queens were not associated with violence or conflict, but its opposite, often acting as intercessors on behalf of those threatened with punishment.[24] Just as they were not supposed to deal in violence, so they did not attract violence, even from their enemies. The difference with their less fortunate sixteenth-century successors was a political one. Jane Grey and Mary Stuart both represented a direct threat to the crown, as rival claimants to the throne. The only direct parallel in medieval history of a woman claiming the crown in her own right was that of the Empress Matilda, and that conflict was ended by negotiation, so no blood needed to be shed. As for Anne Boleyn, she had been convicted of treason; more to the point, Henry VIII's plans for remarriage and need for a male heir required her to be eliminated. Later fear that she had been unfaithful to him led to Katherine Howard's downfall and execution. The nearest medieval parallel did not lead to such extreme measures: Henry V's accusations of necromancy against Joan of Navarre were an expedient to allow him to acquire her lands, and as such were hardly likely to be taken to the lengths of requiring her death.

Henry VIII's execution of Anne Boleyn allowed him to marry Jane Seymour. Her fate – death in childbirth – was a far more common one than Anne Boleyn's, yet no reigning medieval queen of England suffered this death (although Richard II's second wife, Isabella of France, died in this way in a later marriage, and Katherine de Valois, Henry V's queen, may have died in childbirth after her marriage to Owen Tudor. Henry's mother, Mary de Bohun, also died giving birth, but she was not queen at the time, as her husband, the future Henry IV, was merely earl of Derby).[25] This is most surprising, in the light the dangers that childbirth posed to women until recent times, and given that the most important role of a medieval queen was to give birth to royal heirs. John's second wife, Isabella of Angoulême, had no fewer than sixteen children, five by him and eleven by her second husband, without suffering any mishap, and lived to be nearly sixty.

It is debatable whether we should read any significance into the sturdiness of medieval queens of England – maybe they were simply fortunate never to die in this agonising way – although some possible reasons may be advanced. Dynastic marriages were not carried out without research into the child-bearing record of the girl's female relatives, so an element of selection – or even selective breeding – may have been at work. Although marriages were often celebrated when the bride was very young (Isabella of Angoulême married John when she was just twelve; Isabella of France married Richard II at the age of only six), there is evidence that Plantagenet kings and queens were dissuaded from consummating their marriages until the wife had reached physical maturity, minimising the dangers of childbirth.[26] Isabella of Angoulême, for example, did not give birth to her first-born until she was nineteen, seven years into her marriage to John. Such medical knowledge as existed at the time would have been available to the royal physicians. The *Trotula*, a compendium of women's medicine, was available to medieval doctors from the twelfth century and was widely circulated in England. This was an example of the superior medical knowledge of Muslim Sicily becoming available to the Christian world (it was traditionally attributed to a Sicilian woman, Trotula of Salerno, who does actually appear to have written one section of the work).[27]

One point to consider is medieval obstetric practice. Jane Seymour died after a caesarean section was performed, in order to save her child (the future Edward VI, who would turn out to be Henry VIII's sole male heir). Her medieval forerunners were less likely to be sacrificed in order to save the child. Medieval manuals always advocated saving the mother's life before the baby's, even to the extent of killing and dismembering the foetus. Caesarean sections were only performed on a dead woman, in order to extract the foetus, and this was primarily intended to allow the child's baptism before it too died. The fifteenth-century English writer John Mirk, in his 'Instructions for Parish Priests', advocated that

> ... yef the wommon thenne dye,
> Teche the mydwyf that scho hye
> For to vndo hyre wyth a knyf,
> And for to saue the chyldes lyf
> And hye that hyt crystened be,
> For that ys a dede of charyte.[28]

In addition, royal women, and female members of the aristocracy, were able to give birth in more hygienic conditions than their counterparts in the lower classes. The risk of infection and puerperal fever would have been reduced by having dedicated attendants (instead of having to share the village midwife with other mothers), a good diet and private quarters. These factors meant that the rate of death in childbirth among the medieval English aristocracy may well have been less than we imagine. A study of fifty-five countesses in the period 1066–1230 reveals that only one died from complications surrounding childbirth.[29]

Leaving the subject of the deaths of queens themselves, the role of the queen was important in the aftermath of a king's death. The queen was often younger than her royal husband, so could be expected to outlive him. As her position was defined by being the wife of the king, she was left in an anomalous position by his death. But if she was no longer *the* queen, she did not cease to be *a* queen simply because her royal husband was dead. It is important to remember that a medieval queen was anointed and crowned alongside her husband, or in a separate ceremony if she married him after his own coronation. Joan of Navarre, the second wife of Henry IV (and his only queen, as his first wife died before he seized the throne), enjoyed an almost kingly coronation, complete with orb and sceptre (the usual practice was for the queen to hold a sceptre only – and that a smaller one than the king's – the orb being the symbol of temporal power).[30] The anointing of queens developed because as the dynastic principle of hereditary kingship became established it was increasingly desirable for a king to be the son of not one but two anointed monarchs.[31] Therefore, although a queen derived her title from her marriage to a king, she derived her queenly status through the coronation ceremony. Just as no one could wash the balm from an anointed king, neither did a crowned queen cease to enjoy royal status on her husband's death. If she had successfully produced a surviving male heir, she would still have an important status as queen mother. If her son were a minor, she might even hold real power as regent or guardian of the young king and the kingdom. There was never a formal regency by an English queen, although there were many elsewhere in Europe. One of the most notable such occasions was the rule of Blanche

of Castile, who was regent of France on behalf of her young son Louis IX
(the future St Louis) from 1226 to 1234, when she dealt with internal
political problems with aplomb, and proved a great and beneficial
influence on the young king. She resumed this role when the adult Louis
was captured on crusade in 1250. There is no such parallel in England,
but two English queens did wield real power on behalf of their sons in
more disturbed political circumstances. Isabella of France, after the
murder of her husband Edward II, ruled England with her lover Mortimer in the name of her son, the young Edward III, from 1327 to 1330.

The incapacitating mental illness of Henry VI in the 1450s created a
situation not unlike that of a minority. It allowed his queen, Margaret
of Anjou, to play a leading role in the politics of the period, a position
strengthened by her being mother to the heir to the throne, Prince
Edward, who was born in 1453, the same year as the first attack of
madness suffered by her husband. She was at times effectively a regent,
a role often carried out in other kingdoms by a royal widow on behalf
of her son, if the latter was a minor. The claims of the queen as the
mother of the heir could not be ignored in a situation where Henry
was, like a minor, incapable of governing the kingdom himself. This
gave her, and her supporters, great influence. Margaret's career was,
however, ultimately disastrous and she died in obscurity. After her defeat
by Edward IV's armies at Tewkesbury in 1471 and the death of her son
on the battlefield, followed by the murder of Henry VI upon Edward's
return to London, Margaret's hopes were crushed and her political
power finished. She was held captive by Edward until 1476, when she
was handed over to her cousin Louis XI of France as part of the terms
of the treaty of Picquigny of the previous year. Louis forced her to sign
over her rights in Anjou, and she lived on a meagre pension until her
death in 1482.[32] She was buried at Angers Cathedral, in her father's
ancestral lands.

Many queens, far from wielding power, found themselves in a strange
limbo after the death of the king. With their formal role as queen ended,
they were often surplus to requirements, a not altogether welcome relic
from the previous reign. Customs of land tenure and inheritance provided one reason why a new king might be impatient to see his mother
out of the way. Upon marriage, a woman received a portion of her
husband's lands, the marriage-portion or dower, not to be confused

with the dowry, which was the lands or money received by the husband from the bride's family. Upon marrying a king, a queen would receive a portion of the royal estates. She would hold this land for her lifetime, providing her with an income of her own in marriage and in widow-hood. On her death, it would pass to her son and heir if she had one, or revert to the crown. The survival of the queen from the previous reign was therefore an obstacle to the new king coming entirely into his own. The dowry could also be a matter for contention: if the queen had produced no heir, her family was entitled to claim back the dowry, which her family by marriage were understandably equally eager to retain.

The widowhood of Elizabeth Woodville was a case where a dowager queen was treated with hostility. The death of her husband Edward IV in 1483 led to the succession of their twelve-year-old son Edward V. In such a situation, the queen mother became an obvious candidate to play a part in the governance of the realm. Elizabeth, however, was a controversial figure. She was drawn not from one of the great noble families of England, nor from a royal house of Europe, but from a family of minor nobles. She was a widow before her marriage to Edward, having previously been married to a Lancastrian knight, further reason to make her suspect in the eyes of the Yorkists. Her humble origins should not, however, be exaggerated. Her mother was Jacquetta of Luxembourg, from one of the great houses of Europe and one which had at some time held the imperial throne and the kingship of Bohemia. Before marrying Elizabeth's father, Jacquetta had been married to John, duke of Bedford, the brother of Henry V and governor of the English lands in France. Jacquetta had been forbidden from remarrying without royal consent, and was fined £1000 for her marriage to Richard Wood-ville in 1436. Her sister, and therefore Woodville's sister-in-law, married Charles of Anjou, the uncle of Henry VI's queen.[33]

Elizabeth's Woodville relatives, notably her brother Anthony, Lord Rivers, were deeply unpopular among the nobility on account of the power and influence they had gained in the reign of Edward IV. The young king's uncle, Richard, duke of Gloucester, was able to exploit the unpopularity of the Woodvilles to arrest Rivers and take the young Edward V into his custody, and later to remove him from the throne and declare himself king as Richard III. Elizabeth's role as royal widow,

which could have given her great influence, in fact turned her into
something of a liability because of her relatives. She was never able to
attain the status of previous queens of higher birth; her dower was less
than that of Margaret of Anjou, and this small income was seized by
Richard in 1484. As Richard based his claim to the throne on the
supposed illegitimacy of Edward IV's sons, it followed that Elizabeth
was not a legitimate queen.[34] Following Richard's coup, she fled into
sanctuary at Westminster, but was persuaded to surrender her younger
son, Richard (the second 'Prince in the Tower'), to his uncle. This
incident has been interpreted by Richard III's modern supporters to
show that Elizabeth had no reason to fear for her sons' safety, but in
fact it occurred while Richard's soldiers surrounded the abbey and is
an indication of just how powerless Elizabeth was.[35]

Elizabeth, like many royal widows, retired to a convent, at Bermondsey
in 1487. In her case this was a semi-enforced retirement, due to her
suspected role in the revolt of Lambert Simnel against Henry VII.[36]
Elizabeth's position in the politics of Henry's reign was anomalous.
Although she was the mother of Henry's queen, Elizabeth of York, she
was also associated with the Yorkist dynasty that Henry had ousted.
Upon her death in 1492, she enjoyed a prestigious resting-place, being
buried alongside her husband in St George's Chapel, Windsor. She
benefited from the overthrow of Richard III in 1485, and the 'rehabilitation' of Edward IV and his legacy by Henry VII, who married
Elizabeth's daughter. Her position was nevertheless demonstrated by the
fact that her body was taken 'prevely' to Windsor, and she was given
only a small and low-key funeral.[37] She had a more lasting legacy: her
daughter who married Henry VII was also named Elizabeth, and Henry's
son, Henry VIII, in turn named his daughter Elizabeth in her honour,
so ultimately Elizabeth Woodville's name was given to that of a ruling
queen of England.

If a queen was a second or subsequent wife of the dead king, and was
not the mother of his successor, she had even less of a role to play. The
widowhood of Joan of Navarre, the second wife of Henry IV, saw
the most extreme example of the conflicts associated with a widowed
queen's property. She had been endowed by Henry with a very generous
dower in 1403, an income of 10,000 marks per annum (£6666 13s. 8d.),
and also possessed a considerable private income from her previous

marriage to the duke of Brittany.[38] She was therefore a valuable asset to any king who could lay his hands on this fortune, which was, unfortunately for her stepson Henry V, hers to dispose of as she wished in her lifetime. Henry therefore had her accused of necromancy in 1419, and cancelled the payment of her dower. Charges of sorcery, necromancy or witchcraft were often used in the later middle ages against political opponents, as they were hard to disprove and cast the accused beyond the pale of society.[39] The suppression of the Templars by Philip IV of France in 1307–14, an act that considerably enriched the French crown, is the most famous example of this type of process. In England necromancy was also associated with treason, as in many cases (including Joan's) the accused was said to have attempted to calculate the date of the king's death.

Joan was also vulnerable as a foreigner, a situation which queens, who were usually from foreign royal houses, often found themselves in. As the former duchess of Brittany, and mother of its pro-French duke, Joan was under suspicion, and there were complaints that members of her household were passing secrets to the enemy.[40] Her son, Arthur, even fought on the French side at Agincourt, being captured and taken to England, where he was reunited with his mother.[41]

Given the seriousness of the charges, Henry made surprisingly little effort to bring Joan to trial, merely keeping her in comfortable custody and enjoying the use of her dower for three years, until he repented his actions and restored it to her on his death-bed. His unwillingness to prosecute the case demonstrates that the charges were trumped up, an excuse to cancel Joan's income and use the money to pay for Henry's French wars.[42] Joan's later years were uneventful: she lived in obscurity at Langley, and died at one of her dower manors at Havering in Essex.

The prospect for widowed queens was not, however, entirely bleak. As an unmarried woman of status and property, an aristocratic widow enjoyed a freedom unusual for those of her sex. Although a widowed queen was to some extent limited in her actions by political considerations, she might be free to remarry. If this subsequent marriage produced offspring, it might have important political results, as these children would be blood relatives of the king.

In medieval religious thought, it was believed that a widow should if possible not remarry. There was no canon law sanction against remarriage, but theologians considered chastity the ideal state, with marriage as an acceptable second best. Therefore, although there was no reason for a widow not to remarry, there was a strong moral pressure on her to remain chaste, to live a quiet and pious life, or ideally to enter a religious order. There were also political reasons favouring a queen choosing not to remarry, as this might lead to her new husband and his family gaining undue political influence, to her dower lands being alienated to possibly hostile rival dynasties, and to the birth of children who could claim blood-affinity with the royal house, if only through the maternal line. Consequently, several medieval queens of England remained unmarried, often during long periods of widowhood, although their later careers seldom matched the image of the submissive and pious widow.

Eleanor of Aquitaine is perhaps the most famous of the medieval queens of England, and one who had a long and active widowhood. She married Henry, count of Anjou – the future King Henry II of England – in 1152, having previously been married to Louis VII of France, a marriage that had been annulled on the grounds of consanguinity. Although eleven years Henry's senior, she outlived him by fifteen years, dying in 1204. Her widowhood was an active one, spanning the reign of one son, Richard I, and part of that of a second, John. She played a leading role in organising Richard's marriage to Berengaria of Navarre, and went as far as Sicily to take her to him after he had departed on crusade.[43] She performed a similar role in escorting her granddaughter Blanche of Castile through Aquitaine, for the latter's marriage to Louis, the eldest son of the French king Philip II. Eleanor also toured Aquitaine in 1199, an assertion that she still held a measure of ducal authority in her ancestral lands, for which she had performed homage to the king of France.[44] It should be remembered that her husband and, until her death in 1204, her sons only held Aquitaine through Eleanor, not outright.[45] She therefore derived her authority not only from her position as queen of England by marriage, but in her own right as duchess of Aquitaine. Much has been written of Eleanor's supposedly spirited character, mostly derived from the legends – both medieval and modern – that have gathered around her. It is difficult to know whether her active involvement in politics, particularly during John's reign when she was entering her eighties, was due to personal choice or the force of circumstances. Eleanor entered the abbey of Fontevrault in 1201 (although without taking holy orders), but if this was intended as a peaceful retirement it was disturbed by revolt of Arthur of Brittany, her grandson and John's nephew. Leaving Fontevrault to assist John, she was besieged by Arthur at Mirebeau in 1202. She died in 1204, probably at Fontevrault, where she was buried.[46] Perhaps significantly, she was buried not alongside her husband Henry II but her son Richard, a possible reflection of the strained relations between her and Henry in the later part of his reign.

Berengaria of Navarre, the wife of Richard I, was a widow for thirty-one years, and never remarried. The traditional view of her as quiet and unremarkable, a historical footnote to the career of her famous husband, has recently been challenged.[47] In some ways, she fits the image of the quiet, pious widow; she remained unmarried, and, as her marriage had produced no issue, she was unable to play any political role as regent for a young heir or as queen mother. She devoted her later years to the promotion of favoured religious houses, notably the Cistercian abbey of L'Epau near Le Mans, where she was to be buried.[48] She also played a minor but important political role as the lady of Le Mans. The lordship of this city had been granted to her as the outcome of a familiar problem that faced widows, and royal widows in particular: the struggle to obtain her dower lands. She had been promised dower lands in Gascony on her marriage to Richard, and expected to inherit the dower of her mother-in-law, Eleanor of Aquitaine, in England and northern France. In the event she had to wait until 1204 before Eleanor died, and even then her brother-in-law, King John, did all in his power to prevent or delay her receiving the lands. Berengaria was forced to appeal to Pope Innocent III and Philip II of France (her ultimate feudal overlord), and eventually received Le Mans in lieu of the dower lands.[49]

Eleanor of Provence, the wife of Henry III, came from a notable noble family. She was one of four daughters of Raymond Berengar of Provence and Beatrice of Savoy who all married kings; her other sisters married Louis IX of France, Richard of Cornwall (Henry III's brother), titular king of the Romans, and the king of Sicily, Charles of Anjou. She was a strong-minded woman who played in important political role in the troubled reign of her husband. By promoting her Savoyard relatives, she became unpopular at a time when baronial reformers were targeting their criticisms of Henry's rule at the many 'aliens' in his government.

Eleanor outlived Henry by nineteen years, dying in 1291. Henry's death in 1272 did not end her role as queen, as she continued to style herself 'queen of England'.[50] Eleanor's letters to her son, written as queen to king, imply an equality of status. She also continued to play a political role in her own right, seeking Edward's assistance in her attempts to pursue her claim to the county of Provence.[51] Her life as a dowager illustrates many of the problems inherent in the relationship between the new king, Edward I, and the queen mother. The period between the death of her husband and her retirement into the cloister in 1286 also saw her in conflict with her son over her dower lands. Although she received these in 1273, she struggled to gain her full entitlement.[52]

Toward the end of her life, Eleanor followed a path that was common for royal or aristocratic widows and became a nun. As with kings who retired into monasteries, taking up the life of a religious was viewed as a political death: by forsaking the world, a man or woman was supposed to forsake its cares and its politics. For Eleanor, however, her entry into the order of Fontevrault was not such a simple end to her active life. She entered the house of Amesbury in Wiltshire in 1286, a year after two of her daughters. This hardly suggest a woman in a hurry to take the veil, and she retained many of her estates, suggesting that she may not have taken the full vows of a nun. In instances such as this, we might regard the move into a religious house as a form of retirement more than a genuine desire to give up the world. Whatever her exact status may have been, she described herself in these years as 'a humble nun of the order of Fontevrault of the convent of Amesbury'.[53] The choice of a house of Fontevrault may reflect personal devotion, but it also had a dynastic significance. This Angevin abbey, an unusual double house enclosing both male and female religious, had close associations with the Plantagenet dynasty. Henry III's paternal grandparents Henry II and Eleanor of Aquitaine were buried there, as were his uncle Richard I and mother Isabella of Angoulême. Although she was not herself buried in Fontevrault, Eleanor was interred in the Amesbury house of the order. After her death, her husband Henry's heart was reburied at Fontevrault.

Eleanor's death and burial in 1291 were intertwined with those of her namesake and daughter-in-law, Edward I's queen Eleanor of Castile, who had died the previous year. The younger Eleanor seems to have usurped her mother-in-law's position in death, as she was buried in Westminster Abbey at the foot of Henry III's tomb. This place would perhaps have been more fitting for Henry's wife, an impression that is strengthened by the fact that Eleanor of Castile's effigy was in the same style as Henry's. Eleanor of Provence's burial at Amesbury contradicted her earlier plan to be buried alongside her husband in Westminster.[54]

Not all queens who outlived their royal husbands were content to end their lives in a nunnery. It was relatively common for widows to remarry, an act that could have important political and dynastic implications.

John was survived by two wives: Isabella of Gloucester, whose marriage to the king had been annulled, lived until 1217; his second wife, Isabella of Angoulême, died in 1230. The former married twice after the end of her marriage to John; first Geoffrey de Mandeville, earl of Essex, and secondly, following Geoffrey's death in 1213, Hubert de Burgh, earl of Kent, the justiciar and one of the leading figures in the kingdom. The latter marriage occurred only a few days before her death, so appears blatantly to have been a financial arrangement. As daughter of the powerful earl of Gloucester, Isabella was a high-status bride even without her royal connections. John's second wife, Isabella of Angoulême, made a second marriage that had important political consequences in the reign of his son, Henry III. She married the Poitevin lord Hugh of Lusignan, to whom she had been betrothed before her marriage to the English king. Her many children by this marriage rose to important positions in the England of their half-brother King Henry, a fact that caused much resentment among the Anglo-Norman aristocracy who felt their own role was being usurped by these 'foreigners'.

Following the death of his first wife Anne of Bohemia, Richard II was betrothed in 1396 to Isabella, the six-year-old daughter of Charles VI of France. As Richard was deposed and murdered in 1399–1400, when Isabella was only nine, the marriage was never consummated. It is hard to credit a girl so young with political guile, but she nevertheless had a significant role to play in subsequent events, if only as a symbol of Richard's kingship. Thomas Walsingham reported that the Ricardian loyalists who rebelled against Henry in 1400 rallied to the child-queen at Sonning.[55] As a crowned and anointed queen, she was a tangible representative of Richard's kingship.

A French delegation negotiated her return to her home country in the autumn of 1400. They were faced with the common problem of negotiations over the widowed queen's dower and dowry, which Henry IV refused to release. Henry also had plans to remarry Isabella to his own son. A treaty was finally negotiated in May 1401, by which Henry kept her dower but pledged to return her with her jewels (a not insignificant item in such negotiations, on account of their value), movable property and dowry, in return for which she was to abstain from any future involvement in English politics. English sources portray Isabella, although still only eleven years old at the time of her return to France in 1401, as a symbol of French enmity. Adam of Usk has her returning to France dressed in mourning and 'scowling with deep hatred at King Henry', and reported popular mutterings 'that she would, in her burning desire for revenge for the death of her former husband ... stir up even more trouble' for Henry.[56] This did not happen, but the French found it useful in 1404, when they occupied the Isle of Wight, to maintain the fiction that Richard still lived, so as to demand tribute from the island in the name of Richard and his French queen.[57] On her return to France, Isabella married her cousin Charles, duke of Orléans, in 1404, and died in childbirth in 1409 – ending a tragically short but eventful life.

One of the most significant remarriages made by a widowed queen was that of Katherine of Valois, Henry V's French wife, to Owen Tudor in about 1429. This match produced Edmund Tudor, the father of Henry VII, who was thereby able to claim descent from the royal house of France as well as that of England (by his mother, Margaret Beaufort). The presence of Katherine in England after the death of Henry V in 1422 demonstrated some of the fears associated with a royal widow. England at that time was ruled by a council on behalf of the infant Henry VI, Henry and Katherine's son. In this delicate political situation, made worse by factional disputes between the king's cousins, the Beaufort family, and his uncle, Humphrey, duke of Gloucester, any subsequent marriage by Katherine might have serious effects. Who-ever married the queen could, by becoming the boy king's stepfather, claim a guiding role in the kingdom. The queen had already been courted by Edmund Beaufort, but this match had been blocked by Gloucester and his supporters on the council.[58] Parliament decreed that Katherine could not remarry without its permission.[59] The marriage of Katherine and Owen Tudor was therefore carried out in secret, which has led to it often being portrayed in romantic terms.

The Welsh chronicle of Ellis Griffith tells a colourful story of their first meeting. Owen had been courting a lady in Katherine's retinue, but his affections were not reciprocated. In order to shield her from his advances, Katherine disguised herself as the lady-in-waiting and went to meet Owen that night. She rebuffed his advances, and received a scratch on the face for her pains. The truth was revealed the following day, when a horrified Owen saw a scratch on the queen's face and realised the truth.[60] This romantic tale need not be taken seriously; the motif of the queen swapping places with her maid is a common one in medieval romance, as in the Tristan and Iseult legend, where Iseult's maid Brangaine takes her lady's place on her wedding night with King Mark, so that Iseult does not have to lie with him.[61]

However unreliable such sources may be, the circumstances surrounding Katherine and Owen's marriage suggest it was a genuine love-match. The marriage was celebrated in secret, and there was no political gain for Katherine, the king or the council in an alliance with a relatively obscure figure. (The same cannot be said for Owen, for whom marriage to the mother of the king of England, and sister of the king of France, was an extraordinary coup.) The secrecy surrounding the marriage was necessary on account of the ban on Katherine' remarriage, which could have led to Owen being dispossessed. A further impediment to the marriage was Owen's nationality, as discriminatory legislation introduced in the wake of the Glyn Dwr revolt would have prevented him, as a Welshman, from marrying Katherine. Owen was naturalised as an Englishman in 1432. But his position was never secure, and after Katherine's death in 1437 his enemies moved against him for having breached the ban on her remarriage. He was arraigned before the council, acquitted, but subsequently rearrested and deprived of his possessions. He was eventually pardoned in 1439. Despite the disapproval of Owen's enemies, nobody ever suggested that the secret marriage was invalid, or the offspring it produced illegitimate.[62]

Owen was executed much later, in the course of the Wars of the Roses, when, as a leading Lancastrian partisan, he was captured by the Yorkists after the battle of Mortimer's Cross in 1461. Another famous story, reflecting the romantic view of Owen and Katherine's relationship, is told of Owen's death. It is said that, when he placed his head on the block, he remarked wistfully that that same head had once lain in the lap of a queen.[63] Although Owen's ultimate fate was directly related to his marriage, his earlier troubles, and the resentment directed towards him, illustrate the dangers facing anyone contemplating marriage to a royal widow.

Notes

Notes to Introduction

1. Henry of Huntingdon, *Historia Anglorum*, ed. and trans. D. Greenway (Oxford, 1996), p. vii.
2. Paul Strohm, *Hochon's Arrow: The Social Imagination of Fourteenth-Century Texts* (Princeton, 1992), p. ix.
3. Bernard Hamilton, *Religion in the Medieval West* (London, 1986), p. 93.
4. Strohm, *Hochon's Arrow*, p. 3.
5. Henry of Huntingdon, *Historia Anglorum*, pp. 366–69.
6. Alfred Smyth, *King Alfred the Great* (Oxford, 1995), p. 177.
7. Robert Phillips, *History Teaching, Nationhood and the State* (London, 1998), p. 129.
8. Clifford Brewer, *The Death of Kings: A Medical History of the Kings and Queens of England* (London, 2000).
9. Speaking to the local Historical Association in Canterbury on the subject of the deaths of kings, I was careful to explain at the beginning of my talk that I was not going to speculate on such matters. Nevertheless, I was asked by a member of the audience whether I thought Richard III had killed the princes. Such is the fascination with Richard, and such also the understandable desire to know the 'truth' even when it is impossible to do so.
10. David Carpenter, *The Reign of Henry III* (London, 1996), pp. 430–35.
11. Romans 13: 1.
12. I Samuel 10: 1, II Samuel 2: 4, I Kings 1: 39.
13. E. H. Kantorowicz, *The King's Two Bodies: A Study in Medieval Political Theology* (Princeton, 1957), pp. 47–48.
14. Paul Binski, *Medieval Death: Ritual and Representation* (London, 1996), pp. 39–43; C. Daniell, *Death and Burial in Medieval England, 1066–1550* (London, 1997), pp. 37–38, 40.
15. Binski, *Medieval Death*, pp. 40–41.
16. David Crouch, 'The Culture of Death in the Anglo-Norman World', in

Anglo-Norman Political Culture and the Twelfth-Century Renaissance, ed. C. W. Hollister (Woodbridge, 1997), pp. 157–80.

17. Binski, *Medieval Death*, pp. 35–36; Jean de Joinville, 'The Life of St Louis', in *Chronicles of the Crusades*, ed. M. R. B. Shaw (Harmondsworth, 1963), pp. 347–49.

18. Christopher Daniell, *Death and Burial in Medieval England, 1066–1550* (London, 1997), p. 6.

19. L. Dugarde Peach and John Kenney, *Warwick the Kingmaker* (Loughborough, 1966).

Notes to Chapter 1: Death and Burial

1. M. T. Clanchy, *England and its Rulers, 1066–1272* (London, 1983), p. 49.

2. William of Malmesbury, *De gestis regum Anglorum*, ed. and trans. R. A. B. Mynors, R. M. Thomson and M. Winterbottom, 2 vols (Oxford, 1998–99), i, pp. 510–13.

3. Orderic Vitalis, *The Ecclesiastical History*, ed. Marjorie Chibnall, 6 vols (Oxford, 1969–80), iii, p. 248–49.

4. Orderic, *Ecclesiastical History*, v, pp. 286–93; William of Malmesbury, *De gestis regum*, i, p. 575.

5. Discussed by C. Warren Hollister, 'The Strange Death of William Rufus', *Speculum*, 48 (1973), pp. 637–53.

6. William of Malmesbury, *De gestis regum Anglorum* ed. and trans. R. A. B. Mynors, R. M. Thomson, M. Winterbottom, 2 vols (Oxford, 1998–99), i, pp. 758–63; Henry of Huntingdon, *Historia Anglorum*, pp. 466–67, 594–95; Orderic, *Ecclesiastical History*, vi, pp. 298–303.

7. Henry of Huntingdon, *Historia Anglorum*, ed. and trans. Diana Greenway (Oxford, 1996), pp. 490–91, 702–5.

8. The Winchester chronicler commented that he was buried 'in the place to which his merits had led him'. This may be an ironic comment on Stephen's record as king, but his most recent biographer rejects this interpretation. Donald Matthew, *King Stephen* (London, 2002), p. 271 n. 60.

9. Gervase of Canterbury, *Chronicle of the Reigns of Stephen, Henry II and Richard I*, ed. William Stubbs, 2 vols (London, 1879), i, p. 159.

10. John Gillingham, *Richard I* (New Haven, Connecticut, and London, 1999), pp. 321–32.

11. Roger of Wendover, *Flores historiarum*, ed. H. G. Hewlett, 2 vols (London, 1886–89), ii, pp. 195–97; Ralph de Coggeshall, *Chronicon Anglicanum*, ed. J. Stevenson (London, 1875), pp. 183–85.

12. *The Brut or Chronicles of England*, ed. F. W. D. Brie, 2 vols (London, 1906, 1908), i, pp. 202–3.

13. Geoffrey le Baker, *Chronicon Galfridi le Baker de Swynebeck*, ed. E. Maunde Thompson (Oxford, 1889), pp. 30–31, 33–34.

14. Thomas Walsingham, *Chronicon Angliae, 1328–88*, ed. E. Maunde Thompson (London, 1874), pp. 143–44.

15. John Capgrave, *Chronicle of England*, ed. F. C. Hingeston (London, 1858), p. 291.

16. *The Chronicle of Adam Usk, 1377–1421*, ed. and trans. C. Given-Wilson (Oxford, 1997), pp. 242–43.

17. Christopher Allmand, *Henry V* (2nd edn, New Haven and London, 1997), p. 58; Keith Dockray, *William Shakespeare, the Wars of the Roses and the Historians* (Stroud, 2002), pp. 55–56.

18. Thomas Walsingham, *Historia Anglicana*, ed. H. T. Riley, 2 vols (London, 1863–64), ii, p. 289.

19. *The Brut*, ii, pp. 429–30, 493, 496.

20. Dockray, *Shakespeare*, p. 39.

21. Dominic Mancini, *The Usurpation of Richard the Third*, ed. and trans. C. A. J. Armstrong (2nd edn, Oxford, 1969), pp. 66–67.

22. Keith Dockray (ed.), *Richard III Sourcebook*, pp. 129–30.

23. *The Anglo-Saxon Chronicle*, ed. and trans. Michael Swanton (London, 1996), p. 162.

24. Paul Binski, *Medieval Death: Ritual and Representation* (London, 1996), p. 58.

25. Ibid., p. 72.

26. Ibid., p. 78.

27. For a study of Westminster Abbey and its significance to the Plantagenets, see Paul Binski, *Westminster Abbey and the Plantagenets: Kingship and the Representation of Power* (London, 1995).

28. Sergio Bertelli, *The King's Body: Sacred Rituals of Power in Medieval and Early Modern Europe*, trans. R. Burr Litchfield (University Park, Pennsylvania, 2001), pp. 214–15.

29. See David Carpenter, 'King Henry III and the Cosmati Work at Westminster Abbey' and 'The Burial of King Henry III, the *Regalia* and Royal Ideology', in *The Reign of Henry III* (London, 1996), pp. 409–25 and 427–59.

30. Carpenter, 'Henry III and the Cosmati Work'.

31. Binski, *Westminster Abbey and the Plantagenets*, p. 92.

32. Allmand, *Henry V*, pp. 173, 178.

33. Binski, *Westminster Abbey and the Plantagenets*, p. 107.

34. Allmand, *Henry V*, p. 174.

35. D. Gordon, *Making and Meaning: The Wilton Diptych* (London, 1993), p. 18.

Notes to Chapter 2: Death as Divine Punishment

1. William of Poitiers, *Gesta Guillelmi*, ed. and trans. R. H. C. Davis and Marjorie Chibnall (Oxford, 1998), pp. 136–37.
2. *The Carmen de Hastingae Proelio of Guy, Bishop of Amiens*, ed. and trans. Frank Barlow (Oxford, 1999), pp. 32–33.
3. *The Gesta Normannorum Ducum of William of Jumièges, Orderic Vitalis and Robert of Torigni*, ed. and trans. E. M. C. Van Houts, 2 vols (Oxford, 1995), ii, pp. 168–69.
4. *The Anglo-Saxon Chronicle*, ed. and trans. Michael Swanton (London, 1996), pp. 198 ('E' text), 199 ('D' text).
5. D. Bernstein, 'The Blinding of Harold and the Meaning of the Bayeux Tapestry', in *Anglo-Norman Studies*, 5, ed. R. Allen Brown (Woodbridge, 1983), p. 49.
6. Ibid., p. 47.
7. Ibid., p. 42.
8. N. P. Brooks and H. E. Walker, 'The Authority and Interpretation of the Bayeux Tapestry', *Anglo-Norman Studies*, 1, ed. R. A. Brown (Woodbridge, 1979), p. 2.
9. William of Poitiers, *Gesta Guillelmi*, pp. 136–37.
10. Brooks and Walker, 'The Authenticity and Interpretation of the Bayeux Tapestry', pp. 3–4.
11. William of Malmesbury, *Historia Novella*, ed. E. King, trans. K. R. Potter (Oxford, 1998), pp. 22–23; John of Worcester, *Chronicle*, ed. R. R. Darlington and P. McGurk, trans. J. Bray, 3 vols (Oxford, 1995–98), iii, p. 37.
12. R. M. Stein, 'The Trouble with Harold: The Ideological Context of the *Vita Haroldi*', *New Medieval Literatures*, 2 (1998), p. 186.
13. Ibid., p. 188.
14. William of Poitiers, *Gesta Guillelmi*, pp. 140–41.
15. Stein, 'The Trouble with Harold', p. 184.
16. *Anglo-Saxon Chronicle*, p. 199.
17. 'The Life of King Harold Godwinson', in Michael Swanton ed. and trans., *Three Lives of the Last Englishmen* (London and New York, 1984), pp. 3–40.
18. *The Anglo-Saxon Chronicle*, p. 164; *Vita Aedwardi Regis* (*The Life of King Edward*), ed. and trans. Frank Barlow (London, 1962), pp. 79–80.
19. William of Poitiers, *Gesta Guillelmi*, pp. 118–19.
20. Bernstein, 'The Blinding of Harold', p. 54.

21. Ibid., pp. 56–57.

22. For a sceptical review of the theories, see C. Warren Hollister, 'The Strange Death of William Rufus', *Speculum*, 48 (1973), pp. 637–53.

23. Orderic Vitalis, *The Ecclesiastical History of Orderic Vitalis*, ed. and trans. Marjorie Chibnall, 6 vols (Oxford, 1969–80), v, pp. 286–93; William of Malmesbury, *De gestis regum*, i, p. 575.

24. Frank Barlow, *William Rufus* (Bungay, 1983), p. 300.

25. Ibid., pp. 110–12.

26. Margaret A. Murray, *God of the Witches* (Oxford, 1921).

27. Orderic Vitalis, *The Ecclesiastical History*, v, pp. 286–87.

28. Ibid., v, pp. 286–89.

29. Ibid., v, pp. 288–89.

30. Ibid., v, pp. 292–93.

31. Ibid., v, p. 292 and n. 5.

32. *Biothanatus* is defined in the *British Academy Dictionary of Medieval Latin from British Sources*, ed. R. E. Latham and D. R. Howlett (Oxford, 1997-), *A-L*, as 'one dying (deservedly) a violent death (esp. suicide)'. The reference to Judas occurs in Cassian, vii, 14, 2, 'Iudas vitam ipsam communi exitu finire meruit eamque biothanati morte conclusit'. *Thesaurus Linguae Latinae*, ii, *Atusiri-Byzeres*, p. 1999a.

33. Alexander Murray, *Suicide in the Middle Ages*, 2 vols (Oxford, 1998, 2000), ii, pp. 475–76.

34. Orderic, *Ecclesiastical History*, iii, pp. 176–77.

35. Ibid., iv, pp. 246–47.

36. Ibid., vi, pp. 492–93.

37. Antonia Gransden, *Historical Writing in England*, i, *c. 550 to c. 1307* (London, 1974), pp. 151–55. See below, Chapter 2.

38. Ibid., pp. 151, 154.

39. Orderic, *Ecclesiastical History*, v, pp. 282–83.

40. Ibid., iii, pp. 114–15.

41. Ibid., v, pp. 284–85.

42. *Anglo-Saxon Chronicle*, p. 221.

43. William of Newburgh, *A History of English Affairs*, book 1, ed. and trans. P. G. Walsh and M. J. Kennedy (Warminster, 1988), p. 51.

44. William of Malmesbury, *De gestis regum*, i, pp. 504–5.

45. II Samuel, 18: 9.

46. William of Malmesbury, *De gestis regum*, i, pp. 572–73.

47. Ibid., i, pp. 572–73.

48. Ibid., i, pp. 572–73.

49. See Chapter 2 for a discussion of the symbolism of dismemberment versus

the intact body in death. The saints were often described as miraculously overcoming dismemberment.

50. Matthew Paris, *Chronica majora*, ed. H. R. Luard, 7 vols (London, 1872–83), ii, p. 113. The he-goat was also associated with licentiousness.

51. William of Malmesbury, *De gestis regum*, i, pp. 566–67.

52. Ibid., i, pp. 574–75.

53. *Anglo-Saxon Chronicle*, pp. 235–36.

54. Eadmer, *Life of Saint Anselm*, ed. and trans. R. W. Southern (London, 1962), p. 123.

55. Eadmer, *History of Recent Events in England*, ed. and trans. G. Bosanquet (London, 1964), p. 120.

56. Ibid., p. 121.

57. Orderic, *Ecclesiastical History*, iii, pp. 114–15.

58. *Gesta Stephani*, ed. and trans. K. R. Potter and R. H. C. Davis (Oxford, 1976), pp. 24–25.

59. Ibid., pp. 146–49.

60. Henry of Huntingdon, *Historia Anglorum*, ed. and trans. Diana Greenway (Oxford, 1996), pp. 602–3.

61. Suger, *The Deeds of Louis the Fat*, ed. and trans. R. Cusimano and J. Moorhead (Washington, 1992), p. 144.

62. Eadmer, *History*, p. 120.

63. Orderic, *Ecclesiastical History*, v, pp. 292–93.

64. Ibid., iv, pp. 106–9; Thomas Walsingham, *Chronicon Angliae, 1328–88*, ed. E. M. Thompson (London, 1874), pp. 143–44.

65. William of Newburgh, *A History of English Affairs*, book 1, ed. and trans. P. G. Walsh and M. J. Kennedy (Warminster, 1988), p. 45.

66. Suger, *The Deeds of Louis the Fat*, pp. 149–50.

67. *Chronique de Morigny*, ed. L. Mirot (Paris, 1909), pp. 55–57.

68. Snorri Sturluson, *Heimskringla: History of the Kings of Norway*, ed. and trans. L. M. Hollander (Austin, Texas, 1994), pp. 240–41.

69. Orderic, *Ecclesiastical History*, vi, pp. 420–23.

70. Walter Map, *De nugis curialium*, ed. and trans. M. R. James (1923; revised edn by C. N. L. Brooke and R. A. B. Mynors, Oxford, 1983), pp. 456–57.

71. Gaimar, quoted in Gransden, *Historical Writing*, i, pp. 210–11.

72. Geoffrey Gaimar, *L'estoire des Engleis*, ed. A. Bell (Oxford, 1960), lines 6337, 6345–46.

73. Miri Rubin, *Corpus Christi: The Eucharist in Late Medieval Culture* (Cambridge, 1991), p. 177.

74. Bernard Hamilton, *Religion in the Medieval West* (London, 1986), p. 116.

75. Hollister, 'The Strange Death of William Rufus', pp. 637–53.

76. Christopher Tyerman, *Who's Who in Early Medieval England* (London, 1986), p. 50.

77. Orderic, *Ecclesiastical History*, v, p. 290.

78. Ibid., v, pp. 288–91.

79. John Gillingham, *Richard I* (New Haven, Connecticut, and London, 1999), pp. 321–32.

80. Roger of Howden, *Chronica*, ed. William Stubbs, 4 vols (London, 1868–71), iii, pp. 288–89.

81. John Gillingham, *The Life and Times of Richard I* (London, 1973), p. 17.

82. Gillingham, *Richard I*, p. 321.

83. Ibid., p. 328.

84. Gervase of Canterbury, *Chronicle of the Reigns of Stephen, Henry II and Richard I*, ed. William Stubbs, 2 vols (London, 1879–80), i, pp. 592–93.

85. Howden, *Chronica*, iv, pp. 84–85.

86. Ralph de Coggeshall, *Chronicon Anglicanum*, ed. J. Stevenson (London, 1875), pp. 331–32.

87. William of Newburgh, *A History of English Affairs*, pp. 69–73.

88. Ibid., pp. 69–71.

89. For example, Margaret of Beverley, who used a cooking-pot for a helmet while defending the walls of Jerusalem. P. G. Schmidt, '*Peregrinatio Periculosa:* Thomas von Froidmont über die Jerusalem-Fahrten seiner Schwester Margareta', in *Sonderdruck aus Kontinuität und Wandel: lateinische Poesie von Naevius bis Baudelaire*, ed. U. Justus Stache, W. Maaz and F. Wagner (Hildesheim, 1986), p. 478.

90. J. Madaule, *The Albigensian Crusade*, trans. B. Wall (New York, 1967), p. 84.

91. Gillingham, *Richard I*, pp. 325–32.

92. Ibid., p. 327.

93. William of Malmesbury, *Historia novella*, pp. 22–27.

94. Ibid., pp. 26–27.

95. Gervase of Canterbury, *Chronicle*, i, 159.

96. *Gesta Regis Henrici Secundi et Regis Ricardi*, ed. W. Stubbs, 2 vols (London, 1867), ii, p. 71.

97. Michael Prestwich, *Edward I* (2nd edn, New Haven, Connecticut, and London, 1997), pp. 557–58; Christopher Allmand, *Henry V* (2nd edn, New Haven, Connecticut, and London, 1997); Paul Strohm, *England's Empty Throne: Usurpation and the Language of Legitimation, 1399–1422* (New Haven, Connecticut, and London, 1998), p. 158.

98. Coggeshall, *Chronicon Anglicanum*, pp. 94–96.

99. Howden, *Chronica*, iv, pp. 82–84.

100. Gervase of Canterbury, *Chronicle*, i, pp. 592–93.

101. *Annales Monastici*, ed. H. R. Luard, 5 vols (London, 1864–9), ii, p. 71.

102. Gillingham, *Richard I*, p. 331.

103. *Richard III*, Act 5, Scene 3.

104. *The Crowland Chronicle Continuations, 1459–1486*, ed. N. Pronay and J. Cox (Gloucester, 1986), p. 181.

105. A. Hanham (ed.), *Richard III and his Early Historians* (London, 1985), pp. 123–24.

106. Keith Dockray (ed.), *Richard III Sourcebook*, pp. 129–30.

107. *The Great Chronicle of London*, ed. A. H. Thomas and I. D. Thornley (London, 1938), pp. 237–38.

108. Robert Fabyan, *The New Chronicle of England and France ... Named by Himself the Concordance of Histories*, ed. H. Ellis (London, 1811), p. 673.

109. Antonia Gransden, *Historical Writing in England*, ii, *c. 1307 to the Early Sixteenth Century* (London, 1982), pp. 231, 245–48.

Notes to Chapter 3: The Corruption of the Body

1. Orderic Vitalis, *The Ecclesiastical History*, ed. and trans. Marjorie Chibnall, 6 vols (Oxford, 1969–80), iv, pp. 106–7.

2. Henry of Huntingdon, *Historia Anglorum*, ed. and trans. Diana Greenway (Oxford, 1996), pp. 702–5.

3. Henry of Huntingdon, *Epistola ad Walterum de contemptu mundi*, in ibid., pp. 604–5.

4. Henry of Huntingdon, *Letter to Henry I*, in ibid., pp. 501–2, 556–57.

5. Ibid., pp. 703–4.

6. Quoted in David Carpenter, *The Reign of Henry III* (London, 1996), p. 454.

7. Orderic, *Ecclesiastical History*, iv, pp. 106–9.

8. Ibid., vi, pp. 450; iv, p. 106.

9. Sellar and Yeatman include this among the 'memorable deaths' of medieval kings: 'He was extremely fond of his son, William, who was, however, drowned in the White City. Henry tried to console himself for his loss by eating of surfeit of palfreys. This was a Bad Thing since he died of it and *never smiled again*.' W. C. Sellar and R. J. Yeatman, *1066 and All That* (London, 1930), p. 27.

10. Henry of Huntingdon, *Historia Anglorum*, pp. 490–91.

11. Ibid., pp. 501–2.

12. Ibid., pp. 530–31.

13. *The Siege of Jerusalem*, ed. E. Kolbing and M. Day (Oxford, 1932), lines 941–42.

14. Henry of Huntingdon, *De contemptu mundi*, pp. 606–7.

15. Paul Binski, *Medieval Death: Ritual and Representation* (London, 1996).

16. Roger of Wendover, *Flores historiarum*, ed. H. G. Hewlett, 2 vols (London, 1886–89), ii, pp. 195–97.

17. Ralph de Coggeshall, *Chronicon Anglicanum*, ed. J. Stevenson (London, 1875), pp. 183–85 (my translation). 'Sed ibidem, ut dicitur, ex nimia voracitate qua semper insatiabilis erat venter eius, ingurgitatus usque ad crapulam, ex ventris indigeries solutus est in dysenterium.'

18. Ibid., p. 184.

19. Matthew Paris, *Chronica maiora*, ed. H. R. Luard, 7 vols (London, 1872–83), iii, p. 121.

20. *King John*, Act 5, Scenes 6–7.

21. Dominic Mancini, *The Usurpation of Richard the Third*, ed. and trans. C. A. J. Armstrong (2nd edn, Oxford, 1969), pp. 66–67.

22. Einhard, *The Life of Charlemagne*, in *Two Lives of Charlemagne*, ed. and trans. Lewis Thorpe (Harmondsworth, 1969), p. 76.

23. Mancini, *Usurpation of Richard the Third*, pp. 58–59.

24. Ibid., p. 107 n. 5.

25. *The Crowland Chronicle Continuations, 1459–1486*, ed. and trans. N. Pronay and J. Cox (Gloucester, 1986), pp. 150–51.

26. Henry of Huntingdon, *De contemptu mundi*, pp. 604–5.

27. Ibid., pp. 698–701.

28. Gransden, *Historical Writing*, i, p. 153.

29. Orderic, *Ecclesiastical History*, v, pp. 284–85.

30. Ibid., v, pp. 292–93.

31. R. Morse, *Truth and Convention in the Middle Ages: Rhetoric, Representation and Reality* (Cambridge, 1991), p. 1.

32. Jacobus de Voragine, *The Golden Legend*, ed. and trans. W. G. Ryan, 2 vols (1993), i, pp. 58–59.

33. Josephus, *The Jewish War*, ed. and trans. G. A. Williamson (Harmondsworth, 1959), p. 110.

34. Acts, 12: 23.

35. Lactantius, *On the Deaths of the Persecutors*, ed. and trans. J. L. Creed (Oxford, 1984), 33: 1–8.

36. Janet L. Nelson, 'La mort de Charles le Chauve', *Médiévales*, 31 (1996), p. 61.

37. Ibid., pp. 61–62.

38. *Gesta Stephani*, ed. and trans. K. R. Potter and R. H. C. Davis (Oxford, 1976), pp. 150–53.

39. Christopher Daniell, *Death and Burial in Medieval England, 1066–1550* (London, 1997), pp. 69, 184–85, 195.

40. *The Chronicle of Adam Usk*, ed. and trans. C. Given-Wilson (Oxford, 1997), pp. 242–43.

41. *Chronicles of the Revolution, 1397–1400*, ed. and trans. C. Given-Wilson (Manchester, 1993), pp. 201–2.

42. Ibid., p. 6.

43. Carpenter, *The Reign of Henry III*, p. 435.

44. John Capgrave, *Chronicle of England*, ed. F. C. Hingeston (London, 1858), p. 291.

45. BL MS Cotton Claudius A. viii, fol. 17, quoted in P. Strohm, *England's Empty Throne: Usurpation and the Language of Legitimation, 1399–1422* (New Haven, Connecticut, and London, 1998), p. 116.

46. *Chronicle of Adam of Usk*, p. 168.

47. Thomas de Cantimpré, *The Life of Christina the Astonishing*, ed. and trans. M. H. King (Toronto, 1999).

48. *Golden Legend*, i, pp. 385.

49. Caroline Walker Bynum, *The Resurrection of the Body* (New York, 1995), pp. 221–24.

50. '*La descente de Saint Paul en Enfer*, poème français composé en Angleterre', ed. P. Meyer, in *Romania*, 24 (1895), pp. 357–75.

51. Ronald Finucane, *Miracles and Pilgrims: Popular Beliefs in Medieval England*, (2nd edn, Basingstoke, 1995), p. 34.

52. William of Newburgh, *A History of English Affairs*, book 1, ed. and trans. P. G. Walsh and M. J. Kennedy (Warminster, 1988), p. 51.

53. Bynum, *The Resurrection of the Body*, pp. 210–11.

54. Finucane, *Miracles and Pilgrims*, p. 35.

55. Antonia Gransden, 'Legends and Traditions Concerning the Origins of the Abbey of Bury St Edmunds', *English History Review*, 100 (1985), p. 4.

56. Ibid., p. 5.

57. Jocelyn of Brakelond, *Chronicle, Concerning the Acts of Samson, Abbot of the Monastery of St Edmund*, ed. and trans. H. E. Butcher (London, 1949), p. 114.

58. *The Life of King Edward who Rests at Westminster*, ed. and trans. Frank Barlow (2nd edn, Oxford, 1992), pp. 92–95.

59. Frank Barlow, 'The King's Evil', *English History Review*, 95 (1980), pp. 4–5.

60. Bynum, *The Resurrection of the Body*, p. 205.

61. Gransden, 'Legends of Bury', p. 6.

62. William of Poitiers, *Gesta Guillelmi*, ed. and trans. R. H. C. Davis and Marjorie Chibnall (Oxford, 1998), pp. 136–41.

63. R. M. Stein, 'The Trouble with Harold: The Ideological Context of the *Vita Haroldi*', *New Medieval Literatures*, 2 (1998), p. 184.

64. *The Carmen de Hastingae Proelio of Guy, Bishop of Amiens*, ed. and trans. Frank Barlow (Oxford, 1999), pp. 32–33.
65. Stein, 'The Trouble with Harold', pp. 184–85.
66. *Carmen de Hastingae*, pp. 34–35.
67. Paul Strohm discusses this in the later context of Richard II and the Lancastrians. See *England's Empty Throne*, pp. 101–27, and below, Chapter 5.
68. Stein, 'The Trouble with Harold', pp. 185–86.
69. *Carmen de Hastingae Proelio*, pp. 34–35.
70. Thomas Walsingham, *Historia Anglicana*, ed. H. T. Riley, 2 vols (London, 1863–64), ii, pp. 270–71.
71. Henry Knighton, quoted in *The Peasants' Revolt of 1381*, ed. R. B. Dobson (2nd edn, Basingstoke, 1983), p. 314.
72. R. Jouet, *La résistance à l'occupation Anglaise en Basse-Normandie, 1418–1450* (Caen, 1969), p. 25.
73. *Chronicle of Adam of Usk*, pp. 82–83.
74. *Chronicles of the Revolution*, p. 97.
75. Orderic, *Ecclesiastical History*, vi, pp. 448–51.
76. Roger of Howden, *Chronica*, ed. William Stubbs, 4 vols (London, 1868–71), iv, p. 84.
77. Paul Binski, *Medieval Death: Ritual and Representation* (London, 1996), p. 63.
78. Carpenter, *The Reign of Henry III*, p. 428.
79. *Political Songs of England, from the Reign of John to that of Edward II*, ed. Thomas Wright (London, 1839), p. 247; Christopher Tyerman, *England and the Crusades* (Chicago, 1988), p. 233.
80. Daniell, *Death and Burial in Medieval England*, p. 122.
81. Froissart, *Chronicles*, ed. and trans. T. Johns (London, 1839), p. 38.
82. Daniell, *Death and Burial in Medieval England*, p. 88.
83. Ibid., p. 122.

Notes to Chapter 4: Father and Son

1. Henry of Huntingdon, *De contemptu mundi*, in *Historia Anglorum*, ed. and trans. Diana Greenway (Oxford, 1996), pp. 604–5.
2. Orderic Vitalis, *The Ecclesiastical History*, ed. Marjorie Chibnall, 6 vols (Oxford, 1969–80), vi, pp. 212–15.
3. Ibid., vi, pp. 40–41.
4. Ibid., vi, pp. 212–13.
5. Ibid., vi, pp. 278–79.

6. D. Bernstein, 'The Blinding of Harold and the Meaning of the Bayeux Tapestry', in R. Allen Brown (ed.), *Anglo-Norman Studies*, 5 (1983), pp. 56–57.

7. Ralph de Coggeshall, *Chronicon Anglicanum*, ed. J. Stevenson (London, 1875), pp. 139–41.

8. *King John*, Act 4, Scenes, 1, 3.

9. Bernstein. 'The Blinding of Harold', p. 54.

10. Hans Eberhard Mayer, *The Crusades*, trans. John Gillingham (2nd edn, Oxford, 1988), pp. 74–75.

11. Henry of Huntingdon, 'Book on the Present Times', in *Historia Anglorum*, pp. 698–99.

12. M. T. Clanchy, *England and its Rulers 1066–1272: Foreign Lordship and National Identity* (London, 1983), p. 73.

13. Charlotte A. Newman, *The Anglo-Norman Nobility in the Reign of Henry I* (Philadelphia, 1988), p. 42.

14. Orderic, *Ecclesiastical History*, vi, pp. 422–23.

15. Marjorie Chibnall, 'Women in Orderic Vitalis', *Haskins Society Journal*, 2 (1990), p. 113.

16. Orderic, *Ecclesiastical History*, vi, pp. 278–79.

17. Newman, *The Anglo-Norman Nobility*, p. 56.

18. Chibnall, 'Women in Orderic Vitalis', 105–21.

19. Orderic, *Ecclesiastical History*, vi, pp. 402–5.

20. Newman, *The Anglo-Norman Nobility*, p. 42.

21. Megan McLaughlin, 'The Woman Warrior: Gender, Warfare and Society in Medieval Europe', *Women's Studies*, 17 (1990).

22. David Carpenter, *The Minority of Henry III* (London, 1990), p. 36.

23. See, for example, Lorraine K. Stock, 'Arms and the (Wo)man in Medieval Romance: The Gendered Arming of Female Warriors in the *Roman d'Eneas* and Heldris's *Roman de Silence*', *Arthuriana* (1995), pp. 56–83.

24. See Michael R. Evans, '"Unfit to Bear Arms": The Gendering of Arms and Armour in Accounts of Women on Crusade', in *Gendering the Crusades*, ed. Susan B. Edgington and Sarah Lambert (Aberystwyth, 2001), pp. 45–58.

25. Frank Barlow, *William Rufus*, p. 272.

26. Orderic, *Ecclesiastical History*, iv, pp. 212–15.

27. Ibid., iv, pp. 212–13.

28. Ibid., vi, pp. 294–95.

29. Ibid., vi, pp. 296–97.

30. William of Malmesbury, *Gesta regum Anglorum*, ed. and trans. R. A. B. Mynors, R. M. Thomson, M. Winterbottom, 2 vols (Oxford, 1998–99), i, pp. 758–59.

31. I Kings 12.

32. Jonah 1:4–17.

33. Caroline Walker Bynum, *The Resurrection of the Body in Western Christendom, 200–1336* (New York, 1995), pp. 117–55.

34. Samantha Riches, *St George; Hero, Martyr, and Myth* (Stroud, 2000), p. 25.

35. Henry of Huntingdon, *Historia Anglorum*, pp. 466–67, 594–95.

36. William of Malmesbury, *Gesta regum Anglorum*, i, pp. 762–63, quoting Statius.

37. Orderic, *Ecclesiastical History*, vi, pp. 302–3.

38. *The Anglo-Saxon Chronicle*, ed. and trans. Michael Swanton (London, 1996), p. 249.

39. Aelred of Rievaulx, *Life of St Edward the Confessor*, ed. and trans. J. Bertram (Southampton, 1990), p. 38.

40. Ibid., p. 39.

41. William of Newburgh, *A History of English Affairs*, book 1, ed. and trans. P. G. Walsh and M. J. Kennedy (Warminster, 1988), pp. 69–71.

42. *Annales Monastici*, ed. H. R. Luard, 5 vols (London, 1864–9), i, p. 27.

43. Orderic, *Ecclesiastical History*, vi, pp. 298–99.

44. Wace, *Roman de Rou*, ed. H. Andersen (Heilbronn, 1877), lines 10203–34.

45. Quotations all from Orderic, *Ecclesiastical History*, vi, pp. 300–1.

46. Ibid., vi, pp. 302–3.

47. Gransden, *Historical Writing*, i, p. 167.

48. William of Malmesbury, *Gesta regum Anglorum*, i, pp. 758–59.

49. Ibid., i, pp. 760–61.

50. Ibid., i, pp. 762–63.

51. Ibid., ii, pp. xvii.

52. Ibid., i, pp. 722–25.

53. *The Life of King Edward who Rests at Westminster*, ed. and trans. Frank Barlow (2nd edn, Oxford, 1992), pp. 75–76.

54. Malmesbury, *Gesta regum Anglorum*, i, pp. 758–59.

55. Orderic, *Ecclesiastical History*, vi, pp. 296; C. Warren Hollister (ed. and completed A. C. Frost), *Henry I* (New Haven, Connecticut, and London, 2001), p. 277.

56. I am grateful to Judith Green for this suggested reading.

57. Henry Huntingdon, *Historia Anglorum*, pp. 466–67.

58. Ibid., pp. 482–83.

59. Ibid., pp. 592–95.

60. Orderic, *Ecclesiastical History*, vi, pp. 302–3.

61. John of Worcester, *Chronicle*, ed. R. R. Darlington and P. McGurk, trans. J. Bray, 3 vols (Oxford, 1995–98), iii, pp. 202–3.

62. Ibid., iii, pp. 210–11.
63. W. L. Warren, *Henry II* (2nd edn, New Haven, Connecticut, and London, 2000), pp. 117–18.
64. Ibid., pp. 591–93.
65. Thomas M. Jones, 'The Generation Gap of 1173–74: The War of the Two Henries', *Albion*, 5 (1973), p. 32; *Fasti Ecclesiae Anglicanae*, ed. J. Le Neve, 3 vols (Oxford, 1854), i, p. 158, records a 'Thomas' who was archdeacon *c.* 1175–85.
66. Thomas de Agnellis, *De morte et sepultura Henrici Regis Junioris*, in Ralph de Coggeshall, *Chronicon Anglicanum* (London, 1875), pp. 266–67.
67. 'Gaufredi Prioris Vosiensis ...' in *Recueil des historiens des Gaules et de France*, xviii, p. 218.
68. Ibid., p. 218.
69. Ralph de Diceto, *Opera historica*, ed. William Stubbs, 2 vols (London, 1876), ii, pp. 19–20.
70. Henry of Huntingdon, *Historia Anglorum*, p. 704.
71. Roger of Howden, *Gesta Regis Henrici Secundi et Regis Ricardi*, ed. William Stubbs, 2 vols (London, 1867), ii, pp. 301–2.
72. *L'histoire de Guillaume le Maréchal*, ed. P. Meyer, 3 vols (Paris, 1896–1901), lines 6869–72. 'But fortune, which is ever-changing and makes all things strange, became to them a stranger and in a short time was changed.'
73. William of Newburgh, in *Chronicles of Stephen, Henry II and Richard I*, p. 234; Howden, *Gesta Regis*, i, pp. 300–1.
74. Walter Map, *De nugis curialum*, ed. and trans. M. R. James (1923; revised edn by C. N. L. Brooke and R. A. B. Mynors, Oxford, 1983), pp. 280–81.
75. David Abulafia, *Frederick II: A Medieval Emperor* (London, 1988), p. 241.
76. Malcolm Barber, *The Two Cities* (London, 1992), p. 219.
77. Map, *De nugis curialum*, pp. 282–83.
78. Ibid., pp. 280–81.
79. T. Callahan, 'Sinners and Saintly Retribution: The Timely Death of King Stephen's Son Eustace, 1153', *Studia monastica*, 18 (1976), pp. 109–17.
80. William of Newburgh, *Chronicle*, pp. 125–27.
81. *Histoire de Guillaume le Maréchal*, lines 6884–85.
82. Roger of Wendover, *Flores historiarum*, ed. H. G. Hewlett, 2 vols (London, 1886–89), ii, pp. 195–97.
83. Howden, *Chronica*, ii, p. 278.
84. Diceto, *Opera historica*, ii, pp. 19–20.
85. *Histoire de Guillaume le Maréchal*, lines 6891–911.
86. Ibid., line 6898.
87. Geoffrey de Vigeois, p. 218.
88. Ibid., p. 218.

89. Thomas de Agnellis, *De morte Henrici Regis*, pp. 267–68.
90. Ibid., pp. 268–69.
91. D. W. Rollason, 'The Cults of Murdered Saints of Anglo-Saxon England', *Anglo-Saxon England*, 11 (1983), pp. 4, 13.
92. Thomas de Agnellis, *De morte Henrici Regis*, pp. 269–71.
93. Matthew, 12: 9–14, the curing of a man with a withered arm.
94. Antonia Gransden, 'Legends and Traditions Concerning the Origins of the Abbey of Bury St Edmunds', *English Historical Review*, 100 (1985), p. 5.
95. *Histoire de Guillaume le Maréchal*, lines 2443ff.
96. David Crouch, *William Marshal: Court, Career and Chivalry in the Angevin Empire* (Harlow, 1990), p. 51 n. 16; William of Newburgh, *Chronicle*, p. 234.
97. Ecclesiastes, 1: 15.
98. Pius Bonifacius Gams, *Series episcoporum ecclesiae catholicae* (Regensburg, 1873), p. 614.
99. D. Spear, 'Les doyens du chapitre cathédral de Rouen, durant la période ducale', *Annales de Normandie*, 33 (1983), pp. 102–3; *Fasti Ecclesiae Gallicanae*, 2, *Diocèse de Rouen*, ed. V. Tabbagh (Turnhout, 1998), p. 77.
100. BL, MS Harley 2261, in Ranulf Higden, *Polychronicon.*, ed. C. Babington, 9 vols (London, 1865–86), viii, pp. 325–27.
101. Diceto, *Opera historica*, ii, p. 20. Thanks to Dr Nicholas Vincent and Dr Roger Smith for this reference.
102. Colin Morris, *The Papal Monarchy: The Western Church from 1050 to 1250* (Oxford, 1989), p. 349.
103. Geoffrey de Vigeois, p. 219.
104. Ibid., p. 338; *Gesta Regis Henrici*, i, pp. 301.
105. Howden, *Gesta Regis Henrici*, ii, p. 71.
106. Ibid., ii, p. 71; Roger of Howden, *Chronica*, ed. William Stubbs, 4 vols (London, 1868–71), ii, p. 367.
107. Richard of Devizes, *Chronicle of Richard of Devizes of the Time of King Richard the First*, ed. and trans. J. T. Appleby (London, 1963), pp. 75–78.

Notes to Chapter 5: Killing the King

1. A. J. Pollard, *The Wars of the Roses* (Basingstoke, 1988), provides a good survey of the civil wars of the later fifteenth century.
2. A. Tuck, *Crown and Nobility, 1272–1461* (London, 1985), pp. 308, 316, 334.
3. *The Crowland Chronicle Continuations, 1459–1486* ed. N. Pronay and J. Cox (Gloucester, 1986), pp. 181, 183.
4. I Samuel 1: 13–16.

5. Romans, 13: 3.

6. S. Walker, 'Political Saints in Later Medieval England', in R. H. Britnell and A. J. Pollard (ed.), *The McFarlane Legacy: Studies in Late Medieval Politics and Society* (Stroud, 1995), pp. 87–88.

7. A. E. Goodman, 'Killing the King in Medieval England', unpublished conference paper, Edinburgh, May 1999.

8. Richard Kieckhefer, *Magic in the Middle Ages* (Oxford, 1989), pp. 187–88.

9. *England in the Later Middle Ages: Portraits and Documents*, ed. D. Baker (London, 1968), pp. 38–39.

10. Trinity College, Cambridge, MS R.5.41, fos 125r–126r, quoted in N. Fryde, *The Tyranny and Fall of Edward II, 1321–1326* (Cambridge, 1979), p. 234.

11. *England in the Later Middle Ages*, ed. Baker, pp. 39–40.

12. Ibid., p. 49.

13. *Chronicles of the Revolution, 1397–1400*, ed. and trans. C. Given-Wilson (Manchester, 1993), pp. 144–45.

14. *England in the Later Middle Ages*, ed. Baker, pp. 45–46.

15. Ibid., pp. 47–48.

16. W. C. Sellar and R. J. Yeatman, *1066 and All That* (London, 1930), p. 45.

17. Bertram Wolff, *Henry VI* (London, 1981), pp. 129–31.

18. Ibid., p. 17; PRO, KB 9/256/12.

19. *Three Fifteenth-Century Chronicles*, ed. J. Gairdner (Camden Society, 1880), p. 103.

20. BL, MS Cotton Vitellius A XVI, in *Chronicles of London*, ed. C. L. Kingsford (Oxford, 1905), p. 157.

21. *The Great Chronicle of London*, ed. A. H. Thomas and I. D. Thornley (London, 1938), p. 179.

22. Georges Chastellain, *Oeuvres*, 8 vols, ed. Kervyn de Lettenhove (Brussels, 1863–66; reprint in 4 vols Geneva, 1971), vii, p. 87. 'couché tout nud sur une table, lié de cordes … Faison regrets et gémissemens pour percer les cieux, et, couché sur ces coustes à genoux, monstra avoir au fondement un cornet de vache percé au bout, et parmy cellui coulant une ardant broche de fer, férant jusques au coeur, affin de faire sembler sa mort venir de nature, car il fut mis depuis au lit entre deux draps tout nud pour faire le personnage'.

23. *Chronicles of London*, p. xvi.

24. This theme was used, for example, by Chaucer in his *Monk's Tale*, and by John Lydgate, who received patronage from Duke Humphrey.

25. Geoffrey le Baker, *Chronicon Galfridi le Baker de Swynebeck*, ed. E. Maunde Thompson (Oxford, 1889), pp. 30–31, 33–34.

26. Adam Murimuth, *Continuatio chronicarum Robertus de Avesbury de gestis mirabilis Regis Edwardi Tertii*, ed. E. Maunde Thompson (London, 1889), p. 54.

27. Robert Fabyan, *The New Chronicle of England and France ... Named by Himself the Concordance of Histories*, ed. H. Ellis (London, 1811), p. 619.

28. Antonia Gransden, *Historical Writing in England*, ii, *c. 1307 to the Early Sixteenth Century* (London, 1982), p. 40.

29. Fryde, *Tyranny and Fall*, p. 206.

30. Tuck, *Crown and Nobility*, pp. 292–93.

31. Gransden, *Historical Writing in England*, ii, p. 222.

32. John Whethamsted, *Register*, 2 vols, ed. H. T. Riley (London, 1872–73), i, pp. 178–83.

33. Gransden, *Historical Writing in England*, ii, p. 381.

34. K. H. Vickers, *Humphrey, Duke of Gloucester* (London, 1907), pp. 329–31.

35. Whethamsted, *Register*, i, p. 179.

36. Gransden, *Historical Writing in England*, ii, pp. 41–42.

37. For the cult of Thomas of Lancaster, see Ranulf Higden, *Polychronicon*, ed. C. Babington, 9 vols (London, 1865–86), viii, pp. 313–15. For pilgrims to tomb of Edward II, see *Historia et cartularium monasterii Sancti Petri Gloucestriae*, ed. W. H. Hart, 3 vols (London, 1863) i, p. 46.

38. John Stow, *Survey of London*, ed. H. B. Wheatley (London, 1956), p. 300.

39. BL, MS Harley 2261, in Higden, *Polychonicon*, viii, pp. 325–27.

40. Geoffrey Chaucer, *The Canterbury Tales*, ed. A. C. Cawley (London, 1958), p. 102; *Miller's Tale*, lines 3809–13.

41. Ibid., lines 3798, 3806.

42. Ibid., lines 3734–35.

43. Higden, *Polychronicon*, viii, p. 327.

44. *The Paston Letters*, ed. N. Davis, 2 vols (Oxford, 1971–76), ii, p. 2.

45. Adam of Usk, *The Chronicle of Adam Usk*, ed. C. Given-Wilson (Oxford, 1997), pp. 62–63.

46. Murimuth, *Continuation chronicarum*, p. 54.

47. C. L. Kingsford, 'An Historical Collection of the Fifteenth Century', *English Historical Review*, 29 (1914), p. 513.

48. *An English Chronicle of the Reigns of Richard II, Henry VI, Henry V and Henry VI*, ed. J. S. Davies, Camden Society, old series, 64 (1856), p. 63.

49. Fryde, *Tyranny and Fall*, p. 201.

50. Ibid., p. 202.

51. R. R. Florescu and R. T. McNally, *Dracula, Prince of Many Faces: His Life and his Times* (Boston, Toronto and London, 1989), p. 104.

52. Ibid., pp. 195–202.

53. R. J. Mitchell, *The Spring Voyage: The Jerusalem Pilgrimage in 1458* (London, 1965), p. 121.

54. John Warkworth, *A Chronicle of the First Thirteen Years of the Reign of King Edward IV*, ed. J. O. Halliwell, Camden Society (1839), p. 9.

55. Henry of Huntingdon, *Epistola ad Walterum de contemptu mundi*, 11, in *Historia Anglorum*, ed. and trans. Diana Greenway (Oxford, 1996), pp. 602–3.

56. *Self and Society in Medieval France: The Memoirs of Abbot Guibert of Nogent*, ed. J. F. Benton, trans. C. C. Swinton Bland (New York and Evanston, 1970), p. 185.

57. Suetonius, *The Twelve Caesars*, trans. R. Graves, revised edn, ed. M. Grant (London, 1990), p. 158.

58. *Rotuli parliamentorum*, ed. R. Blyke et al., 6 vols (London, 1767–77), iii, p. 453. '[They] seized the said duke of Gloucester lying on a bed, and the said William Serle and Fraunceys placed a featherbed over him; and ... they lay over the mouth of the duke of Gloucester in such a way that he died.'

59. Thomas More, *The History of King Richard III*, ed. R. S. Sylvester (New Haven, 1976), p. 86.

60. *Chronique des ducs de Bourgogne*, ed. P. Buchon (Paris, 1827), p. 45, quoted in Vickers, *Humphrey, Duke of Gloucester*, p. 451. '[They placed him] in a vat full of wine rather than strangle him, believing by giving him this bath that his death would not be apparent.'

61. Vickers, *Humphrey, Duke of Gloucester*, p. 451.

62. Michael Hicks, *False, Fleeting, Perjur'd Clarence: George, Duke of Clarence 1449–78* (revised edn, Bangor, 1990), p. 184.

63. Adam of Usk, pp. 90–91.

64. *Historia vitae et regni Ricardi Secundi*, ed. G. B. Shaw (Philadelphia, 1977), p. 166.

65. Whalley Abbey Chronicler, in *Chronicles of the Revolution*, p. 51; John Hardyng, *Chronicle*, ed. H. F. Ellis (London, 1812), p. 357.

66. Adam of Usk, pp. 94–95.

67. *Chronicles of the Revolution*, pp. 233–34.

68. Nigel Saul, *Richard II* (New Haven, 1997), p. 425.

69. Keith Dockray, *William Shakespeare, the Wars of the Roses and the Historians* (Stroud, 2002), p. 39.

70. *Richard II*, Act 5, Scene 5.

71. Dockray, *Shakespeare*, p. 137.

72. Ibid., p. 23.

73. *History of the Arrivall of Edward IV in England and the Finall Recouerye*

of his Kingdomes from Henry VI, ed. J. Bruce, p. 38; repr. in *Three Chronicles of the Reign of Edward IV*, ed. K. Dockray (Stroud, 1988), p. 184.

74. *An English Chronicle*, p. 63.
75. *Arrivall of Edward IV*, p. 46.
76. Warkworth, *Chronicle of Edward IV*, p. 21.
77. Fabyan, *Concordance of Histories*, p. 662.
78. *Arrivall of Edward IV*, p. 47.
79. *Crowland Continuations*, pp. 128–31.
80. Warkworth, *Chronicle of Edward IV*, p. 43.
81. I write this a few days after the massacre of most of the Nepalese royal family, where lack of hard facts led to civil unrest as rumours and conspiracy theories circulated.
82. *Crowland Continuations*, p. 145.
83. Dominic Mancini, *The Usurpation of Richard the Third*, ed. and trans. C. A. J. Armstrong (2nd edn, Oxford, 1969), pp. 62–63.
84. *Richard III: A Source Book*, ed. Keith Dockray (Stroud, 1997), pp. 24, 26–28.
85. Charles Ross, *Richard III* (London, 1981), p. xxxviii.
86. Mancini, *Usurpation of Richard the Third*, pp. 66–67.
87. Snorri Sturluson, *Heimskringla: History of the Kings of Norway*, ed. and trans. L. M. Hollander (Austin, Texas, 1994), pp. 14–15.
88. *Crowland Continuations*, pp. 162–63.
89. Mancini, *Usurpation of Richard the Third*, p. 93.
90. Dockray, *Richard III: A Sourcebook*, p. 79; Fabyan, *Concordance of Histories*, p. 670; Polydore Vergil, *Three Books of Polydore Vergil's English History*, ed. H. Ellis, Camden Socirty (1844), pp. 187–90.
91. *Great Chronicle*, pp. 236–37.
92. Polydore Vergil, *English History*, pp. 683–84.
93. BL, MS Cotton Vitellius A XVI.
94. A. J. Pollard, *Richard III and the Princes in the Tower* (Stroud, 1991), pp. 17–20.
95. Mancini, *Usurpation of Richard the Third*, p. 93.
96. D. W. Rollason, 'The Cults of Murdered Royal Saints in Anglo-Saxon England', *Anglo-Saxon England*, 11 (1983), pp. 10, 13.
97. Ibid., p. 13.
98. P. Strohm, *England's Empty Throne: Usurpation and the Language of Legitimation, 1399–1422* (New Haven, Connecticut, and London, 1998), pp. 116–18.
99. Ibid., pp. 117–18.
100. *Crowland Continuations*, pp. 132–33.
101. Dockray, *Shakespeare*, pp. 138–39.

102. Ibid., p. 40; *Henry V*, Act 4, Scene 1.
103. *Crowland Continuations*, pp. 182–83.
104. May McKisack, *The Fourteenth Century* (Oxford, 1959), p. 202 and n. 2.
105. Adam of Usk, pp. 94–95.
106. Warkworth, p. 21.
107. *Arrival of Edward IV*, p. 39.
108. Fabyan, *Concordance of Histories*, p. 662.
109. Dockray, *Richard III: A Sourcebook*, pp. 123–24.
110. Ross, *Richard III*, pp. 225–26.
111. Ibid., p. 225; Goodman, 'Killing the King in Medieval England.'
112. *Crowland Continuations*, pp. 184–85.
113. *Richard III*, Act 1, Scene 1.

Notes to Chapter 6: Once and Future Kings

1. Norman Cohn, *The Pursuit of the Millennium* (2nd edn, London, 1970), pp. 31–32, 72–73, 90, 93, 113, 142–43.
2. Michael Ashdown, 'An Icelandic Account of the Survival of Harold Godwinson', in P. Clemoes (ed.), *The Anglo-Saxons* (London, 1959), p. 135.
3. Richard Barber, *King Arthur: Hero and Legend* (New York, 1990), p. 16.
4. R. S. Loomis, 'The Legend of Arthur's Survival', in *Arthurian Literature in the Middle Ages* (Oxford, 1959), p. 64.
5. Barber, *King Arthur*, p. 42.
6. *Selections from Layamon's* Brut, ed. G. L. Brook (Oxford, 1903), p. 127n.
7. Antonia Gransden, 'The Growth of the Glastonbury Traditions and Legends in the Twelfth Century', *Journal of Ecclesiastical History*, 27 (1976), pp. 337–58.
8. Gerald of Wales, *Speculum Ecclesiae*, ii, 8–10, in *The Journey through Wales, and the Description of Wales*, ed. and trans. Lewis Thorpe (Harmondsworth, 1978), pp. 285–85.
9. The association of Glastonbury with Arthur was by no means entirely a product of Plantagenet propaganda. The abbey had its own motives, and it was a Welshman, Caradoc of Llancarfan, who first made the association in his *Life of St Gildas*, which was commissioned by the abbey. Gransden, 'Glastonbury Traditions', pp. 346–47.
10. Barber, *King Arthur*, pp. 131–35.
11. Ibid., p. 131.
12. Ibid., pp. 132, 134.
13. Einhard, *The Life of Charlemagne*, in *Two Lives of Charlemagne*, ed. and trans. Lewis Thorpe (Harmondsworth, 1969), p. 76; 'The Monk of Caen',

in William of Jumièges, *Gesta Normannorum ducum*, ed. J. Marx (Rouen and Paris, 1914), pp. 145–59.

14. David C. Douglas, *William the Conqueror* (London, 1969), p. 369.
15. Cohn, *The Pursuit of the Millennium*, p. 72.
16. This tale is classified by folklorists as type 766 in the Aarne-Thompson index.
17. Ashdown, 'An Icelandic Account', pp. 134–35.
18. Michael R. Evans, '*Robynhill* or Robin Hood's Hills? Place-Names and the Evolution of the Robin Hood Legends', *Journal of the English Place-Name Society*, 30 (1998), pp. 43–52.
19. Cohn, *The Pursuit of the Millennium*, p. 72.
20. *The Song of Roland*, ed. and trans. G. Burgess (Harmondsworth, 1990), p. 34.
21. Cohn, *The Pursuit of the Millennium*, pp. 31–32 and passim.
22. Ibid., p. 72.
23. Malcolm Barber, *The Two Cities: Medieval Europe, 1050–1320* (London, 1992), pp. 438–39.
24. Malcolm Lambert, *Medieval Heresy* (2nd edn, Oxford, 1992), p. 199.
25. Cohn, *The Pursuit of the Millennium*, pp. 111–13.
26. Hans Eberhard Mayer, *The Crusades*, trans. J. Gillingham (2nd edn, Oxford, 1988), p. 226.
27. Cohn, *The Pursuit of the Millennium*, pp. 113–18.
28. Barber, *King Arthur*, p. 137.
29. *Beowulf*, ed. and trans. D. Wright (Harmondsworth, 1957), pp. 79–91.
30. Koch, *Die Siebenschlafereigende, ihr Ursprung und ihre Verbreitung* (Leipzig, 1883), pp. 24–40.
31. 'The Life of King Harold Godwinson', in *Three Lives of the Last Englishmen*, ed. and trans. Michael Swanton (London and New York, 1984), pp. 3–40.
32. Ibid., p. 13.
33. Ibid., pp. 13–14.
34. Ibid., pp. 27–32.
35. Ibid., pp. 39–40.
36. Cohn, *The Pursuit of the Millennium*, pp. 90–93, 113–114.
37. Reifenberg (ed.), *Philippe Mouskes: chronique rimée* (Brussels, 1838). For comments on the nature of vernacular rhymed histories, see above, pp. 50–51 on Geoffrey Gaimar.
38. R. M. Stein, 'The Trouble with Harold: The Ideological Context of the *Vita Haroldi*', *New Medieval Literatures*, 2 (1998), p. 201.
39. Jacqueline De Weever, *Sheba's Daughters: Whitening and Demonizing the Saracen in Medieval French Epic* (New York and London, 1998), p. 32.

40. Gottfried von Strassburg, *Tristan, with the 'Tristan' of Thomas*, ed. and trans. A. T. Hatto (Harmondsworth, 1960), pp. 246–48.

41. Ashdown, 'An Icelandic Account', p. 135.

42. Natalie Fryde, *The Tyranny and Fall of Edward II* (Cambridge, 1979), pp. 204–5.

43. G. P. Cuttino and T. W. Lyman, 'Where is Edward II?', *Speculum*, 43 (1978), pp. 522–43.

44. Cohn, *The Pursuit of the Millennium*, pp. 111–12.

45. Gerald of Wales, pp. 198–99.

46. Walter Map, *De nugis curialium*, ed. and trans. M. R. James (1923; revised edn by C. N. L. Brooke and R. A. B. Mynors, Oxford, 1983), pp. 481–83.

47. Ashdown, 'An Icelandic Account', pp. 122–136.

48. Ibid., p. 122.

49. Ibid., pp. 122–23.

50. Ibid., p. 123.

51. Ibid., p. 124.

52. This tradition occurs in the *Formanna Sögur*; ibid., pp. 131–32.

53. Snorri Sturluson, *Heimskringla: History of the Kings of Norway*, ed. and trans. L. M. Hollander (Austin, Texas, 1994), pp. 240–41.

54. Ibid., p. 241.

55. Ashdown, 'An Icelandic Account', p. 132.

56. *Heimskringla*, pp. 522–33.

57. Ibid., p. 522.

58. *Myths and Legends of the British Isles*, ed. Richard Barber (Woodbridge, 1999), p. 71.

59. *Richard II*, Act 3, Scene 2.

60. Clovis was 'marked in holy chrism' at his baptism; Gregory of Tours, *The History of the Franks*, ed. and trans. Lewis Thorpe (Harmondsworth, 1974), p. 144.

61. Ibid., p. 181.

62. Ibid., p. 156.

63. Ibid., p. 182.

64. Cohn, *The Pursuit of the Millennium*, p. 126.

65. Ashdown, 'An Icelandic Account', p. 135.

66. Roger of Howden, *Chronica*, ed. William Stubbs, 4 vols (London, 1868–71), iii, pp. 288–89, translation in John Gillingham, *The Life and Times of Richard I* (London, 1973), p. 43.

67. BL, MS Harley 3776, fos 1–24; *The Waltham Chronicle: An Account of the Discovery of our Holy Cross at Montacute and its Conveyance to Waltham*, ed. and trans. Leslie Watkiss and Marjorie Chibnall (Oxford, 1994).

68. 'Life of King Harold', p. xxv.
69. *Waltham Chronicle*, pp. xxxiii, xlvii.
70. S. J. Ridyard, *The Royal Saints of Anglo-Saxon England* (Cambridge, 1988), p. 10.
71. 'Life of King Harold', p. 3.
72. *Waltham Chronicle*, p. xxxiii.
73. Frank Barlow, ed and trans., *The Life of King Edward who Rests at Westminster* (Oxford, 1992), pp. 75–76.
74. Stein, 'The Trouble with Harold', pp. 191–95.
75. 'Life of King Harold', pp. 6–7.
76. Ibid., pp. 7–8.
77. Stein, 'The Trouble with Harold', pp. 200.
78. 'Life of King Harold', p. 10
79. Ibid., pp. 34–35.
80. Ibid., pp. 38–40.
81. I. W. Walker, *Harold, the Last Anglo-Saxon King* (Stroud, 1997), pp. 181–82.
82. 'Life of King Harold', pp. 11, 338–40.
83. Ibid., p. 3.
84. Cohn, *The Pursuit of the Millennium*, p. 93.
85. A. Tuck, *Crown and Nobility, 1272–1461* (London, 1985), pp. 225–27.
86. Paul Strohm, *England's Empty Throne: Usurpation and the Language of Legitimation, 1399–1422* (New Haven and London, 1998), p. 102.
87. Ashdown, 'An Icelandic Account', p. 133.
88. *Heimskringla*, pp. 240–41.
89. *Beowulf*, p. 82.
90. William of Poitiers, *Gesta Guillelmi*, ed. and trans. R. H. C. Davis and Marjorie Chibnall (Oxford, 1998), pp. 140–41.
91. Stein, 'The Trouble with Harold', pp. 183–84.
92. William of Malmesbury, *Gesta regum Anglorum*, 2 vols, ed. and trans. R. A. B. Mynors, R. M. Thomson, M. Winterbottom, (Oxford, 1998–99), i, p. 461.
93. *Waltham Chronicle*, pp. 52–57.
94. 'Life of King Harold', p. 34.
95. *Waltham Chronicle*, pp. 46–47.
96. 'Life of King Harold', p. 35.
97. *The Anglo-Saxon Chronicle*, ed. and trans. Michael Swanton (London, 1996), pp. 198 ('E' text), 199 ('D' text).
98. Fryde, *The Tyranny and Fall of Edward II*, pp. 202–3.
99. Tuck, *Crown and Nobility*, p. 93.
100. Fryde, *The Tyranny and Fall of Edward II*, p. 203.

101. Strohm, *England's Empty Throne*, p. 104.

102. Tuck, *Crown and Nobility*, p. 226.

103. *The Great Chronicle of London*, ed. A. H. Thomas and I. D. Thornley (London, 1938), pp. 237–38.

104. Robert Fabyan, *The New Chronicle of England and France ... Named by Himself the Concordance of Histories*, ed. H. Ellis (London, 1811), p. 673.

105. A. Fletcher and D. MacCulloch, *Tudor Rebellions* (4th edn, London and New York, 1997), pp. 14–15.

106. Ibid., pp. 15–16.

107. S. B. Chrimes, *Henry VII* (London, 1972), p. 72.

108. Ibid., p. 88.

109. Polydore Vergil, p. 24.

110. Thompson, *Motif-Index*, D24.1, ii, 9.

111. S. Thompson, *The Folktale* (Berkeley, Los Angeles and London, 1977), p. 268.

112. *The Crowland Chronicle Continuations, 1459–1486*, ed. N. Pronay and J. Cox (Gloucester, 1986), pp. 132–33. This story has been described as 'colourful but not wholly improbable', Charles Ross, *Richard III* (London, 1981), p. 28.

Notes to Chapter 7: Royal Saints and Martyrs

1. *The Times*, 1 September 1997.

2. William Rees-Mogg, *The Times*, 3 September 1997.

3. Quoted by John Lloyd in *The Times*, 5 September 1997.

4. *Gesta Henrici Quinti*, ed. and trans. F. Taylor and J. S. Roskell (Oxford, 1975), pp. 106–8; S. Walker, 'Political Saints in Later Medieval England', in *The McFarlane Legacy: Studies in Late Medieval Politics and Society*, ed. R. H. Britnell and A. J. Pollard (Stroud, 1995), p. 87.

5. Christopher Allmand, *Henry V* (2nd edn, New Haven, Connecticut, and London, 1997), p. 173.

6. Samantha Riches, *St George: Hero, Martyr, and Myth* (Stroud, 2000), p. 112.

7. D. W. Rollason, 'The Cults of Murdered Royal Saints in Anglo-Saxon England', *Anglo-Saxon England*, 11 (1983), p. 14.

8. The following saints are discussed by Rollason, 'The Cult of Murdered Royal Saints', pp. 2–11.

9. Riches, *St George*, pp. 101–13.

10. Henry himself was buried there, and was later joined by Edward I, Richard II (belatedly), Henry V, Henry VII, and a number of post-Reformation monarchs.

11. *The Life of King Edward who Rests at Westminster*, ed. and trans. Frank Barlow (2nd edn, Oxford, 1992), pp. xviii, 92–95.
12. Frank Barlow, 'The King's Evil', *English Historical Review*, 95 (1980), pp. 3–27.
13. *Life of King Edward*, p. xvii.
14. Riches, *St George*, pp. 22, 109.
15. *Life of King Edward*, p. xxv.
16. Aelred of Rievaulx, *Life the St Edward the Confessor*, ed. and trans. J. Bertram (Southampton, 1990), pp. 108–9.
17. Ibid., pp. 32–33. Thanks also to Emily O'Brien, whose ideas in an unpublished paper given at Kalamazoo 1999 have informed my views on this question considerably.
18. Ibid., pp. 37–39.
19. Frank Barlow, *Edward the Confessor* (London, 1970), pp. 81–82.
20. Ibid., p. 82; *Life of King Edward*, pp. 122–23.
21. Aelred, *Life of St Edward the Confessor*, pp. 34–36.
22. *Life of King Edward*, pp. 6–7. Barlow points out that this is a reference to Vergil on Augustus, ibid., p. 6 n. 8.
23. Ibid., pp. 116–18; Aelred, *Life of St Edward the Confessor*, pp. 87–89, 91–92.
24. See section on Rufus, where the idea of the Conquest as divine punishment also occurs.
25. *Life of King Edward*, p. 119; Aelred, *Life of St Edward the Confessor*, pp. 87–89.
26. *Life of King Edward*, p. 118 n. 302.
27. Aelred, *Life of St Edward the Confessor*, pp. 91–92.
28. *Life of King Edward*, pp. xxix–xxxiii.
29. Ibid., pp. 91–101.
30. Ibid., pp. 126–27.
31. Ibid., pp. 124–25.
32. Ibid., pp. 151–52; Aelred, *Life of St Edward the Confessor*, pp. 108–9.
33. Ibid., p. 163.
34. Ibid., p. 158.
35. E. H. Kantorowicz, *The King's Two Bodies: A Study in Medieval Political Theology* (Princeton, 1957), pp. 46–56. *Christos* is Greek for 'the anointed', a translation of the Hebrew *Mashiah*, Messiah.
36. *Life of King Edward*, pp. 92–95.
37. Ibid., pp. 96–97.
38. David Carpenter, *The Reign of Henry III* (London, 1996), pp. 422–24; Margaret Howell, *Eleanor of Provence: Queenship in Thirteenth-Century England* (Oxford, 2001), p. 306.
39. Carpenter, *The Reign of Henry III*, p. 424.

40. Claire Valente, 'Simon de Montfort, Earl of Leicester, and the Utility of Sanctity in Thirteenth-Century England', *Journal of Medieval History*, 21 (1995), pp. 27–49.

41. *The Miracles of Simon de Montfort*, in *Chronicle of William de Rishanger of the Barons War*, ed. J. O. Halliwell, Camden Society, old series, 15 (1840).

42. Rishanger, *Miracles of Simon de Montfort*, p. 47.

43. Valente, 'Simon de Montfort', pp. 42–43.

44. *Furness Chronicle* in *Chronicles of the Reigns of Stephen Henry II and Richard I*, ed. R. Howlett, 4 vols (London, 1884–89), ii, pp. 543; Roger of Wendover, *Flores historiarum*, ed. H. G. Hewlett, 2 vols (London, 1886–89), ii, pp. 495.

45. Matthew Paris, *Chronica maiora*, ed. H. R. Luard, 7 vols (London, 1872–83), iv, pp. 5, 98, 629; *Calendar of Entries in the Papal Registers Relating to Great Britain and Ireland, AD 1198–1304: Letters*, i, ed. W. H. Bliss (London, 1893), p. 394.

46. *Annales Monastici*, ed. H. R. Luard, 5 vols (London, 1864–69), iv, pp. 173–75.

47. *Miracles of Simon de Montfort*, pp. 109–10.

48. J. R. Maddicott, *Simon de Montfort* (Cambridge, 1994), p. 344.

49. *Chronicon de Lanercost*, ed. J. Stevenson (Edinburgh, 1839), p. 77.

50. Valente, 'Simon de Montfort', p. 30.

51. William Stubbs, *Select Charters and Other Illustrations of English Constitutional History from the Earliest Times to the Reign of Edward the First*, 9th edn, rev. by H. W. C. Davis (Oxford, 1929), p. 409.

52. *Miracles of Simon de Montfort*, pp. 109–10.

53. Valente, 'Simon de Montfort', pp. 30–31; *Miracles of Simon de Montfort*, pp. 83–84.

54. David Carpenter, 'English Peasants in Politics, 1258–67', *Past and Present*, 136 (1992), pp. 3–42.

55. Valente, 'Simon de Montfort', pp. 34–35.

56. Ronald Finucane, *Miracles and Pilgrims: Popular Beliefs in Medieval England* (2nd edn, Basingstoke, 1995), pp. 133–35.

57. J. R. Maddicott, *Thomas of Lancaster, 1307–1322: A Study in the Reign of Edward II* (Oxford, 1970), p. 312.

58. Ranulf Higden, *Polychronicon.*, ed. C. Babington, 9 vols (London, 1865–86), viii, pp. 312–15.

59. J. C. Russell, 'The Canonisation of Opposition to the King in Angevin England', in *Haskins Anniversary Essays in Medieval History* (Boston and New York, 1929), p. 284.

60. Riches, *St George*, pp. 105–6.

61. Walker, Political Saints in Later Medieval England', p. 83.

62. *Polychronicon*, viii, pp. 313–15.

63. *Vita Edwardi Secundi*, ed. and trans. N. Denholm-Young (London, 1957), p. 18.

64. Ibid., p. 44.

65. 'The Office of St Thomas of Lancaster', in *The Political Songs of England, from the Reign of John to that of Edward III*, ed. Thomas Wright, Camden Society, old series, 6 (1839), p. 268. 'Rejoice, Thomas, glory of chieftains, the light of Lancaster, who by thy death imitatest Thomas of Canterbury; whose head was broken on account of the peace of the Church, and thine was cut off for the cause of the Peace of England …'

66. Ibid., p. 268. 'O God, who, for the peace and tranquillity of the inhabitants of England, willed that the blessed Thomas thy martyr and earl should fall by the sword of the persecutor …'

67. 'The Lament of Simon de Montfort', in *Political Songs*, pp. 125–26: 'by his death the Earl Montfort gained the victory, like the martyr of Canterbury he finished his life; the good Thomas would not suffer holy Church to perish, the Earl fought in a similar cause, and died without flinching …'

68. *Political Songs*, pp. 124, 270.

69. Ibid., pp. 269–70.

70. Maddicott, *Thomas of Lancaster*, pp. 323, 329.

71. Henry Knighton, *Chronicon*, ed. J. R. Lumby (London, 1889–95), i, p. 426.

72. See Chapter 4.

73. *Historia et cartularium monasterii Sancti Petri Gloucestriae* (3 vols), ed. W. H. Hart (London, 1863–64), i, p. 46.

74. Nigel Saul, *Richard II* (New Haven, Connecticut, and London, 1997).

75. BL, MS Harley 2261, in Higden, *Polychonicon*, viii, pp. 325–27.

76. Paul Strohm, *Hochon's Arrow* (Princeton, 1992), p. 55; R. B. Dobson, *The Peasants' Revolt of 1381* (2nd edn, Basingstoke, 1983), pp. 179, 203.

77. Dobson, *The Peasants' Revolt*, pp. 180–81.

78. Ibid., pp. 167, 179–80, 204, 208, 211.

79. Ibid., p. 199.

80. Ibid., p. 130.

81. Geoffrey Chaucer, *The Canterbury Tales*, ed. A. C. Cawley (London, 1958), p. 2: *General Prologue*, lines 45–46.

82. Dobson, *The Peasants' Revolt*, p. 164.

83. Ibid., p. 258.

84. *Witnesses to the Russian Revolution*, ed. R. Pethybridge (London, 1964), p. 27.

85. *Guardian*, 15 August 2000.

86. Colin Thubron, *In Siberia* (Harmondsworth, 2000), p. 27.

87. Dobson, *The Peasants' Revolt*, p. 371.

88. Adam of Usk, p. 25.
89. A. Tuck, *Crown and Nobility, 1272–1461* (London, 1985), p. 217.
90. Ibid., p. 308.
91. Ibid., pp. 313–14.
92. A. Fletcher and D. MacCulloch, *Tudor Rebellions* (4th edn, London and New York, 1997), pp. 15–16.
93. *The Crowland Chronicle Continuations, 1459–1486*, ed. N. Pronay and J. Cox (Gloucester, 1986), pp. 146–47.
94. Walker, 'Political Saints in Later Medieval England', pp. 77–106.
95. Ibid., p. 86.
96. Ibid., p. 83.
97. Natalie Fryde, *Tyranny and Fall of Edward II* (Cambridge, 1979), pp. 203–6.
98. Paul Strohm, *England's Empty Throne: Usurpation and the Language of Legitimation, 1399–1422* (New Haven, 1998), pp. 106–7.
99. Ibid., pp. 107–8.
100. Saul, *Richard II*, p. 427.
101. Thomas Walsingham, *Historia Anglicana*, 2 vols, ed. H. T. Riley (London, 1863–64), ii, pp. 270–71.
102. John Stow, *Survey of London*, ed. H. B. Wheatley (London, 1956), p. 300.
103. *History of the Arrivall of Edward IV in England and the Finall Recouerye of his Kingdomes from Henry VI*, ed. J. Bruce, p. 38, repr. in *Three Chronicles of the Reign of Edward IV*, ed. Keith Dockray (Gloucester, 1988), p. 184.
104. *Crowland Continuations*, pp. 128–31.
105. Ibid., pp. 130–31.
106. Bertram Wolffe, *Henry VI* (London, 1981), p. 6.
107. Michael Hicks, *Who's Who in Late Medieval England (1272–1485)* (London, 1991), p. 269.
108. Wolffe, *Henry VI*, p. 5.
109. *Crowland Continuations*, pp. 128–31.
110. *Henry VI Part 3*, Act 2, Scene 5.
111. *The Fabric Rolls of York Minster with an Appendix of Illustrative Documents*, ed. J. Raine, Surtees Society, 35, p. 208. I would like to thank Dr Miriam Gill for her assistance in allowing me to read an unpublished section from her Ph.D. thesis, which provides much of the material in the following section.
112. *The Miracles of King Henry VI*, ed. R. Knox and S. Leslie (Cambridge, 1923).
113. B. Spencer, 'King Henry of Windsor and the London Pilgrim', in *Collectanea Londiniensia*, Special Paper no. 2, London and Middlesex Archaeological Society (London, 1978), p. 241.
114. Rollason, 'The Cults of Murdered Royal Saints', pp. 2–3, 13–14.

115. Wolffe, *Henry VI*, pp. 356–57.

116. *Richard III: A Source Book*, ed. Keith Dockray (Stroud, 1997), pp. 123–24.

117. Spencer, 'King Henry of Windsor', p. 241.

118. Ibid., p. 240.

119. Ibid., p. 239.

120. Wolffe, *Henry VI*, p. 12.

121. Antonia Gransden, *Historical Writing in England*, ii, *c. 1307 to the Early Sixteenth Century* (London, 1982), pp. 41–42.

122. Knox and Leslie, *The Miracles of Henry VI*, p. 6.

123. John 20: 15.

124. Wolffe, *Henry VI*, pp. 6–7.

Notes to Chapter 8: Queens

1. For example, (ed.), *Queens and Queenship in Medieval Europe*, ed. Anne J. Duggan (Woodbridge, 1997); *Medieval Queenship*, ed. John Carmi Parsons (Stroud, 1994); Pauline Stafford, *Queen Emma and Queen Edith* (Oxford, 1997).

2. William of Malmesbury, *Gesta regum Anglorum*, ed. and trans. R. A. B. Mynors, R. M. Thomson, M. Winterbottom, 2 vols (Oxford, 1998–99), i, pp. 758–63.

3. Adam of Usk, *The Chronicle of Adam of Usk*, ed. and trans. C. Given-Wilson (Oxford, 1997), pp. 20–21.

4. John Carmi Parsons, '"Never was a Body Buried in England with Such Solemnity and Honour": The Burials and Posthumous Memorials of English Queens to 1500', in Duggan (ed.), *Queens and Queenship*, p. 323.

5. John Carmi Parsons, *Eleanor of Castile: Queen and Society in Thirteenth-Century England* (Oxford, 1985), p. 206.

6. Ibid., p. 209.

7. Ibid., p. 220.

8. Ibid., pp. 223–24.

9. Adam of Usk, pp. 18–19 and n.

10. Nigel Saul, *Richard II* (New Haven, Connecticut, and London, 1997), p. 456.

11. Ibid., p. 456.

12. Parsons, 'Never was a Body Buried', pp. 321–33.

13. Paul Binski, *Medieval Death: Ritual and Representation* (London, 1996), p. 105; Saul, *Richard II*, plate 20, between pp. 242 and 243.

14. Paul Strohm, *England's Empty Throne: Usurpation and the Language of Legitimation, 1399–1422* (New Haven, Connecticut, and London, 1998), pp. 158–59.

15. Parsons, 'Never was a Body Buried', p. 321.
16. Ibid., pp. 330–31.
17. Orderic Vitalis, *The Ecclesiastical History*, ed. and trans. Marjorie Chibnall, 6 vols (Oxford, 1969–80), iv, pp. 44–47.
18. Henry of Huntingdon, *Historia Anglorum*, ed. and trans. Diana Greenway (Oxford, 1996), pp. 400–1.
19. Orderic, *Ecclesiastical History*, vi, pp. 188–89.
20. John of Worcester, *Chronicle*, ed. R. R. Darlington and P. McGurk, trans. J. Bray, 3 vols (Oxford, 1995–98), ii, pp. 142–43.
21. William of Malmesbury, *Gesta regum Anglorum*, eds and trans. R. A. B. Mynors, R. M. Thomson, M. Winterbottom, 2 vols (Oxford, 1998–99), i, pp. 758–59.
22. Huntingdon, *Historia Anglorum*, pp. 462–63.
23. Parsons, *Eleanor of Castile*, p. 216.
24. Paul Strohm, *Hochon's Arrow: The Social Imagination of Fourteenth-Century Texts* (Princeton, 1992), pp. 95–119.
25. *The Westminster Chronicle, 1381–1394*, ed. and trans. L. C. Hector and Barbara F. Harvey (Oxford, 1982), pp. 520–21.
26. 'Mothers, Daughters, Marriage, Power: Some Plantagenet Evidence, 1150–1500', in *Medieval Queenship*, ed. John Carmi Parsons (New York, 1993). My thanks to Miriam Shadis for pointing out this reference.
27. *The Trotula: A Medieval Compendium of Women's Medicine*, ed. and trans. Monica H. Green (Philadelphia, 2001).
28. John Mirk, '*Instructions for Parish Priests*: Edited from MS Cotton Claudius A II and Six Other Manuscripts with Introduction, Notes and Glossary', ed. Gillis Kristensson, *Lund Studies in English*, 49 (Lund, 1974), pp. 72–73; Monica H. Green, 'Obstetrical and Gynecological Texts in Middle English', *Studies in the Age of Chaucer*, 14 (1992), pp. 53–88. My thanks to Monica Green and to Karl Tobias Steel for this reference, and to Monica Green for the background information on obstetric practice.
29. RaGena DeAragon, email to the author, 1 October 2002.
30. Strohm, *England's Empty Throne*, p. 159.
31. Parsons, 'Never was a Body Buried', p. 325.
32. Charles Ross, *Edward IV* (2nd edn, New Haven, Connecticut, and London, 1997), pp. 237–38.
33. David Baldwin, *Elizabeth Woodville: Mother of the Princes in the Tower* (Stroud, 2002), p. 2.
34. Charles Ross, *Richard III* (2nd edn, New Haven, Connecticut, and London, 1999), p. 184.
35. Baldwin, *Elizabeth Woodville*, pp. 105–6.
36. Ibid., pp. 124–25, 131–32.

37. Ibid., p. 136.

38. Strohm, *England's Empty Throne*, p. 157.

39. Richard Kieckhefer, *Magic in the Middle Ages* (2nd edn, Cambridge, 2000), pp. 187–88.

40. Strohm, *England's Empty Throne*, pp. 164–65.

41. Ibid., p. 167.

42. Ibid., pp. 163–64.

43. D. D. R. Owen, *Eleanor of Aquitaine: Queen and Legend* (Oxford, 1993), pp. 81–83.

44. Ibid., p. 95.

45. W. L. Warren, *King John* (3rd edn, Cambridge, Massachusetts and London, 1997), p. 64.

46. Owen, *Eleanor of Aquitaine*, p. 102.

47. Ann Trindade, *Berengaria: In Search of Richard the Lionheart's Queen* (Dublin, 1999).

48. Ibid., pp. 184–89.

49. Ibid., 150–57.

50. Margaret Howell, *Eleanor of Provence: Queenship in Thirteenth-Century England* (Oxford, 2001), p. 288.

51. Ibid., pp. 295–96.

52. Ibid., pp. 288, 292.

53. Ibid., pp. 300–3.

54. Ibid., pp. 301–10.

55. Thomas Walsingham, *Historia Anglicana*, ed. H. T. Riley, 2 vols (London, 1863–64), ii, pp. 243–44.

56. Adam of Usk, pp. 132–33.

57. Walsingham, *Historia Anglicana*, ii, pp. 260–61.

58. R. A. Griffiths, *The Reign of Henry VI* (2nd edn, Stroud, 1998), p. 61.

59. H. T. Evans, *Wales and the Wars of the Roses* (2nd edn, Stroud, 1998), p. 41.

60. Ibid., pp. 44–43.

61. Gottfried von Strassburg, *Tristan*, ed. A. T. Hatto (Harmondsworth, 1960), p. 205–13.

62. Griffiths, *Henry VI*, p. 61.

63. Ibid., p. 871.

Select Bibliography

PRIMARY SOURCES

Aelred of Rievaulx, *Life the Saint Edward the Confessor*, ed. and trans. J. Bertram (Southampton, 1990).

Adam Murimuth, *Continuatio chronicarum Robertus de Avesbury de gestis mirabilis Regis Edwardi Tertii*, ed. E. Maunde Thompson (London, 1889).

Adam of Usk, *The Chronicle of Adam Usk*, ed. and trans. C. Given-Wilson (Oxford, 1997).

The Anglo-Saxon Chronicle, ed. and trans. Michael Swanton (London, 1996).

Annales Monastici, ed. H. R. Luard, 5 vols (London, 1864–69).

Beowulf, ed. and trans. D. Wright (Harmondsworth, 1957).

The Brut or Chronicles of England, ed. F. W. D. Brie, 2 vols (London, 1906–8).

John Capgrave, *Chronicle of England*, ed. F. C. Hingeston (London, 1858).

The Carmen de Hastingae Proelio of Guy, Bishop of Amiens, ed. and trans. Frank Barlow (Oxford, 1999).

Georges Chastellain, *Ouevres*, ed. Kervyn de Lettenhove, 8 vols (Brussels, 1863–66; reprint in 4 vols, Geneva, 1971).

Geoffrey Chaucer, *The Canterbury Tales*, ed. A. C. Cawley (London, 1958).

Chronicles of London, ed. C. L. Kingsford (Oxford, 1905).

Chronicles of the Reigns of Stephen Henry II and Richard I, ed. R. Howlett, 4 vols (London, 1884–89).

Chronicles of the Revolution, 1397–1400. ed. and trans. Chris Given-Wilson (Manchester, 1993).

Chronicon de Lanercost, ed. J. Stevenson (Edinburgh, 1839).

Chronique de Morigny, ed. L. Mirot (Paris, 1909).

The Crowland Chronicle Continuations, 1459–1486, ed. and trans. N. Pronay and J. Cox (Gloucester, 1986).

Eadmer, *History of Recent Events in England*, ed. and trans. G. Bosanquet (London, 1964).

Eadmer, *Life of Saint Anselm*, ed. and trans. R. W. Southern (London, 1962).

Einhard, *The Life of Charlemagne*, in *Two Lives of Charlemagne*, ed. and trans. Lewis Thorpe (Harmondsworth, 1969).

England in the Later Middle Ages: Portraits and Documents, ed. D. Baker (London, 1968).

An English Chronicle of the Reigns of Richard II, Henry IV, Henry V, and Henry VI, ed. J. S. Davies, Camden Society, original series, 64 (1856).

Fasti Ecclesiae Anglicanae, ed. J. Le Neve, 3 vols (Oxford, 1854).

Geoffrey le Baker, *Chronicon Galfridi le Baker de Swynebeck*, ed. E. Maunde Thompson (Oxford, 1889).

Gerald of Wales, *The Journey Through Wales, and the Description of Wales*, ed. and trans. Lewis Thorpe (Harmondsworth, 1978).

Gervase of Canterbury, *Chronicle of the Reigns of Stephen, Henry II and Richard I*, ed. William Stubbs, 2 vols (London, 1879–80).

Gesta Henrici Quinti, eds and trans. F. Taylor and J. S. Roskell (Oxford, 1975).

The Gesta Normannorum Ducum of William of Jumièges, Orderic Vitalis, and Robert of Torigni, ed. and trans. E. M. C. Van Houts, 2 vols (Oxford, 1995).

Gesta Stephani, ed. and trans. K. R. Potter and R. H. C. Davis (Oxford, 1976).

Gottfried von Strassburg, *Tristan, with the 'Tristan' of Thomas*, ed. and trans. A. T. Hatto (Harmondsworth, 1960).

The Great Chronicle of London, eds A. H. Thomas and I. D. Thornley (London, 1938).

Gregory of Tours, *The History of the Franks*, ed. and trans. Lewis Thorpe (Harmondsworth, 1974).

John Hardyng, *Chronicle*, ed. H. F. Ellis (London, 1812).

Henry of Huntingdon, *Historia Anglorum*, ed. and trans. Diana Greenway (Oxford, 1996).

Ranulf Higden, *Polychronicon.*, ed. C. Babington, 9 vols (London, 1865–86).

L'histoire de Guillaume le Maréchal, ed. P. Meyer, 3 vols (Paris, 1896–1901).

Historia et cartularium Monasterii Sancti Petri Gloucestriae, ed. W. H. Hart, 3 vols (London, 1863–64).

Historia Vitae et Regni Ricardi Secundi, ed. G. B. Shaw (Philadelphia, 1977).

History of the Arrivall of Edward IV in England and the Finall Recouerye of his Kingdomes from Henry VI, ed. J. Bruce; reprinted in *Three Chronicles of the Reign of Edward IV*, ed. Keith Dockray (Stroud, 1988).

Jacobus de Voragine, *The Golden Legend*, ed. and trans. W. G. Ryan, 2 vols (1993).

Jocelyn of Brakelond, *Chronicle, Concerning the Acts of Samson, Abbot of the Monastery of St Edmund*, ed. and trans. H. E. Butcher (London, 1949).

John of Worcester, *Chronicle*, ed. R. R. Darlington and P. McGurk, trans. J. Bray, 3 vols (Oxford, 1995–98).

Josephus, *The Jewish War*, ed. and trans. G. A. Williamson (Harmondsworth, 1959).

Henry Knighton, *Chronicon*, ed. J. R. Lumby (London, 1889–95).

Lactantius, *On the Deaths of the Persecutors*, ed. and trans. J. L. Creed (Oxford, 1984).

The Life of King Edward who Rests at Westminster, ed. and trans. Frank Barlow (2nd edn, Oxford, 1992).

'The Life of King Harold Godwinson', in *Three Lives of the Last Englishmen*, ed. and trans. Michael Swanton (London and New York, 1984).

'A London Chronicle 1446–50', in C. L. Kingsford, 'An Historical Collection of the Fifteenth Century', *English Historical Review*, 29 (1914), pp. 513–15.

Dominic Mancini, *The Usurpation of Richard the Third*, ed. and trans. C. A. J. Armstrong (2nd edn, Oxford, 1969).

Matthew Paris, *Chronica maiora*, ed. H. R. Luard, 7 vols (London, 1872–83).

The Miracles of King Henry VI, ed. R. Knox and S. Leslie (Cambridge, 1923).

The Miracles of Simon de Montfort, in *Chronicle of William de Rishanger of the Barons War*, ed. J. O. Halliwell, Camden Society, original series, 15 (1840).

Thomas More, *The History of King Richard III*, ed. R. S. Sylvester (New Haven, 1976).

Myths and Legends of the British Isles, ed. Richard Barber (Woodbridge, 1999).

Orderic Vitalis, *The Ecclesiastical History*, ed. and trans. Marjorie Chibnall, 6 vols (Oxford, 1969–80).

The Paston Letters, ed. Norman Davis, 2 vols (Oxford, 1971–76).

The Peasants' Revolt of 1381, ed. R. B. Dobson (2nd edn, Basingstoke, 1983).

The Political Songs of England, from the Reign of John to that of Edward III, ed. Thomas Wright (London, 1839).

Polydore Vergil, *Three Books of Polydore Vergil's English History*, ed. H. Ellis (London, 1844).

Ralph de Coggeshall, *Chronicon Anglicanum*, ed. J. Stevenson (London, 1875).

Ralph de Diceto, *Opera historica*, ed. William Stubbs, 2 vols (London, 1876).

Richard of Devizes, *Chronicle of Richard of Devizes of the Time of King Richard the First*, ed. and trans. J. T. Appleby (London, 1963).

Robert Fabyan, *The New Chronicle of England and France ... Named by Himself the Concordance of Histories*, ed. H. Ellis (London, 1811).

Roger of Howden, *Chronica*, ed. William Stubbs, 4 vols (London, 1868–71).

Roger of Howden, *Gesta Regis Henrici Secundi et Regis Ricardi*, ed. William Stubbs, 2 vols (London, 1867).

Roger of Wendover, *Flores historiarum*, ed. H. G. Hewlett, 2 vols (London, 1886–89).

Rotuli parliamentorum, ed. R. Blyke et al., 6 vols (London, 1767–77).

Richard III: A Source Book, ed. Keith Dockray (Stroud, 1997).

Riverside Chaucer, ed. Larry D. Benson (3rd edn, Oxford, 1987).

Self and Society in Medieval France: The Memoirs of Abbot Guibert of Nogent, ed. J. F. Benton, trans. C. C. Swinton Bland (New York and Evanston, 1970).

Snorri Sturluson, *Heimskringla: History of the Kings of Norway*, ed. and trans. L. M. Hollander (Austin, Texas, 1994).

The Song of Roland, ed. and trans. G. Burgess (Harmondsworth, 1990).

John Stow, *Survey of London*, ed. H. B. Wheatley (London, 1956).

Suetonius, *The Twelve Caesars*, trans. Robert Graves, revised edn, ed. Michael Grant (London, 1990).

Suger, *The Deeds of Louis the Fat*, ed. and trans. R. Cusimano and J. Moorhead (Washington, 1992).

Three Fifteenth-Century Chronicles, ed. J. Gairdner, Camden Society (1880).

Thomas de Cantimpré, *The Life of Christina the Astonishing*, ed. and trans. Margot H. King (Toronto, 1999).

Vita Edwardi Secundi, ed. and trans. N. Denholm-Young (London, 1957).

Wace, *Roman de Rou*, ed. H. Andersen (Heilbronn, 1877).

Thomas Walsingham, *Chronicon Angliae, 1328–88*, ed. E. Maunde Thompson (London, 1874).

Thomas Walsingham, *Historia Anglicana*, ed. H. T. Riley, 2 vols (London, 1863–64).

The Waltham Chronicle: An Account of the Discovery of our Holy Cross at Montacute and its Conveyance to Waltham, ed. and trans. Leslie Watkiss and Marjorie Chibnall (Oxford, 1994).

Walter Map, *De nugis curialium*, ed. and trans. M. R. James (1923; revised edn by C. N. L. Brooke and R. A. B. Mynors, Oxford, 1983).

John Warkworth, *A Chronicle of the First Thirteen Years of the Reign of King Edward IV*, ed. J. O. Halliwell, Camden Society (1839).

The Westminster Chronicle, 1381–1394, ed. and trans. L. C. Hector and Barbara F. Harvey (Oxford, 1982).

John Whethamsted, *Register*, ed. H. T. Riley, 2 vols (London, 1872–73).

William of Jumièges, *Gesta Normannorum ducum*, ed. J. Marx (Rouen and Paris, 1914).

William of Malmesbury, *De gestis regum Anglorum*, ed. and trans. R. A. B. Mynors, R. M. Thomson, M. Winterbottom, 2 vols (Oxford, 1998–99).

William of Malmesbury, *Historia novella*, ed. E. King, trans. K. R. Potter (Oxford, 1998).

William of Newburgh, *A History of English Affairs*, book 1, ed. and trans. P. G. Walsh and M. J. Kennedy (Warminster, 1988).

William of Poitiers, *Gesta Guillelmi*, ed. and trans. R. H. C. Davis and Marjorie Chibnall (Oxford, 1998).

SECONDARY WORKS

Christopher Allmand, *Henry V* (2nd edn, New Haven and London, 1997).

Philippe Ariès, *In the Hour of Our Death*, trans. Helen Weaver (London, 1981).

Michael Ashdown, 'An Icelandic Account of the Survival of Harold Godwinson', in *The Anglo-Saxons*, ed. P. Clemoes (London, 1959).

Malcolm Barber, *The Two Cities: Medieval Europe, 1050–1320* (London, 1992).

Richard Barber, *King Arthur, Hero and Legend* (New York, 1990).

Frank Barlow, *Edward the Confessor* (London, 1970).

—, 'The King's Evil', *English Historical Review*, 95 (1980), pp. 3–27.

—, *William Rufus* (Bungay, 1983).

D. Bernstein, 'The Blinding of Harold and the Meaning of the Bayeux Tapestry', in *Anglo-Norman Studies*, 5, ed. R. Allen Brown (Woodbridge, 1983).

Sergio Bertelli, *The King's Body: Sacred Rituals of Power in Medieval and Early Modern Europe*, trans. R. Burr Litchfield (University Park, Pennsylvania, 2001).

Paul Binski, *Medieval Death: Ritual and Representation* (London, 1996).

—, *Westminster Abbey and the Plantagenets: Kingship and the Representation of Power, 1200–1400* (New Haven, Connecticut and London, 1995).

Clifford Brewer, *The Death of Kings: A Medical History of the Kings and Queens of England* (London, 2000).

N. P. Brooks and H. E. Walker, 'The Authority and Interpretation of the Bayeux Tapestry', *Anglo-Norman Studies*, 1, ed. R. A. Brown (Woodbridge, 1979).

Caroline Walker Bynum, *The Resurrection of the Body* (New York, 1995).

T. Callahan, 'Sinners and Saintly Retribution: The Timely Death of King Stephen's Son Eustace, 1153', *Studia Monastica*, 18 (1976), pp. 109–17.

David Carpenter, 'English Peasants in Politics, 1258–67', *Past and Present*, 136 (1992), pp. 3–42.

—, *The Reign of Henry III* (London, 1996).

Marjorie Chibnall, 'Women in Orderic Vitalis', *Haskins Society Journal*, 2 (1990).

S. B. Chrimes, *Henry VII* (London, 1972).

M. T. Clanchy, *England and its Rulers, 1066–1272: Foreign Lordship and National Identity* (London, 1983).

Norman Cohn, *The Pursuit of the Millennium* (2nd edn, London, 1970).

David Crouch, 'The Culture of Death in the Anglo-Norman World', in *Anglo-Norman Political Culture and the Twelfth-Century Renaissance*, ed. C. Warren Hollister (Woodbridge, 1997), pp. 157–80.

—, *William Marshal: Court, Career and Chivalry in the Angevin Empire* (London and New York, 1990).

G. P. Cuttino and T. W. Lyman, 'Where is Edward II', *Speculum*, 43 (1978).

Christopher Daniell, *Death and Burial in Medieval England, 1066–1550* (London, 1997).

R. H. C. Davis, *King Stephen* (3rd edn, London and New York, 1990).

Jacqueline De Weever, *Sheba's Daughters: Whitening and Demonizing the Saracen in Medieval French Epic* (New York and London, 1998).

Keith Dockray, *William Shakespeare, the Wars of the Roses and the Historians* (Stroud, 2002).

David C. Douglas, *William the Conqueror* (London, 1964).

Ronald Finucane, *Miracles and Pilgrims: Popular Beliefs in Medieval England* (2nd edn, Basingstoke, 1995).

A. Fletcher and D. MacCulloch, *Tudor Rebellions* (4th edn, London and New York, 1997).

R. R. Florescu and R. T. McNally, *Dracula, Prince of Many Faces: His Life and his Times* (Boston, Toronto and London, 1989).

Natalie Fryde, *The Tyranny and Fall of Edward II, 1321–1326* (Cambridge, 1979).

John Gillingham, *The Life and Times of Richard I* (London, 1973).

—, *Richard I* (New Haven, Connecticut, and London, 1999).

Antonia Gransden, *Historical Writing in England*, i, *c. 550 to c. 1307* (London, 1974).

—, *Historical Writing in England*, ii, *c. 1307 to the Early Sixteenth Century* (London, 1982).

—, 'Legends and Traditions Concerning the Origins of the Abbey of Bury St Edmunds', *English Historical Review*, 100 (1985).

—, 'The Growth of the Glastonbury Traditions and Legends in the Twelfth Century', *Journal of Ecclesiastical History*, 27 (1976), pp. 337–58.

R. A. Griffiths, *The Reign of Henry VI* (2nd edn, Stroud, 1998).

R. M. Haines, 'Edwardus Redivivus: The 'Afterlife' of Edward of Caernarvon', *Transactions of the Bristol and Gloucestershire Archaeological Society*, 114 (1996).

Bernard Hamilton, *Religion in the Medieval West* (London, 1986).

Michael Hicks, *False, Fleeting, Perjur'd Clarence: George, Duke of Clarence, 1449–78* (revised edn, Bangor, 1990).

—, *Who's Who in Late Medieval England (1272–1485)* (London, 1991).

C. Warren Hollister (ed. and completed A. C. Frost), *Henry I* (New Haven, Connecticut, and London, 2001).

—, 'The Strange Death of William Rufus', *Speculum*, 48 (1973), pp. 637–53.

Margaret Howell, *Eleanor of Provence: Queenship in Thirteenth-Century England* (Oxford, 2001).

R. Jouet, *La résistance à l'occupation Anglaise en Basse-Normandie, 1418–1450* (Caen, 1969).

E. H. Kantorowicz, *The King's Two Bodies: A Study in Medieval Political Theology* (Princeton, 1957).

Richard Kieckhefer, *Magic in the Middle Ages* (Oxford, 1989).

Malcolm Lambert, *Medieval Heresy* (2nd edn, Oxford, 1992).

R. S. Loomis, 'The Legend of Arthur's Survival', in *Arthurian Literature in the Middle Ages* (Oxford, 1959).

May McKisack, *The Fourteenth Century* (Oxford, 1959).

J. R. Maddicott, *Simon de Montfort* (Cambridge, 1994).

—, *Thomas of Lancaster, 1307–1322: A Study in the Reign of Edward II* (Oxford, 1970).

Donald Matthew, *King Stephen* (London, 2002).

Hans Eberhard Mayer, *The Crusades*, trans. John Gillingham (2nd edn, Oxford, 1988).

R. J. Mitchell, *The Spring Voyage: The Jerusalem Pilgrimage in 1458* (London, 1965).

R. Morse, *Truth and Convention in the Middle Ages: Rhetoric, Representation and Reality* (Cambridge, 1991).

Alexander Murray, *Suicide in the Middle Ages*, 2 vols (Oxford, 1998 and 2000).

Janet L. Nelson, 'La mort de Charles le Chauve', *Médiévales*, 31 (1996), pp. 53–66.

Charlotte A. Newman, *The Anglo-Norman Nobility in the Reign of Henry I* (Philadelphia, 1988).

John Carmi Parsons, *Eleanor of Castile: Queen and Society in Thirteenth-Century England* (Oxford, 1985).

—, ed. *Medieval Queens* (New York, 1993).

—, '"Never was a Body Buried in England with Such Solemnity and Honour": The Burials and Posthumous Memorials of English Queens to 1500', in *Queens and Queenship in Medieval Europe*, ed. A. J. Duggan (Woodbridge, 1997).

Robert Phillips, *History Teaching, Nationhood, and the State* (London, 1998).

A. J. Pollard, *Richard III and the Princes in the Tower* (Stroud, 1991).

—, *The Wars of the Roses* (Basingstoke, 1988).

Michael Prestwich, *Edward I* (2nd edn, New Haven, Connecticut, and London, 1997).

Samantha Riches, *St George: Hero, Martyr and Myth* (Stroud, 2000).

S. J. Ridyard, *The Royal Saints of Anglo-Saxon England* (Cambridge, 1988).

D. W. Rollason, 'The Cults of Murdered Royal Saints in Anglo-Saxon England', *Anglo-Saxon England*, 11 (1983), pp. 1–22.

Charles Ross, *Edward IV* (2nd edn, New Haven, Connecticut, and London, 1997).

—, *Richard III* (2nd edn, New Haven, Connecticut, and London, 1999).

Miri Rubin, *Corpus Christi: The Eucharist in Late Medieval Culture* (Cambridge, 1991).

J. C. Russell, 'The Canonisation of Opposition to the King in Angevin England', in *Haskins Anniversary Essays in Medieval History* (Boston and New York, 1929).

Nigel Saul, *Richard II* (New Haven, Connecticut, and London, 1997).

Alfred Smyth, *King Alfred the Great* (Oxford, 1995).

R. M. Stein, 'The Trouble with Harold: The Ideological Context of the *Vita Haroldi*', *New Medieval Literatures*, 2 (1998).

Paul Strohm, *England's Empty Throne: Usurpation and the Language of Legitimation, 1399–1422* (New Haven and London, 1998).

—, *Hochon's Arrow: The Social Imagination of Fourteenth-Century Texts* (Princeton, 1992).

Ann Trindade, *Berengaria: In Search of Richard the Lionheart's Queen* (Dublin, 1999).

A. Tuck, *Crown and Nobility, 1272–1461* (London, 1985).

Christopher Tyerman, *England and the Crusades* (Chicago, 1988).

—, *Who's Who in Early Medieval England* (London, 1986).

K. H. Vickers, *Humphrey, Duke of Gloucester* (London, 1907).

Claire Valente, 'Simon de Montfort, Earl of Leicester, and the Utility of Sanctity in Thirteenth-Century England', *Journal of Medieval History*, 21 (1995), pp. 27–49.

I. W. Walker, *Harold, the Last Anglo-Saxon King* (Stroud, 1997).

Simon Walker, 'Political Saints in Later Medieval England', in R. H. Britnell and A. J. Pollard (ed.), *The McFarlane Legacy: Studies in Late Medieval Politics and Society* (Stroud, 1995).

W. L. Warren, *Henry II* (2nd edn, New Haven, Connecticut and London, 2000).

—, *King John* (3rd edn, New Haven, Connecticut and London, 1997).

Bertram Wolffe, *Henry VI* (London, 1981).

Index

Osbert de Clare 181, 182, 183, 184,
185
Oswald, St, king of Northumbria 26,
177, 180
Oswine, St, king of Deira 177
Oswiu, king of Bernicia 177
'Ottonian System' 38
Ovid 64

Paciferi (peace movement) 114
Paglia, Camille 175
Papacy, popes 19, 27, 35, 39, 156
Paris 26, 49, 94, 175, 179
—, parlement 120
Parliament 125, 168, 170, 227
Pavia 156
Paul, St 120
Peasants' Revolt (1381) 11, 193
Pelagius, Cardinal 153
Penda, king of Mercia 177
Pepin the Short, king of the Franks
160
Percy family 198
—, Henry, earl of Northumberland
123
Perkin Warbeck 16, 169, 171, 172
Perrers, Alice 11
Peter, St 70, 184
Peter of Maule 41–42
Petrus Berchorius 27
Philippa of Hainault, queen of
England 214
—, burial 209–10
Philippe de Commines 58, 67, 137,
138
Picquigny, treaty of (1475) 218
Piers Gaveston 10, 84
Poitiers 72
Poitou 24
Polydore Vergil 59, 137, 138, 140, 171

Pontefract 169, 189, 191
—, castle 11, 24, 135
—, Franciscan church 143
'Princes in the Tower' (Edward V,
and Richard, duke of York, son of
Edward IV) xx, 15, 16, 58, 133,
137, 139–42, 145, 170, 171, 220,
229n.
—, *see also* Edward V; Richard, duke
of York (son of Edward IV)
Prophecies of Hannan 153
Protestantism 209
Provence 224
Pseudo-Methodius 152
Pugachev rising (Russia) 148, 198

Rainer, lieutenant of Geoffrey de
Mandeville 98
Ralph de Diceto 107, 110, 113
Ralph de Gael 94
Ralph de Tosny 93
Ralph Harenc 88
Ralph of Coggeshall 53, 54, 55, 56,
57, 66, 89
Rammel mountain (Germany) 151
Ramsey Abbey (Hunts.) 55, 76
Ranulf Higden 113, 129, 130, 189,
192, 197
—, *Polychronicon* 129
Raoul de Varneville 113
Raymond Berengar of Provence 223
Reading Abbey 25, 83, 210
Rees-Mogg, William 175
Regicide xvii, 119–120
Rehoboam, Old Testament King 95
Rhineland 157
Rhodes 132
Richard I 'Lionheart', king of
England 7, 8, 9, 106, 114, 115,
138, 161, 222